Sheryll.

6 - 2pm PST

MODERN POSTCARD.

I sent:

I need to send:

1-800-959-8363
           X 4140

You
Cannot
Be
Serious

# You Cannot Be Serious

G. P. PUTNAM'S SONS

*New York*

John McEnroe

*with James Kaplan*

G. P. Putnam's Sons
Publishers Since 1838
a member of
Penguin Putnam Inc.
375 Hudson Street
New York, NY 10014

Library of Congress Cataloging-in-Publication Data

McEnroe, John, date.
    You cannot be serious / John McEnroe with James Kaplan.
        p.   cm.
    ISBN 0-399-14858-2
    1. McEnroe, John, date.   2. Tennis players—United States—
Biography.   I. Kaplan, James.   II. Title.
GV994.M34    2002                    2002023875
796.342'092—dc21
[B]

Printed in the United States of America

1   3   5   7   9   10   8   6   4   2

This book is printed on acid-free paper. ∞

*Book design by Amanda Dewey*

TO PATTY—

My soul mate, my partner in crime—we *were* meant for each other.

You
Cannot
Be
Serious

# 1

I HATE ALARM CLOCKS. That incessant ticking drives me nuts. And so September 11, 2001, began like any other morning in the McEnroe household, with my seven A.M. call from 540-WAKE. I quickly hung up the phone, let my wife Patty sleep, and dragged myself out of bed to go rouse five of my six children—Ava, the baby of the family at two, was still too young to be part of this daily ritual.

We live at the top of a big apartment building on Central Park West, in what I happen to believe is the best apartment in the most beautiful building in New York City. I think about that, appreciate that, every day. Our house is the top four floors; the kids' rooms are on floors one, two, and three. I smiled as I moved from room to room, mussing hair, scratching backs, patting cheeks. And as my kids fought for that extra minute or two of sleep before the reality of a school day set in, memories of my own boyhood bubbled up.

In my mind's eye, I was fifteen again, just embarking on my four years at the Trinity School on Manhattan's Upper West Side. My mother was struggling to get me out of bed in my upstairs room at 255 Manor Road, Douglaston, Queens, enduring an early-morning grumpiness—sorry, Mom!—caused by the prospect of a commute my own kids couldn't even begin to imagine.

First came the fifteen-minute walk to the Douglaston train station— a walk I made every morning until the glorious day I turned seventeen and finally got my driver's license. Then I'd catch the 7:20 train, show the conductor my monthly pass, and settle in for the thirty-minute ride to Penn Station in Manhattan.

For you out-of-towners, Penn Station is directly under Madison Square Garden, which was a frequent destination for me as a kid: the home of my beloved Knicks and Rangers; the site of the first rock concert I ever attended (Grand Funk Railroad!); as well as of one of the highlights of my adolescence, the New York stop of Led Zeppelin's 1975 world tour. Some of my greatest tennis triumphs, both in singles and doubles, would also take place there just a few years later, in the Masters tournament, just after Christmas.

Getting off the train, I'd walk through the crowded tunnels and catch the subway—the Seventh Avenue IRT, number 2 or 3 express—for the twenty-minute ride to the Upper West Side. Sometimes I'd be traveling with John Ryerson, another Trinity student who commuted from Douglaston, and occasionally John and I would hook up with another classmate, Steven Weitzmann.

I loved the subway. I still do. Being clumped in with masses of my fellow citizens has never bothered me a bit: I'm a New Yorker, after all, through and through, and getting up close (if not personal) is just part of the gig. For another thing, while I get motion sickness reading in a car, the subway doesn't affect me the same way (not that John and Steven and I did a lot of reading down there; I recall a number of paper-clip fights—

sorry, IRT passengers of 1974!). I've also always enjoyed that feeling of rocking and rolling through the dark—it's comforting, in a way that's hard to describe.

I'd get off the subway at 96th Street, climb the steps up to Broadway, with its honking taxi horns and endless street life, and walk the five blocks down to Trinity, at 139 West 91st, between Columbus and Amsterdam Avenues—the very same place to which I now drive Ruby, Kevin, Sean, Emily, and Anna every morning after breakfast.

It's funny—our apartment isn't much more than a half-mile from Trinity, yet despite (or maybe because of) my own arduous commute as a boy, I like to drive them to school. I enjoy having the extra time with them, and I admit it—I like to indulge my children a little. Can you blame me? Having me for a father makes their lives both easy and diffi-cult at the same time, and it's harder than I can tell you to strike exactly the right balance. I want my kids to be happy and secure and comfort-able, to have everything—including what I call the fire in the belly. That's what got me to where I went then, and to where I am today.

But I made that long commute to school, and they get a ride. Am I too easy on them?

I got down to the kitchen around seven-thirty that morning and began lining up the breakfast fruit: apples, grapefruit, strawberries, and can-taloupes. I'm a big believer in eating fruit every morning, and like my parents, I work hard to prepare it for my kids: peeling apples, slicing the grapefruit just right, cutting and de-seeding the cantaloupe.

A few minutes later, the five of them descended like a swarm of lo-custs, and made quick work of the fruit I'd prepared so carefully, with-out so much as a mumbled thank-you (unfortunately, I've been known to be guilty of this now and then myself). Then they wolfed down cereal, waffles, and eggs before we swooped out the door a little after eight.

I got back to my house around 8:45 and decided to switch on one of the morning talk shows. I'm not quite sure what made me do it that

Tuesday morning: I usually like to start my day with coffee, a bagel, and the *Times*. Today, though, I was ready, clicker in hand, for some Diane and Charlie, Katie and Matt, maybe even a little Bryant. I'm a restless clicker.

Then came the news.

There was a fire, they said, in the World Trade Center. Bad luck, I thought, but things appeared to be under control. It was now just past nine, and I was getting ready to head downtown for my weekly therapy session. Anger-management counseling is what the courts call it—or, more specifically in this case, what my ex-wife's lawyer calls it. I've been doing it now for about a year, and while I'm not sure I would've chosen to go if the terms of my divorce hadn't strongly suggested it—and while I don't exactly come out of every session full of calm insight—I have to admit the therapy has done a few things for me. More and more, I'm able to count to ten in certain situations that once would've gotten me going.

What I heard next, though, made me more scared than angry. As I was about to leave, I heard that a plane had just crashed into the World Trade Center's south tower, and that the fire in the north tower reported earlier had also been caused by a plane. It was suddenly clear that we were in the midst of some kind of terrorist attack. My heart was knocking like a hammer.

What should I do? I had absolutely no idea, except to proceed with my usual Tuesday-morning routine. I believe now that I must have been in some kind of shock. When I walked into my therapist's office, I said, almost casually, "Did you hear two planes just crashed into the World Trade Center?" He stared at me, seeming to wonder for a second whether I was serious or not. And then—incredibly enough—we proceeded to have our regular session, without another word about the attacks.

Somehow, the enormity of the situation hadn't yet sunk in. Perhaps it had something to do with my years of traveling as a tennis player, when I'd been forced to put plane crashes out of my mind just so I could keep flying every week. As a group, tennis players never discuss this kind of thing, the way race-car drivers don't like to talk about fatal wrecks. Besides, when you're young, you feel invulnerable.

I don't feel invulnerable anymore.

I got home just before ten and immediately became glued to the TV set. What I watched boggled my mind: first one, then the other tower collapsing, giving downtown Manhattan the look of a surreal war movie—panicked people running for their lives, mountainous clouds of dust—and, where we were on the Upper West Side, only eerie silence. Patty and I just stared at each other, stunned.

As the news came in, we started to worry about our kids. Our phones had gone out—what should we do? What should the school do? What was going to happen next? We came out of our stupor long enough to realize that if there ever was a time to round everyone up and cling together, this was it. I just wanted to hug my four girls and two boys, as much for my sake as for theirs.

Fortunately, Ruby, our sixteen-year-old, had her cell phone with her, and she was able to reach us; soon I was on my way, on foot, to pick up all the kids. As I walked uptown, still in a daze, I kept hearing sirens, seeing fire trucks, ambulances, and police cars shooting by. Other people looked dazed, too, standing around on the sidewalk, talking and staring. The city had been rocked, but it also felt as if it was starting to pull together in a strange new way.

For some reason, as I walked along, I thought about the 2001 U.S. Open, which had just ended a few days before. Now it suddenly felt like six months ago. As always, I'd worked hard doing my commentary for USA and CBS; as always, I'd loved the work. The tournament had ended on a down note for me: an exhibition match between Boris Becker and myself, which had been scheduled to follow the women's singles final between Venus and Serena Williams on Saturday night, had fallen through: Boris claimed an injury.

I had felt angry and disappointed, not just for myself but for Seniors tennis. The exhibition would have marked Becker's entry, at thirty-three, onto the Seniors Circuit—a tour into which I'd thrown myself whole-heartedly for the past six or seven years, but which had been struggling financially of late. Boris's almost casual withdrawal from a big match at the U.S. Open didn't seem like a good sign.

But all at once, all of that felt incredibly trivial and far, far away. I just wanted to see my children, right away, and take them home. Why, I wondered, did it take such a horrific event to make me appreciate what was really important?

ONE NIGHT LAST JULY (in what now seems like an infinitely more innocent time) I went to a Mets game with my son Kevin, his friend Josh, and Josh's father, who's a friend of mine. We took the subway both ways.

I wore a variation of my usual walking-around-New York outfit: leather jacket and baseball cap (Mets or Yankees, Rangers or Knicks). And the whole ride out there, and the whole way back, not a single person bothered me. As we got close to Shea, I saw a guy who seemed to be trying to maneuver to get my autograph, but I just pretended not to see him, and then the crowd pushed us out the door, and that was that.

Part of me really enjoyed being left alone. I thought, *That's exactly what I want. Right?* Then I thought, *Well, maybe that isn't exactly what I want.*

It's hard to describe what it was like to be in my shoes for the fifteen years I spent on the men's tennis tour. It was a pretty wild ride.

It didn't hurt that I happened to come along at exactly the right point in history. For a decade, from the mid '70s to the mid '80s, professional tennis went through a boom the likes of which it had never enjoyed before, or have since. The money in the game was unprecedented, as was the electricity. Starting with Bjorn Borg, tennis players became more than just sports stars. Back then, even rock musicians aspired to be touring tennis pros. (Of course, *we* all aspired to be rock musicians.)

Borg was three years older, but had turned pro at a younger age than I did, and there never seemed to be anything especially boyish about him—even if he did spend his spare time reading comic books. He was remote, soulful, self-contained: The less he showed of himself, the more the girls screamed.

From the start, when I came out of nowhere to reach the semifinals of Wimbledon at the age of eighteen, I was a bad boy in the public's eyes. (I read somewhere that when Thomas Hulce was studying for his role as Mozart in *Amadeus,* he looked at videotapes of me acting up on the tennis court.)

My friends on the tour called me Junior. (My dad is John Patrick McEnroe, Senior.) To the public, I was Super-Brat, McBrat, McNasty— all those snide nicknames—or just plain Johnny Mac, everybody's naughty brother or son or cousin or neighbor, the guy people loved to hate, or (maybe) hated to love. Tennis players had had tantrums before, had yelled at umpires before—Pancho Gonzalez, Ilie Nastase, Jimmy Connors—but no one had done it quite the way I did.

People had an incredible reaction to me right from the start. Maybe my rages stirred up something that they'd had to bury or swallow as kids. I don't know. Whatever it was, the public really sat up and took notice.

Most people dream about being famous, but as the saying goes, be careful what you wish for. There were times when I would have loved to get away from my high visibility. I tried. Once I took a vacation trip to Fiji, thinking that surely, out there in the vast reaches of the South Pacific, I could become an anonymous American citizen for a few days. What I hadn't realized was that 90 percent of the tourists who went to Fiji were Australians—the world's biggest tennis fans. G'day, Mac!

To this day, I often feel as if my name is written across my forehead. It's hard to walk down a street anywhere (and especially in my beloved

Manhattan, where walking down the street is one of my favorite occupations) without being spotted, and called out to, as if the person knew me in the fifth grade.

Most of the time, the experience is positive. Sure, I could live without being asked for my autograph in the middle of dinner. And the fact is, I don't really like to give autographs to anyone over eleven or twelve years old: What can my chicken-scrawl mean to anybody who's not a kid—besides money on the sports memorabilia market? (But don't get me started on that.) And my signature isn't worth that much.

But having someone come up and say, "Hey, John McEnroe, you're the greatest tennis player that ever lived!" is not exactly difficult to swallow. Or, "Hey, tennis isn't the same since you've been gone!" Or "That Davis Cup victory in ninety-two was amazing!" Or "I really appreciate your making that stand on South Africa." (Back in 1980, someone offered me a million dollars—an unbelievable amount at the time—to play a one-day exhibition against Bjorn Borg in Sun City. I turned it down—it didn't feel right—little knowing how many friends I would win in the process.)

I don't get tired of such compliments. I feel proud of having earned them. And—I admit it—there's a part of me that's addicted to the attention.

It's one reason—I'll also admit this—that I'm writing this book. It's not just to get attention, but to do some serious thinking about how much attention I actually need, and why I need it (as you've probably figured out by now, that title on the cover is really half-joking and half-serious). I truly do wonder sometimes: Will I be totally forgotten at some point? Will I end up walking around wishing for what I don't have anymore? People always seem to want what they can't have, which seems a rather pathetic part of human nature to me. Will I be the guy going around saying, "Hey, remember me?"

I hope not.

At worst, I know people have seen me as a kind of caricature: a spoiled, loudmouthed, ill-tempered crybaby. I don't deny I've acted that way a lot (though I've almost always instantly regretted it). However, I sometimes worry that as I get older, that caricature is getting more deeply etched—that maybe it's all I'll get to leave to posterity.

I worry when the best my own agent can seem to do for me is say, "Hey, are you interested in playing Anna Kournikova?" Am I really that much of a caricature that the best gig I can get now is playing Kournikova? Is that what it's come down to for me at forty-three years old? Is that what it's come down to for tennis? I think it shows how many problems there are for the game when the main topic of conversation at the 2000 U.S. Open seemed to be my comments about Venus Williams and whether I was going to play her. (And when I brought up the subject in the first place, in the course of being profiled for the *New Yorker*, was it just a way of promoting myself? I'm still not sure.)

I'll tell you right here and now, though, that I have a lot of other fish to fry besides playing Anna Kournikova or Venus Williams—and I know the same is true for them.

I feel there has to be some real seriousness in my life—in all our lives—since September 11th. It's as if we finally have to face the reality that we've been avoiding for a long time. Those beliefs we all depended on—"Buy any technology stock, it's going to go through the roof"; "No one would ever do anything to the United States of America"—have been shattered. I certainly hope something good will come out of all that's happened—that the new reality is one we can live with.

At forty-three, I'm a father of six. I don't want to be a caricature anymore—in some ways, I feel I've hidden behind that for a long time, or at the very least, I've gotten by without having to be particularly mature.

See, part of the magic of playing tennis for a living is that it lets you act like a kid for as long as you can keep going. Now, some of you will say, and I agree, that it's good to keep that kid in you, but every kid has to grow up sometime, or else wind up a case of arrested development.

I always considered myself more well-rounded than most tennis players: I read, I thought, I looked at the outside world. But I always looked at it from a distance. It was hard to get away from the feeling that everything revolved around my own closed little universe, one I ventured outside of just to get perks—to get good seats at a concert, or meet people I would never have known if I weren't a famous tennis player. And I didn't venture out of it a great deal. In a lot of ways, I was really oblivious to the outside world. And let me tell you: Once you get away from the real world, it's very difficult to make that transition back into it. Look at all the ex-celebrities who wind up sick or angry or burned-out. Or dead.

There was a time—I'll admit it—when my head was so big it barely fit through the door. Having kids, I hope, changed all that for me. Having kids brings you down to earth right away, unless you let other people raise them, which I was never about to do.

Imagine that: Johnny Mac a forty-three-year-old father of six! When I first stepped out onto the world's stage, I was a chubby-faced eighteen-year-old with a mop of curly brown hair and a red headband. Today I'm a lean-faced man with thin graying hair, lines in my cheeks, a small silver hoop in my left earlobe, and a roses-and-thorns tattoo on my right shoulder. I can change a diaper, calm a tantrum, dry tears, make breakfast.

I'm still in good shape. I play tennis almost every day and work out on a stationary bike or jump rope when I can't find the time or want to mix things up. My vision is still sharp enough (around 20/15), and my reflexes quick enough, that on a given day, I can give anyone on the men's tour a run for his money for a set or two. My standards—as you may remember—are rather high on a tennis court, and I put enough work into my game so that I don't disgust myself out there. Until recently, I actually considered going back to playing Davis Cup doubles again, after a break of nearly a decade. But you'll have to ask my brother Patrick about that now.

On the other hand, I'm not kidding myself. No one knows his own body like a professional athlete, and I fully realize that the machine God gave me is nowhere near as flexible as it used to be, that I've lost the inevitable step or two along the way. As somebody who thinks almost obsessively in numerical terms (when I was a little boy I used to amaze my parents' friends by multiplying and dividing large numbers in my head), I'd say, objectively speaking, that I'm about 60 percent of the tennis player I was in my prime.

Which is not too shabby. But then again, I'm not really a tennis player anymore.

So what am I?

For one thing, I've been a tennis commentator for the last ten years, with enough pride in my work to feel that I'm at the top of my profession. This didn't just happen by itself. As you know, I've always had a certain facility for speaking my mind, but commentating demanded that I focus my thoughts, speak in complete sentences, and learn when silence was more valuable than talk. In short, it was (and still is) hard work. And so I had to learn the ropes.

Fortunately—as in my tennis career—I had great teachers. I've always been happier as a team player than as a solo performer, and my work with great broadcasters like Dick Enberg and Ted Robinson (and producers like Gordon Beck and John McGuinness, who gave me the freedom to be myself) has been a joy and an education to me. I believe that the joy comes through on television and over the radio—that my commentary has allowed people to see a different part of me, a far more lighthearted and self-deprecating side than I ever allowed myself to show on the tennis court.

I've done a lot of growing up over the past quarter-century. On the other hand, like most people—maybe even more than most people—I'm still a work in progress. Anyone who's seen me play on the Seniors Tour knows that even if my temper has lost a step or two, I can still get pretty far out there. It doesn't happen nearly as often as it used to—for one thing, because I don't play nearly as much as I used to—but now even a little bit feels like way too much (and the fact that people *expect* me to go too far doesn't make matters any easier).

I'm trying to work it out. One of the things I'm striving to come to terms with is the deep-down part of me that isn't completely willing to give up my anger. After all, I feel certain that it's part of what drove me to the top, and though I may not be at the top of my game anymore, that fire in my belly is still hot. Where would I be if I let it go out?

And what exactly do I need it for now?

PRIDE IS A FUNNY THING. While throughout my playing career, I had a lot to be proud of—and much to regret—I was never one to dwell on things. After all, I'm a serve-and-volley player: my whole game was, and still is, based on moving forward, always forward, then making the winning shot.

But once your career is over you're in a funny place if you've done reasonably well as a professional athlete, namely: Where do you go from here?

During my whole career, I basically went from one thing to another: The next thing always just came around the corner. Make no mistake, I had goals along the way—to win the NCAA's, to win Wimbledon, the U.S.

Open, the Davis Cup; to try to emulate my hero, Rod Laver—and I achieved a lot of them. In the last few years, however, I've given a lot of hard thought to who I was, who I am, and who I want to become.

I'm very proud of my tennis career. I won 77 singles tournaments and 77 doubles—154 tournament titles in all, more than any pro ever to play the game. My singles record puts me in third place, all-time, after Connors and Ivan Lendl, and in doubles titles I'm second only to Tom Okker, who won 78.

Think about how few great players had significant records in both singles and doubles. Not Borg (he almost never played doubles), nor Connors, nor Lendl. Think about how few American stars of the modern era have played Davis Cup. One of my very proudest achievements is having helped resuscitate the Cup in this country, starting in the late '70s, a time when the other top Americans—especially James Scott Connors—weren't especially interested in wasting their energy on playing for practically nothing when there was so much money to be had in tournaments and exhibitions.

Call me corny, but I've always been extraordinarily proud of representing my country: There's simply no thrill in tennis quite like it. You may remember the pictures of me running around the court with an American flag after our dramatic victory over Switzerland in my last Davis Cup tie in the final year of my career, 1992. (A meeting between countries in Davis Cup is called a "tie.") In all, I played for the cup in thirty ties over twelve years, winning forty-one singles matches and fifty-nine overall.

The main point, though, I'd like to think, is not the number of matches I won, but the five cups I helped gain for the U.S.A.

I guess you could say that history, and whatever part I've been able to play in it, has always felt extremely important to me. My idol, Rod Laver, has a rock-solid claim to being one of the greatest tennis players of all time, and for a very good reason: He achieved (not once but twice!) the colossally difficult feat of winning all four major titles—the French Open, Wimbledon, the U.S. Open, and the Australian Open—in a single calendar year.

I was never able to do it. I won three Wimbledons and four U.S. Opens, but never a French or Australian Open.

Pete Sampras has won thirteen Grand Slam titles, and even though the French Open has eluded him, he's won seven Wimbledons, four U.S. Opens, and two Australians—an unbelievable, maybe unbeatable, record.

Like me, André Agassi has seven Grand Slam titles altogether; but unlike me, he's won all four of the majors, even if not in one calendar year. His place in history is secure.

Where does that leave me? I guess only time will tell.

I did win over $12 million in prize money overall, and, with the help of my dad and some other wise heads along the way, invested my winnings and endorsement proceeds intelligently and conservatively enough to be able to support my wife and children in great comfort. The endorsement money came slowly at first, because of my bad-boy image, but it built up fast once Madison Avenue, or Phil Knight, more specifically, learned how to market me. I still have significant endorsement deals today, especially with Nike.

Why, then, do I still feel driven?

A lot of it has to do with my tendency to see the glass as half-empty. I'm smart enough to know that there's no sense thinking about what you didn't do instead of what you did. You lose perspective if you compare yourself to people who are out of reach or who it's inappropriate to compare yourself to.

But sometimes I do it anyway.

I'll confess it: I feel I could have done more. There are nights when I can't get to sleep for thinking about the Australian Opens I passed by when I was at the peak of my game and always felt I'd have another chance; the French Open that I had in the palm of my hand, then choked away.

I can practically hear you saying, "Come on, McEnroe! You're rich, famous, and healthy; you have a loving family, a more-than-comfortable life. You've done amazing things and been to amazing places—things and places most people can barely dream of. Why not just relax and enjoy what you have?"

Here's what I'd say back to you: I'm working on it, hard.

But at the same time—I'm a serve-and-volley player. My style is, as it's always been, to move forward, always forward.

My standards for myself are, as they've always been, extraordinarily high.

Why should I change now?

2

WHERE DID IT COME FROM? That's the question interviewers always work around to asking me. *How did you get that way?* And the first thing I tell them is, I'm a New Yorker. New Yorkers don't hold anything back—sitting in traffic or just walking down the street, we lay it on the line, and we don't whisper when we do it.

My dad's like that. He grew up on the Upper East Side of Manhattan, but not the fancy Upper East Side—it was the patchwork of Irish, German, Italian, Polish, and Hungarian working-class enclaves known as Yorkville. His father, John Joseph McEnroe, immigrated here from Ireland in the early 1900s, and worked as a bank messenger and security guard. (He also made a little money on the side as a trombone player in Irish bands, so I come by my performing interest honestly. My actual musical talent, though—that's another question.)

Coming from such a humble background, my dad did extremely well to be able to go to college at all, let alone work his way through night classes at Fordham Law School and wind up as a partner in one of the biggest law firms in New York.

But Dad has never forgotten his roots: He's full of Irish music and humor; there's nothing he likes better than to get together with friends and have a beer or two, and sing and tell jokes at the top of his lungs (unlike me: I can't remember a joke to save my life). I still remember how boisterous my parents' parties were when I was growing up—and how, the next morning, my dad would always be bright-eyed and full of energy, ready to go at the world again.

As those of you who watched tennis in the '80s may recall, my mother was much quieter: My shyness, I think, comes from her. And some of my edge. My mom, Kay—born Katherine Tresham, the daughter of a Long Island deputy sheriff—tended to see the world in a somewhat harsher light than my father, who always seemed to have a smile and a kind word for everyone. My mom has never been as trusting of outsiders as my dad is; she could hold a grudge with the best of them. Unfortunately, I'm like her in those ways, too.

My parents met in New York City in the mid-'50s, when my father was home on vacation from Catholic University in Washington, D.C., and my mother was working as a student nurse at Lenox Hill Hospital. Typically enough, their relationship started at a bar one night, when a couple of my mother's nurse friends ran into my dad and some buddies of his. Dad didn't hit it off with any of those nurses, but they introduced him to a girl who turned out to be perfect for him. John and Kay got married while Dad was in the Air Force, and I was born on February 16, 1959, at Wiesbaden Air Force Base, in West Germany.

When my father got out of the service, we moved to an apartment in Flushing, Queens, home of La Guardia Airport and home-to-be of the New York Mets. Dad worked during the day as an assistant office manager at an advertising agency and attended Fordham Law by night.

There's a story that's typical of my mother: When Dad finished his first year, he proudly told Mom that he was second in his class. "See, if you had worked harder, you could have been first," she said. (The next year, he was.)

We were still in Flushing when my brother Mark was born in February of 1962, but then, shortly before Dad's graduation, we made the big move to the suburbs, way out east to Douglaston, Queens—first to another apartment, and then to a two-story saltbox house at 241–10 Rushmore Avenue.

Douglaston was a typical New York–area bedroom suburb: nice, safe, clean; nothing fancy. The houses were small, square prewar Cape Cods and Colonials; there were a lot of young families like us, with a station wagon in the driveway, a barbecue grill on the back patio. Kids rode their bikes, played football and stickball in the street and at Memorial Field, played basketball in the driveway. It was *Leave It to Beaver,* Queens style.

I even had a paper route when I was ten and eleven, delivering *Newsday* and the *New York Times* on my bike. It was brutal work: I made about a buck-fifty to two bucks a week, and people didn't exactly throw around the tips—it was four cents from one person, exact change for $1.86 from someone else.

I was seven and a half when my baby brother, Patrick, was born: I took vague notice of the fact and then went on about my business, which, from the time I could stand up and walk, was mainly one thing: sports, sports, and more sports. If it had a ball, I played it—and was good at it. A story my dad likes to tell: When I was four, we were playing in Central Park one day. He was pitching a Wiffle ball to me, and I was whacking some pretty good line drives with my yellow Wiffle bat. An older lady walked up and said, "Excuse me, is that a little boy, or a midget in disguise?"

For a long time, I didn't get much bigger than that—"Runt" was what the big kids at Memorial Field used to call me. But I was good enough that they let me play anyway. Team sports like basketball, football, and baseball were my favorites. In softball games, I learned to hit from both sides of the plate, because of the peculiar configuration of the field at P.S. 98. Soccer came a little later. I always enjoyed the camaraderie of a team. I remember long summer evenings playing stickball out on Rushmore with my good friends Andy Keane, John Martin, and Doug Saputo, evenings that seemed like they'd last forever.

The McEnroe males were a sports-obsessed group, and we were vocal about it, whether we were rooting or playing. We were vocal about everything. We all loved each other, but we were definitely a family of yellers when I was growing up, my father leading the way, blowing off steam or just making friendly noise. We didn't hold back in our household.

At the same time, my parents had a serious and demanding side. They expected achievement.

One day, I fell off my bike. I told my mom, "My arm hurts." She was an operating-room nurse at the time, and she knew about hurt arms. She felt the arm, thought it was just a bruise, and said, "Go back to the tennis court." Three weeks later, it was still hurting, and I was still complaining. Finally my mom took me to the doctor. I had a fractured left arm.

And on moral matters, there were no gray areas: Everything was black and white, either right or wrong, period. They always drummed it into me: "Tell the truth. Be honest at any cost."

My mom and dad knew that education was the ticket to moving up in the world. The public schools in Douglaston were part of the reason a lot of young families moved there from the city, but in my parents' eyes, public school wasn't good enough for the McEnroe boys. I started off at St. Anastasia, a Catholic school not far from our house, but when I was in first grade (as Mom tells the story), one of the teachers said, "You should really get him out—he's much too bright." And so my parents sent me—

on partial scholarship, but at no small financial sacrifice—to Buckley Country Day School, a twenty-five-minute bus ride away in Roslyn, Long Island.

My mom and dad were strivers in every way; they fully bought into the American Dream. It was a restless dream for them, and a big part of it was about where you lived. We lived in four different places during my Douglaston years: the apartment, then three different houses. Once—I swear—we moved next door. Better house, my mom said. But damn, there was less of a yard to play football in!

In the summer of 1967, we made a short move that was significant in more ways than one: a mile north, over Northern Boulevard and the Long Island Railroad tracks from Douglaston to Douglaston Manor.

Just as the name sounds, Douglaston Manor was the right side of the tracks, a step up in the world, and our new house at 252 Beverly Road was also just down the block from a place called the Douglaston Club, which my parents had joined while we still lived on Rushmore.

The Douglaston Club wasn't fancy—just a clubhouse, a pool, and five tennis courts—but it was nice, and it meant something to an upwardly mobile young family. Tennis meant something, too. In those days, it was still very much a country-club game that you played in white clothes, exactly the kind of game a young lawyer for a white-shoe Manhattan law firm ought to be playing. And since Dad knew I loved any game that involved a ball, we both started playing it at the same time. Both of my brothers also began tennis in those early Douglaston Club years: Mark at age five, and little Patrick at three, when he used a two-handed backhand because it was the only way he could lift the racket!

I started taking group lessons with the club pro, a high-school teacher named Dan Dwyer. The family legend—there might even be some truth to it!—is that at the age of eight, when I'd only been playing for about two weeks, I entered the Douglaston Club's 12-and-under tournament and got to the semifinals with three other boys, all of them twelve. I lost, but a few weeks later, in another tournament, I was with the same three guys, and this time I won. At a club banquet, Dan Dwyer gave me a special award—a five-dollar gift certificate at the pro shop—saying, "I'm predicting we're going to see John at Forest Hills someday."

After Dwyer left the club, he was replaced by a nice old guy named George Seewagen, whose son Butch actually played on the circuit for a couple of years. I also took some lessons with Warren McGoldrick, a history teacher at Buckley.

Because I was so small for my age, I wasn't getting a huge amount of power out of my wooden racket. I was fast on my feet, though, and my vision was good enough that I saw the ball very early: I seemed to have an instinct for where my opponent was going to hit his next shot. Between my fast feet and my sharp eyes, I got almost every ball back. I learned very early on that you don't have to overpower the ball to win tennis matches—if you get everything back, you're going to beat just about everybody.

But there was something else, too. From an early age I had good hand-eye coordination, and as soon as I picked up a tennis racket, there was another dimension: In a way I can't totally explain, I could feel the ball through the strings. From the beginning, I was fascinated by all the different ways you could hit a tennis ball—flat, topspin, slice. I loved the way a topspin lob would sail over my opponent's head, dive down just inside the baseline, then go bouncing out of his reach. I loved to take my racket back for a hard forehand or backhand, and then, at the very last millisecond, feather the ball just over the net for an angled drop-shot that would leave the other guy flat-footed and open-mouthed. I hit thousands of practice balls at the Douglaston Club backboard, testing all the possibilities (and sending quite a few balls into the backyard of Dick Lynch, a former defensive back for the New York Giants, who lived right behind the wall).

My parents were both intense in their own ways, and I guess they transmitted that to me through the genes. As the oldest son of two intensely striving people, I felt right away that a lot was expected of me. In 1969, my fifth-grade teacher wrote to my parents: "Johnny is a gifted child with a tremendous urge to do better work than any of his classmates." I had a rage not just to succeed, but to compete and win— whether it was tennis, Ping-Pong, or a Latin test at school, I had to come out on top, or I felt crushed. I was one of the best students at Buckley— my mom and dad didn't disapprove—and now my parents saw a way that I could stand out in sports, too. On George Seewagen's recommendation, they enrolled me in the Eastern Lawn Tennis Association when I was nine.

"Lawn tennis" is what they called it back then, when the three or four major tournaments—Wimbledon, the Australian, and Forest Hills—were still played on grass. It sounds fancy and exclusive, and it was. But things were changing fast. The year I joined the ELTA was 1968, a very significant moment for the game, Year One in the history of open tennis. Ever since the sport had been invented, the four Grand Slam tournaments had been closed to professionals. Amateurism (also known as shamateurism) was a typical bit of hypocrisy in a game that prided itself on its genteel trappings and looked down on anyone who didn't fit in: The top players all made money (though nothing like what they would make later), but the money was under the table. The world changed in a lot of ways in the 1960s, and in the tennis world, the big change in 1968 was that for the first time ever, professionals could now play in the same tournaments with amateurs. The money began to flow in.

I wouldn't see any of it for a while. At nine, I put on my white shorts and shirt and started playing ELTA junior tournaments at clubs around the New York metropolitan area. My mother would almost always drive me. As my results improved, I became eligible to play in national tournaments. My dad would take vacation days from work, and Mom and Dad, or sometimes just Dad, would go with me to these events around the country. I still remember my first national 12-and-unders tournament in Chattanooga, Tennessee. Chattanooga, Tennessee! To a kid from Douglaston, it might as well have been Mars.

I did pretty well in the tournaments. By the time I was eleven, I was number 18 in the country in the 12-and-unders. At twelve, I was number 7. I won matches, I got to the semis and even the finals—but I wouldn't win a national title in singles until I was sixteen. I like to think that a lot of it had to do with my size. Maybe it's lame of me (and maybe it's part of what drives me), but I've never thought, at any level I've ever played, that my opponent was just better. If I lost, there was always a reason (they were bigger, they were from California, etc.).

But losing was the hardest thing to get used to. I was never very good at it. People always ask if I had a temper when I was a kid. There's a famous story about Bjorn Borg: When he was nine or ten years old, he lost a point and threw his racket down, and his father wouldn't let him play for six months. He never threw his racket again.

Maybe that should've happened to me! I didn't throw my racket when I was a kid, though. I was ferocious on a tennis court, but when I lost a match, my usual reaction—until an embarrassingly late age—was to burst into tears. People used to say about me, once I shook hands after a losing match, "Here come the floods."

If I ever got mad at anybody back then, it was myself. When I missed a shot, I would send out a wail that could be heard clear across a tennis club. I just hated playing anything less than the kind of tennis I knew I was capable of. But my temper would have to wait a few years. For one thing, there weren't any umpires or linesmen in junior tennis—you called your own lines, which was obviously a tricky thing. A lot of kids cheated outright. I like to think I was fair—although even back then, I was notorious for claiming to be able to see the lines better than anybody. Still, I would even make calls against myself if I knew my opponent's shot had gone out, but felt galled at the prospect of his questioning my call.

By the time I was twelve, the lessons I'd been taking weren't doing much for me anymore. When my parents heard that a couple of kids from the Douglaston Club were going to a nearby place called the Port Washington Tennis Academy, they decided to check it out for me.

Port Washington was about a twenty-five-minute drive east from Douglaston, and Antonio Palafox was the head pro. Tony had played Davis Cup for Mexico, won the Wimbledon doubles title in 1963, and (very significantly, to me) was one of only two men who beat Rod Laver in 1962, the first year Laver won the Grand Slam. I remember going to meet Tony with my mom—I was so shy that I hid behind her legs.

I hit with Tony a little, and he let me in, but not in the most advanced group: The Academy took kids up to the age of eighteen, and—national ranking or not—I was only twelve, and a small twelve at that. Tony felt I had some work to do. There were a lot of strong players at Port Washington (including another talented twelve-year-old, a kid from Great Neck named Peter Rennert); I would have to establish myself.

There were three groups: The most advanced kids played from five P.M. to seven, the next-best came from seven to nine, and the weakest players came from nine to eleven. Tony started me out in the middle section.

My dad wasn't thrilled about that: What was I doing in the middle when he'd been taking me to all these national tournaments? It didn't sit well with his McEnroe pride. And Port Washington wasn't cheap. Was it worth it for me? Did I stand a chance of making it into the top group?

In his law practice in Manhattan, Dad had met a young Wall Street guy named Chuck McKinley—and it just so happened that McKinley had been one of the best tennis players in the world back in the amateur days of the '50s and '60s. Dad asked McKinley to ask his old friend Tony Palafox if I was a real prospect. Tony took another look at me.

When he looked again, he saw a kid who played very much the way he had played when he'd been at the top of his game: fast feet, good hands, the ability to think a shot or two ahead, and a sense of the court in all its dimensions and angles.

Port Washington wasn't all just tennis. A player spent a lot of time on the court, but he also hung around a fair amount between coaching and matches. There was a lounge on the second floor, with windows that looked down on the courts: I remember staring in awe at Port Washington's star, a blond sixteen-year-old named Vitas Gerulaitis (more about him later)—but you could only spend so much time watching tennis. There was no TV, and the owner, Hy Zausner, wouldn't allow cards on the premises, so we'd amuse ourselves by playing chess. We'd have marathon games, some of them lasting an hour or more. I was never a great player, but I was pretty good: I liked the strategic element of the game, planning ahead a move or two

Tony saw me thinking that way on the court—and getting everything back—and so he became my tennis teacher. He took me under his wing. I still play very much the way he taught me, taking every ball on the rise with a short backswing; moving forward, always forward, whenever possible.

Tony felt that the court wasn't utilized enough. If you watched the old guys play on tape, he said, it looked like they were just standing there and hitting the ball back to each other. Didn't they realize the idea was to hit the ball *away* from the other guy? Maybe it just wasn't considered proper in those stuffy old days of tennis.

Not that players like Bill Tilden, Don Budge, and Jack Kramer, or any of the other trailblazers, weren't great champions in their own right, but the more Tony showed me, the more straight-ahead their strategy seemed to me. I began to look at the court differently—as a mathematical equation, almost. The angles were everything. It wasn't about just hitting a slice and approaching the net. Sometimes you should slice it deep, but sometimes you could come in and slice it off the court—*use the angles.*

. . .

AFTER I'D BEEN at Port Washington for a couple of months, an amazing thing happened: Harry Hopman showed up. Harry was a walking legend of tennis, the great old Aussie coach who'd turned Laver, Roy Emerson, Ken Rosewall, and Lew Hoad, among many others, from raw boys into stars, in the process winning sixteen Davis Cups for Australia between 1939 and 1969. However, once the Open era began in 1968, Hop had a much harder time recruiting young talent, and in 1970, he and the Australian Tennis Federation parted ways. To my eternal benefit: The following year, Mr. H. became tennis director at Port Washington.

Harry Hopman left technique to others; he was only interested in you if you already knew how to play the game. From that foundation, he went to work on your mind and body. His players were famous for two things: never giving up, and being fitter than anybody. The two went hand in hand, he felt. You'd hear about the old days in Australia—the ten-mile runs, the calisthenics, the two-on-one drills. Harry would just work his players to the bone, and they reaped the benefits. By the time he got to Port Washington, however, maybe he'd mellowed with age, because he treated me differently.

I guess he saw something in me right away. He used to bring us in and give us the jumping jacks and double knee-jumps and all the rest of it, which most of the time I would do, but basically, I hated calisthenics and stretching. To me, that wasn't what I was there for. I always wanted to get to the tennis court. Because I was running around all the time anyway, I wasn't out of shape, so whenever I didn't show up for the calisthenics, Harry would just smile and say, "Oh, McEnroe's hiding in the bathroom."

It meant a huge amount to me that he had coached Rod Laver. Laver was the first guy I saw who did everything—hit topspin and slice on both forehand and backhand, served with different spins. He utilized every possible shot, all the angles. I used to have a poster of him on the back of my bedroom door. The fact that he was a lefty like me was a big deal, and that massive Popeye forearm of his just seemed so cool— bizarre, but very cool. I remember trying to figure out how I could make my arm like that.

Just like Laver, I used the same grip on every shot: forehand, back-hand, serve, and volley (I still do—slightly toward the forehand from a Continental grip. I don't think anyone else does it now.) The wristiness of his strokes was supposedly what had built up his forearm, but no mat-ter how hard I tried to play like Laver, no matter how many times I squeezed my wrist-builder, my left arm stayed the same size as my right. No muscles. I swear, I think I'm the only number-one player in history whose two arms are the same size.

I may have been short, but I wasn't short on self-confidence. After I'd been working for a few months at Port Washington, one of the pros set up a challenge match between me and a newly arrived sixteen-year-old from New Jersey named Peter Fleming. Peter must've been at least a foot taller than I was at that point, well on his way to his full height of six-foot-five. There's also a huge difference in strength and maturity between a twelve-year-old and a sixteen-year-old. I knew Peter thought I was an in-sect, beneath contempt, and he confirmed it when he offered me a hand-icap: He'd give me an advantage of 4–0, 30–love a set before we even walked out onto the court.

I beat him five sets in a row. Never get an insect mad! It was the start of a beautiful friendship.

Tony Palafox was a very laid-back guy, so while our playing styles were alike, my intensity was something new to him. I had energy and de-sire—the willingness to do what it takes—and part of that, I was start-ing to realize, was the willingness to set myself apart from other people. It was one of the first lessons I learned in tournament tennis: The better you get, the more you get put on some kind of pedestal. And as my British readers would say, the more people look to take the piss out of you.

I saw early on that there were a lot of great advantages to winning, but there was also one big disadvantage: Once you're on that pedestal, you're alone.

THE FUNNY THING IS, if you'd asked me when I was twelve what I wanted to be when I grew up, I would've said, "A pro basketball player."

I loved basketball, and I was good at it (though whether I could ever have become another John Stockton is another question). It was the same with soccer, football, and baseball: I always enjoyed being part of a team. I loved the camaraderie. It's what I loved about Davis Cup. It's what made doubles so important to me. If you're on a team, and you're angry or upset at something that happened in a game, you have people to share it with. It's the same thing when you win.

If you're not at your peak, you can hide it so much easier in a team sport. In basketball, you can play decent defense or set a pick; you can do a lot of little things to help out that aren't related to scoring. It's the same with soccer. As long as you have a lot of energy, run up and down the field, and keep your head in the game, it doesn't matter if you kick the ball with your toe instead of the side of your foot. I remember scoring a couple of goals that way back in school—it's not the way you're taught how to do it, but I did it anyway, the field was full of people, and no one was watching my form. No one cared; I was part of the team.

On a tennis court, you're out there all alone. People ask why I get so angry: This is a big part of it. I'm out there on the line, by myself, fighting to the death in front of people who are eating cheese sandwiches, checking their watches, and chatting with their friends about the stock market.

To be honest, sometimes, when I look back, I don't know how any of this ever happened to me. Sometimes I think I was pushed into something I didn't really want to do. My parents saw that I was good at it and better all the time; they nudged me, and I went along. I was a good boy, an obedient boy. (For example, throughout my junior-high and early high-school years, I was terrified about trying any type of drug, at a time when a lot of my friends were experimenting with marijuana and other substances. In retrospect, staying away from drugs during those years probably kept my motivation sharp.)

Tennis, obviously, turned out to be an incredible thing for me, an amazing roller-coaster ride, and a lot more good came out of it than bad, but the truth is that I didn't really want to pursue it until it just pursued me. Many athletes seem truly to love to play their sport. I don't think I ever felt that way about tennis. I looked forward to the practice and preparation, but the match itself was a constant battle for me, against two people: the other guy and myself.

Once my professional career began, I certainly enjoyed the *consequences* of playing—the adulation, the feeling of contentment at being a professional athlete and then reaching the peak of my profession, the money that came from it.

I guess I would correlate my story to those you hear about kids learning to play the piano. Every now and then, someone says, "I just loved to play six hours a day." But mostly they say, "God, my parents forced me to play, they forced me to take these lessons; but I'm sure glad they made me do it."

Look at almost any of the great players. Would they have succeeded anyway if they hadn't been pushed? That's the unanswerable question. Would Agassi have been a great champion if he hadn't been pushed by his father? Would Monica Seles, if her father hadn't quit his job and pushed her? It's difficult to say.

I had dinner with Richard Williams during the 2000 French Open (yes, we do speak to each other!), and he told me, "Kids have no idea what they want to do most of the time." Which is true. I had no idea I wanted to be a tennis player when I grew up. Richard's attitude about

Venus and Serena was "Look, I picked something great for them, something that'll give them a tremendous living and a tremendous life. It's crazy to think that they were capable of making that decision when they were young. So of course I pushed them, but they needed to be pushed."

And so my parents pushed me. It wasn't in a bad way—you know the horror stories about tennis parents—but they were the driving force. Somehow, deep in my soul, however, I know there was a positive side to it. I seriously doubt I would've been the player I became if I hadn't been forced into it in some way.

My dad was the one, mainly. He seemed to live for my growing little junior career—he was so excited about having a son with some actual athletic talent. Maybe it had something to do with the fact that he'd been the twelfth man on the varsity basketball team at Catholic University. (Sorry, Dad!)

He worked very hard five days a week, but his real pleasure in life, it seemed, was coming to watch my weekend practice sessions at Port Washington. He'd just stand there with a huge smile on his face—he never seemed to get bored with watching me play tennis. Sometimes (I confess) I'd think, "Come on, take a break, take your wife out to lunch!" But he didn't seem to want to do anything else.

I don't think I ever wanted to quit entirely, but I remember telling my dad that I wasn't enjoying it. I'd say, "Do you have to come to every match? Do you have to come to this practice? Can't you take one off?"

His response would either be to laugh—"Ha-ha! You're kidding!"—or act hurt. There was never an in-between. He never said, "OK, I'll go do something else." It was just, "It'll be all right."

The better I got, the harder it was to think about giving up the game. I know that Harry Hopman—who knew what he was talking about—began to tell people, "This guy could be really good" (interestingly, he even said this to my mom and dad, though he was usually very careful about what he said to parents). I remember when I was thirteen and I lost in the round of 16 at the National Indoors in Chicago, a tennis columnist named George Lott—he'd once been a great doubles player, and had won a couple of Wimbledons back in the '20s and '30s—wrote that I was going to be the next Laver. I was amazed, and a little more hopeful. The next Laver!

My parents were pretty impressed by that! Still, their heads weren't turned—which impresses *me*. They had strong ideas about my future, and in their minds, my future was going to be four years of college and a solid profession. (At one point in my teens, my mother said to me, in all seriousness, "John, why don't you become a dentist? You're so good with your hands.")

Mom and Dad always said, "Get a college scholarship." And then, once they met Hopman, who told them war stories about Davis Cup and playing for your country, it was, "Get a college scholarship and play Davis Cup."

In any case, I didn't play a great deal during the school year—which saved me, I think, from getting burned out. After that one National Indoors, I didn't go again. I would usually play the Orange Bowl in Miami over Christmas break. (My baby brother Patrick started his tournament career—at six!—in the 12-and-unders at the Orange Bowl. Mark was more interested in swimming.) The Easter Bowl was played in the New York area. It wasn't tennis-tennis-tennis. At least I did get breaks from it.

Meanwhile, though, I was still moving up in the rankings. My dad was so excited. He said, "You can do it, you can be the best. You can do it, you can *do* it!"

But I remember saying one smart thing at the time—the most brilliant comment I ever made. I said, "Dad, listen, don't talk to me about rankings. I don't want to be number one until I'm eighteen. Don't ask me to be the best in the fourteens. Just wait 'til the eighteens, because that's when I'll get a college scholarship. I'll work my way up and peak at the right time."

Which is exactly what I did.


IN THE MEANTIME, I got a look at my future when I ballboyed at the U.S. Open, at Forest Hills, for a couple of years, starting when I was twelve. The pay was $1.85 an hour—just minimum wage—but after the paper route, it felt like a major step up. Besides, I loved the work.

Not that it was a breeze, by any means. In fact, the first match I ever ballboyed in my life, I almost fainted on the court. Raul Ramirez was playing a Venezuelan named Jorge Andrew, the sun was blazing, and I started getting dizzy. They used to have orange juice and water on the courts at Forest Hills, so on a changeover, I dragged my way up to get some orange juice. Even then, I just barely made it through this match— which didn't even last that long; Ramirez won in straight sets. I thought, "God, best-of-five is intense."

I remember ballboying for Arthur Ashe against Nicky Pilic, and Pilic was just brutal. He was all over you: "Come on, give me the ball! Bounce the ball right! Here, two balls! Give me the other ball!" You had no idea what to do—you'd just throw anything, and then he'd get pissed off at that. I really felt like punching the guy. I thought, "If I become a tennis player, I'm never going to do that"—and in fact I was always pretty good about not getting on the ballboys. I think that's pushing the envelope. Or is that just the dad in me talking?

However, the match I really remember from those early days is one in which I was just a spectator: Ilie Nastase against a German named Hans Pohmann. I loved the way Nastase played—he was a genius with a tennis racket, plus he brought an incredible energy to a match: both positive and negative energy. To tell the truth, he was basically out of control that day, but I loved it. Probably only four people in the stands were for him—but I was one of them. Nastase just had this quality of making people love to boo him. It's even been said once or twice about me.

As far as I was concerned, Pohmann was just some cocky German guy who was faking cramps. He'd run during the point, and then cramp between points—unbearable! He was really milking it. And the crowd was just eating it up. Nastase was unbelievable, though: He even spat at Pohmann once. Then he tried to shake the umpire's hand after the match, and the umpire wouldn't shake! I loved it!

It was great to see all the guys who were like legends to me. Nastase was poetry in motion. Ashe's backhand was beautiful when he let it go, but to be honest, I thought the rest of his game looked a bit mechanical. He had a sort of herky-jerky serve and a weird chip forehand. I preferred Stan Smith's classic style.

I liked Guillermo Vilas, the Bull of the Pampas, early on. His look was great—the big, hairy chest, the muscular thighs, the flowing hair. There was something beautiful about him: It seemed so cool that he could be both soulful (he wrote poetry; he played guitar) and strong. He was incredibly fit, worked incredibly hard. Even though I didn't play like him, I thought his ground strokes were phenomenal.

I was thrilled to see Laver in person, even if he was in the final act of his career, and the great Ken Rosewall, another of Hopman's boys. It killed me the way he'd act tired in the warmup, mope around the court and look like the world was coming to an end—and four or five hours later he'd still be going strong (and his hair would still be perfectly combed)! People don't remember how much Rosewall, Mr. Understated, used to throw his racket. I'm not talking about once or twice—he used to throw it thirty to forty times in a match! It wasn't with the ferocity that I did it, though—he'd bounce it and toss it and kick it, but in a very, very low-key way.

The first year I was at Forest Hills, I freaked out when I saw Pancho

Gonzalez smoking after his match. I thought, *This can't be! Athletes don't do that!* And then, when I asked him for his autograph, he gave me a look which, if looks could kill, would have dropped me on the spot. He finally gave me the autograph, but he wasn't particularly nice about it. And he definitely had a cigarette in his hand. All I could think was, *Forget the autograph. How can Pancho Gonzalez smoke?*

I PLAYED FOOTBALL until the seventh grade. I was Buckley's quarterback, and played defense, too, until the day I got the wind knocked out of me. I vividly remember the coach yelling, "Get up! Get up!" I couldn't respond, because I couldn't breathe. I thought, for about ten seconds, that I was going to die. Later that day, I staggered home, and my parents said, "Hey, what about soccer?" And I said, "That sounds like a better idea."

The soccer team, however, basically consisted of all the people who couldn't make the football team. The soccer and tennis guys were considered sissies, which I found annoying. Here I was, working my guts out, and other kids thought I was some kind of wimp. In the years since, people have stopped seeing tennis (and soccer, for that matter) as a sissy game—though what hasn't changed is the sense that it's still too inaccessible and expensive. Something needs to be done about that.

In the ninth grade, I left Buckley and started making my commute to Trinity, and practically as soon as I arrived, I became known as "the tennis guy." It was an extremely minor distinction: people didn't exactly come out of the woodwork to watch my high-school matches. The fact that I lived in Queens, while virtually everyone else in the school was from Manhattan, also made me kind of an outsider.

Remember my saying I was a top student at Buckley? Trinity was where I discovered mediocrity, at least academically. Tennis and soccer became increasingly distracting—and so did girls.

Up to that point, my love life, if you want to call it that, had been a bit of a comedy of errors. I take the blame. I was shy and a little arrogant at the same time. I had plenty of athletic confidence, but I certainly didn't think of myself as God's gift to girls. As a result, I made a lot of fairly clumsy moves.

The first girl I ever kissed was Jeannie Gengler, behind the tennis bubble at Port Washington, in the seventh grade. It felt like a very big deal—to me, at least. After all, Jeannie was in the eighth grade! She was also from a big tennis family—her sister Margie was a player, too, who later married Stan Smith. And Jeannie really liked me. I don't know why, but she did.

So what did I do next? Not more than a couple of days after that kiss, I asked another girl in my class, Susan Weinstein, to go steady! I never said a word about it to Jeannie. Susan said she'd think it over.

This happened on a Friday, and I thought I was all set. Then Monday came along, I walked into class, and Susan gave me the big freeze-out: She was already going steady with someone else, she said. What had happened, of course, was that Susan and Jeannie had talked to each other. By Monday, it seemed as if everyone in the class knew what a jerk I'd been. I felt terrible about what I'd done to Jeannie and mortified about what Susan had done to me. It was awful.

By the time I got to Trinity, nothing had happened to bolster my sexual self-confidence (and it didn't help matters that I was one of the smallest kids, boy or girl, in the ninth grade.) I did like a few girls in my class—one, Katrina Vanden Heuvel, now runs the political magazine *The Nation*. I would stare at her, and try to talk to her, but when I opened my mouth to ask her on a date, nothing came out. The humiliation from seventh grade still felt fresh.

Miraculously enough, though, I found my first real girlfriend in tenth grade. Jean Malhame was a Douglaston girl, the younger sister of my buddy Jim Malhame. She was dark-haired and pretty, and she played a very decent game of tennis. God knows why *she* liked me, but God bless her.

In May of my tenth-grade year—this was now 1975—I took my first solo trip, to a resort called Walden on Lake Conroe, outside of Houston, to try to qualify for the Junior Davis Cup team. It would be a tremendous honor to make the team—not to mention the fact that if I did, all my expenses would be covered for the ten weeks I'd play over the summer. My parents had been shelling out a lot of money to take me to tournaments: I wanted to help out, and to feel a bit more independent, too.

There were twelve spots on the team, and most of the guys going out for them were a year or two older than I was, bigger and stronger and more accomplished. Nobody in the 16-and-unders had ever qualified for JDC before.

I was in Texas for a week and a half, and it was unbelievably hot and humid. I'd never felt heat like that before. Primarily because of my light skin, heat has always been my worst enemy on a tennis court. My nerve endings frazzle, my concentration wanders; it's very difficult for me to gather my skills and play my best.

We played nine matches in ten days, and I was four and four going into the final. Everything rested on that last match: If I won, I was on the team; if I lost, I wasn't. I was playing a guy named Walter Redondo, a seventeen-year-old who, as a five-foot-ten fourteen-year-old, had beaten me badly a couple of years before in the national 14-and-unders. Walter was a sort of Hawaiian-looking Hispanic kid from California, still a crucial few inches taller than I was (like everybody else), and built like an Adonis. He had a beautiful game: His serve, volley, and groundstrokes were all picture-perfect. A lot of people thought he'd be the next big star in tennis.

But—probably with Harry Hopman's voice whispering in my ear—I wanted badly to play Junior Davis Cup. When I phoned my parents the night before the match, I told them that no matter how hot it was, I was going to stay out there as long as I had to and win.

And that was just what happened. I beat Walter in a dogfight of a two-setter, 6–3, 7–5. I think, ultimately, that I just wanted it more than he did. As it turned out, he had peaked—both in height and in skill—at four-teen. He wound up playing a year or two in the pros, but he couldn't find his way. It's amazing how many people that happens to: They have the strokes and the fitness, but whatever is driving them isn't driving them hard enough.

That match was a real turning point for me, a huge confidence-booster. The long and short of it was, that day I was just mentally tougher than Walter Redondo. I also learned about myself that even if I didn't par-ticularly enjoy playing tennis matches—I hated losing them much more.

FROM THIS DISTANCE, I can see that at sixteen I was a combustible mix of maturity and immaturity, boldness and shyness. Toughness wrapped around a gooey center. I was an ordinary adolescent, and also— it was beginning to seem—some kind of extraordinary one. However, it's never any picnic to be extraordinary (especially as a teenager), and the contradictions confused me. As graceful as I could feel on a tennis court, I was often staggeringly awkward in the rest of my life.

When I was getting ready to go away for Junior Davis Cup, Jean and I got together one afternoon to say goodbye for a couple of months. We played tennis at the Douglaston Club, then afterward sat by the court holding hands. Jean said, "You're not going to go out with any other girls while you're gone, are you?" And I said, "Look, I'll make a deal with you—I promise I'll only go out with one girl a week."

Now, where in God's name did I get off, saying that to her? And what was she supposed to say to me? Even after all these years, that afternoon is so embarrassing to remember. What on earth was I thinking?

I was feeling my oats, I guess. At the same time, though, I was ridiculously insecure. That summer, when I was on the Junior Davis Cup team, I used to carry six rackets with me onto airplanes, hoping someone would say, "Hey, you're a tennis player?" so I could say—very quietly and modestly, of course—"Yeah, I'm number two in the nation in the sixteens." Something like that. I just wanted some sort of recognition for who I was becoming, what I'd accomplished. But it never happened.

More signs of immaturity: Earlier that year, Port Washington sent a group of players up to a tournament at the Concord Hotel, in the Catskills. During those long, slow evenings after matches, my pal Peter Rennert and I did what kids often do, horsed around a little. One of our tricks was to light a towel on fire and knock on one of the other players' doors, throw the towel in the room and yell, "Fire!" Naturally I'd have a bucket of water ready, and just nail the guy. I know, I know. And it didn't help any when one of the victims told on me.

The straw that broke the camel's back, however, wasn't even my fault. One day, Port Washington went to Princeton to play their team. My matches were over, a few were still being played, and the rest of us were standing around by the bus, just looking for something to do. So Peter Rennert and I decided to go down to the Jadwin Gym and play a little basketball. Before we left, I told another Port Washington boy still playing his match, where we were going—I won't tell you his name. "Just come and get us when the team is finished," I said.

Peter and I got into a pickup game and played for a half-hour or so, and eventually the other player came down. He'd been sent by Hy Zausner, the head of the academy, to bring us back to the bus—but the guy didn't say that. He didn't say anything.

Just as he came in, someone else quit the game, and I said to the guy who'd come to get us, "Hey, we need another player." Now, did he say to me, "Listen, there are people waiting"? No, he just got into the game! So, another ten minutes went by, and in walked Zausner, furious. "How dare you keep everyone waiting?" he screamed at me. Not at anyone else; at me. "I'm sick and tired of your attitude!"

Not long afterward, my parents got a letter saying I was suspended for six months from the Port Washington Tennis Academy for bad behavior. "We've got to set an example," the letter said.

After I explained the situation, my parents were furious at Hy Zausner. "How dare he not tell us face-to-face?" they said. "This is totally outrageous."

Peter Rennert got the same six-month suspension, but his parents were mad at him, not at Zausner, so they went in and apologized, and Zausner dropped Peter's suspension. Meanwhile, my parents refused to go in at all.

It wasn't until much later that Peter told me about that, and meanwhile I'd gotten a whole theory in my mind that it was me against him, because he hadn't been suspended and I had. At the Easter Bowl that spring, Peter and I ended up playing each other in the semifinals, which made it a little more interesting: I thought, *I'm not going to lose to* him. And I swear to God, on the first point of the match—Hy Zausner was sitting right behind Peter—I hit a serve wide, and it went *boom* right into Zausner's forehead!

Anyway, because of the suspension, my parents never looked back to Port Washington. Meanwhile, Harry Hopman had left to go start his own tennis academy in Florida, and Tony Palafox had gone on to become head pro at a club in Glen Cove. So Mom and Dad called Tony up and said, "Listen, John would like to come work with you full-time."

Tony took me on full scholarship. I would get the chance to show my gratitude.

# 3

IN THE ELEVENTH GRADE, I stopped playing basketball. On the
face of it, this may not sound like a big deal, but in fact I was extremely
disappointed. Basketball had been a part of my life for at least as long as
tennis, and it was a chance for me to be part of a team and hang out with
friends. I'd always loved the game, and I was pretty good at it. (I remember scoring one-third of my team's points in an early C.Y.O. game.
Never mind that the final score was 3–2!)

Nor was I any less intense about basketball than about tennis. At
Buckley Country Day, my headmaster, Ted Oviatt, who doubled as the
basketball coach, once benched me for talking back during one of our
most important games. *Me!* I'll admit I probably never saw a shot I didn't
like, but I loved to compete. By tenth grade, I was on Trinity's JV team,
but to my dismay I found myself the nonplaying sixth man (shades of my

dad at Catholic University). I quit in disgust, but was lured back—it didn't take much—and, to my surprise, started the final four games.

Deep down, though, I knew my b-ball days were numbered. I didn't want to be a varsity benchwarmer, and the coach, Dudley Maxim, didn't seem to know my name. So I quit for real. The good news was that for the first time, I was able to play tennis more than two days a week during the winter. My game started showing it right away. Getting taller didn't hurt, either—by the time I turned seventeen, in February of 1976, I had almost reached my full height of five-eleven and three-quarters (which I round off to six feet).

Seventeen was also the blessed age when I got my driver's license, and just a couple of months later came that other huge rite of passage, getting my first car. It was—are you ready?—a secondhand 1972 Ford Pinto, the infamous burst-into-flames-on-contact model, in a color that had once been white. I loved it anyway. My parents bought it for me, for the grand sum of $100, from one of my dad's law partners, Don Moore; Dad and Mr. Moore used to drive it to work. But something definitely had to be done about that crummy exterior, and so Dad very generously took the Pinto to Earl Scheib in Long Island City and had it painted a very snappy shade of red, or at least that's what it was supposed to be. Actually, it came out orange.

An orange '72 Pinto! Add the Pioneer car-stereo system I'd won in a tournament (amateurs could take home prizes, but not cash) and I was all set.

I was also now out of the 16-and-unders and into the 18's—a big step up in terms of competition. I was mostly up to the task. I made the Junior Davis Cup team again, and was inspired once more by the coaching of Bill McGowan. Bill was twenty-four, a former player for Trinity University's national-championship team, and a great, no-nonsense guy. The previous summer, at the National Hardcourts, in Burlingame, California, I'd come down to breakfast one morning and ordered pancakes, scrambled eggs, bacon—and a hot-fudge sundae. Bill took one look at my chunky sixteen-year-old body and told me that henceforth I would be limited to one hot-fudge sundae a day, not three!

I had dropped more than ten pounds in the year since then, and had grown more mature physically and mentally. But Bill was still keeping a close eye on me. In my second summer of JDC, I was in a clay-court event in St. Louis, and the gray-haired, bespectacled umpire in my final match was a little slower with his decisions than I would have liked. I started to make my feelings known—loudly—and Bill called me over to the fence. "John," he said. "If you don't shut up right now, I won't hesitate to yank you out of this match and send you straight home." I shut up.

The other big thing that summer was that at a tournament at Kutscher's, the old Catskills resort, I met Stacy Margolin, a young Californian starting to make her mark on the junior circuit. Stacy was small, cute, athletic, and blond, and we were immediately attracted to each other. Over the next couple of years, we would get together at events around the country; in between, we talked on the phone and exchanged letters.

THAT BICENTENNIAL SUMMER, I was able to win the National Clay Courts, in Louisville, once again. At that point in my career, I was still very much a clay-court player. I'd always been able to get everything back from the baseline. Yet even though I had grown quite a bit, my serve was still suspect, and although I could volley, I wasn't quick or strong enough yet to take advantage of my net play. My doubles results were consistently better back then, and that's why: With only half the court to cover, I got to the ball more often.

Where I differed from most other baseliners was in the shortness of my backswing: Since I hit the ball on the rise, constantly moving forward, I could— theoretically—get to the net more easily and end the point with a volley or an overhead, instead of standing out there all day trading moonballs. Now if I could just get faster, fitter, and stronger!

A parenthetical note: People have always talked about what a good volleyer I was, and I'll accept the compliment. However, I think the most undernoticed of my skills was my speed at backing up and covering the overhead, which allowed me to close in on the net and get the best possible angle for the volley without worrying about the other guy putting a lob over me. I've always worked extensively on my smash. I see a lot of people in practice sessions—even a lot of professionals—go up and hit all of two or three overheads, thank you very much. It's not enough.

I believe firmly that players at every level should practice *every* shot, from any position on the court, using a variety of paces and spins. Lobs, drop-shots, and half-volleys—all shots that are too seldom paid attention to by recreational players—can change the outcome of a match.

And all that is just working up to practicing what has become the most important shot in tennis, the serve. A good server should be able to keep a receiver off-balance the same way a good baseball pitcher (Pedro Martinez is an excellent example) can befuddle hitters by mixing speed, placement, and spin.

When I came into the game, most of the tournaments were on clay, even on the professional level: Most people don't remember that even the U.S. Open was played on clay from 1975 through 1977. As a result, the top players then—Connors, Borg, Vilas, Gerulaitis, Harold Solomon—were mainly baseliners, which meant a lot of matches were excruciatingly long conditioning contests. I thought there was a need to take the game to a new place—but I didn't yet have the serve to do it.

Again, my Achilles' heel was fitness. That summer, I lost the finals of the National Juniors in Kalamazoo to Larry Gottfried, in five sets (I never did win that damn tournament). My conditioning—or lack of it—was a definite factor. I lost almost every best-of-five-set match I ever played in the juniors. As a kid, I'd been able to duck Harry Hopman's calisthenics sessions because I'd felt I was in naturally good shape from playing soccer and basketball and riding my bike. I was still playing soccer, and plenty of tennis, but I was at a different level now. I couldn't just play myself into shape. As I closed in on college age, the stakes were higher—and the opponents tougher.

Larry Gottfried was the younger brother of Brian Gottfried, who got to number five in the world in 1977. Larry was the number-one junior in '75 and '76; he was also my doubles partner, the guy who was always ranked just ahead of me, the super-hard worker. Larry would actually play a match and go practice afterward! I was amazed and appalled. But he never seemed happy with his success; he was one of those people who seemed to peak too early, and he enjoyed the road far too little.

Later that summer, thanks to my old friend and supporter, Gene Scott, an ex-player (and member of the 1963 Davis Cup team) who was the director of a small event in South Orange, New Jersey, I got a wild-card entry into my first ATP (Association of Tennis Professionals) tournament. In the first round, I beat a lefty named Barry Phillips-Moore, whose claim to fame was having invented the spaghetti racket. (Do you remember that crazy string job? It was eventually outlawed.) I won 6–0, 6–2, my first victory ever on the ATP tour. Then I played a guy from New Zealand named Onny Parun, a real character: he wore a string around his neck and would bite it in his mouth while he served, mumbling to himself the whole time. I thought, *I can't lose to this guy. He's horrible!* Well, apparently he wasn't *that* horrible: I did lose to him, 7–6, 6–1. He also happened to be number 18 in the world at the time. Still, the results were encouraging enough to make me think that maybe, just maybe, I had the stuff to play with the pros.

And I got five ATP points for winning one round! At the end of the year, I was the 264th-ranked player in the world.

Because I'd made it to that final in Kalamazoo, I was also given a wild card for the qualifiers of the U.S. Open. (I also played in the U.S. Open juniors, where Ricardo Ycaza of Ecuador beat me in the semis.) I won the first two rounds of the "qualies"—as I had done the year before, when I'd beaten Tony Parun, Onny's brother, before being demolished by one Vladimir Zednik.

This time, I felt more prepared to make a breakthrough. Then, in the third round, I played Zan Guerry.

Guerry was ranked something like 150 in the world, so it was a big round in more ways than one. It turned out to be a really long, contentious match, clay-court tennis at its worst, or best, whichever way you want to look at it.

We'd played for three and a half hours—I had lost the first set, 5–7, and won the second one, 7–5—and I was serving at match point, 5–4 in the third set. We got into an extended rally, and finally, when Guerry approached the net, I hit a backhand that shot by him, a winner, right on the line. The umpire (in the qualies there was one umpire on the court, who called both the score and the lines) said, "Game, set, match, McEnroe." And I thought, *U.S. Open! I'm in!* I broke into a big grin.

But Guerry didn't come up to shake my hand right away. Instead, he went over to the line where my shot had landed. He just stood there looking at the mark, while I waited impatiently to shake hands: I wanted to seal the match, fair and square, and I felt the handshake was a necessity, win or lose. A couple of guys on my Junior Davis Cup team, who'd been there to cheer me on, were calling, "Just walk off the court!" And I was thinking, *No, I'm not walking off the court. Not until I shake this guy's hand.* Meanwhile, Guerry was looking for a mark that showed the ball was out.

A minute went by, which is a long time when you're waiting for that final handshake. Finally, Guerry said, "No, no, no, that ball was out! *This* is the mark." The umpire got off his chair, squatted down, looked at the mark, and said, for the second time, "The ball was in. Game, set, and match, McEnroe."

I was thrilled. But now more people on my team were telling me, "Get off the court. Forget the handshake. Something's bad." Because Guerry was sort of stalling, still refusing to come up to the net. The commotion grew.

By now, a few minutes had gone by, they'd called the match for me twice, and—I'll never forget this—out of nowhere, a woman named Anita Shukow, who happened to be the head referee, came strolling out from behind a fence about 500 feet away. She'd been out of sight of the court, but someone must have heard the uproar and alerted her. She walked over, looked at the mark, and said, "If this is the mark, the ball was out. Deuce."

I was about to lose it—I couldn't believe this was happening. I kept saying (mostly to myself), "I'm not playing. Forget it. That's it. That guy called the match for me twice. This is over, period." But then, another part of me thought, *What if they default me? It's still deuce; I still could win this.* I was just two points away. . . .

So—of course—I folded completely and lost, 5–7. Now it was time for the floods. I totally fell apart in the locker room, crying and crying—I was so humiliated that this had happened, that this had been taken away from me!

But—are you ready for this?—there's a kicker. In the first round of the Open, Guerry came up against an experienced old Aussie pro named Ross Case—his nickname was "Snake"—and the exact same thing happened! Guerry was down 6–5, there was a close call on match point, and he looked for a mark that was out. The difference was: Case walked off the court within ten seconds. It was a lesson I learned the hard way about the differences between the juniors and the pros: When the final score is announced, get off the court.

I would soon learn a few more lessons.

It's funny: I seem to have a memory (and to this day I don't know if it's a real memory or not) that I later played Guerry in another tournament. I always said to myself, *If I ever play this guy again*—especially when I got better and could do a whole lot more on the court—*if I ever play this guy again, he's going to suffer like he's never suffered before. I'm going to drop-shot him and lob him, just keep him out there and make him look like a bum.*

Which is exactly what I did. Unless I did dream it. But I refuse to check the record books, in case it really was a dream.

AS I ENTERED my senior year of high school, I was the number-two junior in the country, but now that Larry Gottfried had moved up out of the category—he would never do as well again—I was the expected number one. My headmaster at Trinity, Robin Lester, was willing to give me a little leeway with my classes and homework so I could travel to a few tournaments. It seemed as if this could be my year.

Accordingly, that fall, I decided to finally try and notch up my conditioning. In addition to my soccer games, I started jogging for the first time in my life, one or two mile-and-a-half laps around the Central Park Reservoir every day after school. It felt like a major distance to this novice runner. It was also unusually cold in New York that autumn—or so it seemed to me. A little cold-weather jogging around the Reservoir, however, wasn't exactly the best preparation for the incredible heat of the Argentine Open, in Buenos Aires, in the Southern Hemisphere spring of November 1976.

I was playing the junior event, but many of the players were tough, up-and-coming, South American clay-court specialists. I'll never forget my semifinal match against one of the best of them, José-Luis Clerc, a tall, slim Argentinian who would later become a top-five player and one of my most formidable Davis Cup opponents. I won the match in what sounds like a routine fashion—6–3, 6–4—but thank God it was only two sets, because the sun was so broiling hot that one more would've done me in.

I spent twenty minutes in the shower after the match, just letting the cold water pour onto my head.

I was in no shape to give my U.S. Open juniors nemesis, Ricardo Ycaza, much of a match in the final. Still, I did have the pleasure of seeing Guillermo Vilas, the fittest guy of them all, win the main tournament. Just looking at him made me realize I would have to work a whole lot harder.

IN DECEMBER, I had a pair of big victories in Miami, winning the Sunshine Cup against Yannick Noah and Gilles Moretton of France in my last doubles match with Larry Gottfried, and winning the Orange Bowl, beating Eliot Teltscher in the singles final. Even though there were no international junior rankings then, the best foreign players all came to the Orange Bowl, so I was now effectively the top junior in the world. The months to come would confirm my status.

In January, I headed back to South America, traveling to Caracas for the Venezuelan Open Juniors, where my most vivid memory is not of the players I beat in a comparatively weak field, but of the soldiers sticking machine guns in the car window before we drove up the hill to the matches. In the world outside the safe old U.S.A., a lot was going on that I'd never dreamed of.

And then in February, I went to Ocean City, Maryland, for an indoor tournament on the Bill Riordan/Gene Scott tour. Riordan managed Jimmy Connors at the time, and he put together a series of non-ATP events that Gene directed. It was there, on my eighteenth birthday, that I coughed and hacked my way to a 5–7, 4–6 loss to Ilie Nastase.

I had bronchitis, a frequent problem with me until my airways matured. Physically and emotionally, I was still a kid. Being able to play one of tennis's greats, however, to such a close loss gave me the feeling again that maybe I really could play with the pros. My nineteenth year would more than bear that feeling out.

All this traveling was starting to make me feel very sophisticated, but my first trip to Brazil, for the Banana Bowl in March, convinced me I still had a lot to learn. I flew alone down to São Paulo, and when nobody showed up to meet me at the airport, I literally couldn't find anyone who spoke English. I'd been given a couple of phone numbers to call, but no one on the other end could understand me, either. If they'd spoken Spanish instead of Portuguese, I might've been able to say or make out a few words, but this might as well have been Chinese.

So I sat by the luggage carousel. And sat. Finally, after about an hour and a half, a fellow saw my rackets and said, "Tennis?"

"Yeah!" I said. He motioned me to follow him. As we walked off, I thought, *This guy could be anybody, anybody at all.* But what were my other options at the moment?

He drove me to the home of a Brazilian junior player named Cassio Motta, which seemed to be a kind of checkpoint for tournament participants. At least now I knew I wasn't being abducted. But the tournament itself was a two-hour drive from there, down to Santos, where Pelé had played soccer.

We were driving, it was absolutely pouring rain, and I swear to God, it felt like our driver was going a hundred miles an hour. It was scary how fast it was, and you couldn't see more than five feet in front of you in the rain. I was sitting in the back, with no seatbelt. Then suddenly, right ahead of us in the fast lane, an orange "Caution" cone appeared, and then another, and another, and then a broken-down car was right in front of us. All this happened in a second or two.

The guy veered right, and we started to skid, and just as we veered, a bus loomed up next to us, going just as fast as we were. We swerved, and skidded, and banged into the bus, but our driver didn't even slow down— he just took off and passed it! When we got to the end of the highway, the bus caught up and cut us off, and the bus driver began opening his door to try to block us; our guy drove up on the curb to get away from him.

Finally we stopped, the bus stopped, and the two drivers stood screaming at each other in the rain. It was a lovely introduction to Brazil.

There was this, too: Over the next few days, as I started to play my rounds, I noticed—there's always a lot of free time at tournaments—that the South American players were constantly going up to the fifth floor. I wondered about that for a while, then I found out what was going on. How can I put this delicately? Let's just say that there were ladies up there, and that money was changing hands. The Banana Bowl indeed! I never visited that fifth floor, however, or any similar establishment.

I won the tournament, by the way, beating a couple of guys named Andrés Gomez and Ivan Lendl in the process. Now no one could challenge my status as the number-one junior in the world.

MEANWHILE I'D APPLIED to college—Stanford, USC, and UCLA. Stanford was my first choice because UCLA and Stanford were the best teams, but I preferred USC to UCLA—George Tolley was the USC coach at the time, and he seemed a little more laid-back than Glen Bassett at UCLA.

I went on a college visit to Los Angeles; it was my first time there. L.A. was also Stacy's home town, and so we got to spend a lovely few days together while she showed me the sights, including the USC and UCLA campuses. At UCLA, I asked Glen Bassett, "So how do you run things here? What's your coaching style?" And he said, "Oh, we work really hard—we practice five hours a day." I said, "Thank you very much." That was it for UCLA!

In April, I played in my second Riordan/Scott event, a clay-court tournament in Virginia Beach, Virginia, that featured both Vilas and Connors; they were numbers two and three in the world at the time. I beat

Charlie Pasarell, who was number 49, and Bob Lutz, who was around number 30. It's true that both of them were more comfortable on fast courts than on clay; still, a victory was a victory.

As I was getting ready to play my semifinal against Nastase— again!—I very shyly (or so it seemed to me) walked out onto a court where Vilas was hitting with his manager, the crazed former Romanian Davis Cupper Ion Tiriac, and asked if I could warm up with them for five minutes. Five minutes was all I ever needed right before a match. For years afterward, however, both Vilas and Tiriac loved to tell the story about the cocky young McEnroe, annoyed that they were on the court at all, demanding to hit with the great Vilas.

Maybe, deep down, I was a little starstruck by Vilas in his greatest year. But even if I did still look like a kid, I was a lot more than a fan.

This time, I took Nastase to three sets.

In May, after Stanford accepted me for the coming fall, the United States Tennis Association gave me $500 and a plane ticket, said "Good luck," and I went off to play the French and Wimbledon Juniors. Since I had a couple of ATP points, I was also going to try to qualify for the main draws, and I planned to meet up with Stacy, who would be playing the juniors in the French.

Soon after I checked in to the players' hotel, the Sofitel, I did a double-take: Somehow I had failed to realize that my hotel bill wasn't going to be taken care of by the USTA, but by yours truly, J.P.M., Jr. That five hundred bucks had seemed like a lot of money . . . until I checked in. Now I did some quick calculations: The players' rate was around thirty dollars a night, and I was going to be in Paris for the three days of the qualifiers, and, whether I qualified or not, the fourteen days until the end of the junior tournament. After that came two weeks before Wimbledon, then two weeks *at* Wimbledon . . . five hundred bucks for seven weeks wasn't exactly going to cut it!

But before I could think about money, I had to play tennis.

In my head, I kept hearing what my Port Washington buddy Vitas Gerulaitis had told me before I came over: "Here's what's going to happen on your first trip to the French—you're going to play some guy from Europe that you've never heard of, and you're going to get your ass kicked."

Thank you, Vitas. Sure enough, the first round in the qualies put me up against someone named Robert Machan, a stiff from Hungary—or so I thought. Before I knew what was happening, the stiff was indeed kicking my ass, 6–3, 2–0. Then it suddenly dawned on me: I was hitting every ball to his backhand. That's common when you don't know someone's game. Out of desperation, I started hitting the ball to his forehand—and, lo and behold, Mr. Machan could not hit a forehand to save his life.

On to the second round.

MY BIGGEST DISCOVERY about tennis so far was that things seemed to get a whole lot more exciting as I went up the ladder. Paris in '77 was my first real taste of the big time, and I'd never seen guys work so hard. I'll never forget watching an American named Norman Holmes playing someone who was the French version of Norman Holmes, in the second round of the qualifiers. It was incredible how hard they were going at it— hustling and diving onto the court until their whites were completely covered with red clay. Maybe all of a hundred people were watching, but it was one of the all-time best matches I've ever seen.

Norman Holmes won the match, qualified, and eventually rose to around 100 in the world. He wasn't a world-beater that afternoon, but that wasn't the point. Watching him made me think, "If this guy can try that hard, there's no reason why I can't."

Who knew how far I could go if I pulled out all the stops?

•   •   •

I WON MY SECOND-ROUND qualifying match. All the while, though, I kept thinking, *I've got to find a cheaper hotel.* I knew a player named Lucia Romanova, one of the tennis-playing Romanov twins from Romania, who spoke some French, and I asked her if she could help me.

God bless her, she went all-out and found a hotel for about three bucks a night. The amenities were roughly what you'd expect, but was it too much to ask that the room have an alarm clock, and that somebody in the place speak English? I didn't have a travel alarm with me. "Could I be awakened?" I asked the man at the front desk. He answered me in French—"Screw you," probably.

Now I was panicking, because while my first two matches had been at five in the afternoon, the last round of qualifying was set for 8:45 in the morning. I was still jet-lagged, even after a couple of days in Paris—I'd been sleeping to noon or one o'clock—and I *thought* the desk clerk had understood that I needed a wake-up call, but I wasn't sure. I thought, *How in God's name am I going to get up in time?* My solution: I didn't sleep a wink the entire night. Just stayed up.

I went to play on zero hours' sleep, and somehow (it helps to be young!) I managed to beat my opponent, a typical clay-courter from Spain. I was in the main draw! Suddenly, a lightbulb went on over my head: If you made it into the main draw, you received sixty dollars a day in expense money. I went right back to that three-dollars-a-night hotel and checked out and checked back into the Sofitel.

I HAD A VERY LUCKY first-round draw—Alvin Gardiner, an Aussie journeyman—and won easily, 6–4, 6–2, and 6–0. Now I was cooking. I'd piled up six more ATP points—one point for qualifying, another five for winning a round. That's when I went up against Phil Dent.

Dent was an Aussie, an ancient twenty-seven years old, a seasoned Davis Cup player, and an extremely tough competitor. Current fans will know him better as Taylor Dent's father. He had a reputation for playing every point to the utmost, even if he was hopelessly down in a match. He came from that true Australian mold: Harry Hopman had driven his players mercilessly, demanding total physical fitness and mental toughness, pitilessly casting aside anyone who didn't measure up. It seemed, to me at least, that Phil Dent measured up.

From the moment our match began, the line calls were abysmal. Dent would hit a shot that was in by six inches, and the linesman would call it out. Every time it happened, I would tell Dent, "I can't take this point, we've got to play a let." I was used to the juniors, where you call your own lines.

All along, though, I kept noticing that no matter what happened on his side, Dent never once asked to play a let. True to form, he was one of the toughest opponents I'd ever faced, and after five hard-fought sets, he was the victor. And when we came to net to shake hands, he put his arm around my shoulder and said, "Sonny, this is the pros now. You play the calls, and if you have something to say, you tell the umpires."

Many people would say I learned that lesson a little too well in the years to come.


I MET UP WITH STACY, and between matches and practice, we got to see a little bit of each other. On the courts, I also bumped into my old Port Washington buddy Peter Fleming, who was in the main draw. Peter had just graduated from UCLA and was out on the tour, doing pretty well. We'd only seen each other a couple of times since he'd gone away to school—one of them was at the 1974 U.S. Open, where he and Vitas Gerulaitis had beaten Tony Palafox and me in doubles—and it was good to come across a familiar face in foreign surroundings on my first trip overseas.

The French juniors started in the second week of the tournament, and Stacy and I both began our rounds. When she was eliminated from the singles, however, she suddenly told me she had to go back to California. Family matters, she said vaguely. Figuring it was something sensitive, I didn't push the subject.

Meanwhile, a piece of luck came my way.

I ran into Mary Carillo, an old friend from Douglaston, who was actually playing in the main women's tournament. Two years older than I was, she had grown up just a couple of blocks away, on Knollwood Avenue, in the Manor. When I think about the odds of three world-class tennis players—myself, my brother Patrick, and Mary—all coming from the same little neighborhood, I shake my head. Her tennis career had followed a similar path to mine: She'd learned to play at the Douglaston Club, where we'd hit together now and then, and gone to the Port Washington Tennis Academy—where, just like me, she'd been coached by Tony Palafox and Harry Hopman.

By the time Mary had graduated from high school, she'd become one of the best women players in the country; instead of going to college, she'd taken a job at Mr. Hopman's new academy in Florida. Then she'd decided to give the women's pro tour a try, and now she actually had a pretty high ranking.

Certainly a lot higher than mine.

And that day at Stade Roland Garros, we had the following historic conversation:

"Want to try the mixed?"

"OK."

Thus are great mixed-doubles teams born. Mary and I had hit balls together, but we had literally never set foot on the same side of a court. What did that matter? When you're a kid, you figure you can do anything.

More important for us, though, was the fact that the mixed-doubles field was the weakest of all the events at the French—primarily because there wasn't much money in it. As the top male players finished the tournament, they left Paris, looking for greener pastures (literally: the grass-court tune-ups for Wimbledon were just beginning in England). Between Mary's ranking and my little handful of ATP points, we were allowed to sign ourselves up.

At the same time, I began playing the juniors, where, because of my successes over the winter and in early spring, I was a strong favorite. This didn't make me nervous—if anything, it had the opposite effect. My confidence was up, and I improved from round to round.

In the meantime, Mary decided that as long as we were in Paris with time on our hands, she'd get a little culture into me. At that point, I didn't know a Matisse from a Michelangelo. Mary did, though, and she took me out a bit—specifically to the Jeu de Paume, at the time a leading Impressionist museum. I wish I could say I was an eager student, but I remember looking at one of Monet's water-lily paintings and saying, "My baby brother Patrick has better than that on the refrigerator door at home."

Still, my eyes were starting to open just a little, and it was amazing to soak up Paris, although that first time, the art and the architecture looked so magnificent that I felt intimidated. The people also seemed unbearable to me, though we've grown to love each other since. I felt as if I was in a *National Lampoon Vacation* movie—Chevy Chase and Beverly D'Angelo are eating their lunch in a restaurant; he's saying, "God, honey, aren't they nice?" and the waiter is saying (in French, with English subtitles), "You stupid American asshole." That's exactly how it felt.

But not on the tennis court. None of my matches in the juniors was as tough as that five-setter with Dent, not even the semifinal against Ivan Lendl, whose number I seemed to have at the time. And amazingly enough, Mary and I were cruising, too: Our roughest match was a three-setter in the semis against Tomas Koch of Brazil and Cynthia Durner of Australia. In the final—which took place just an hour after my victorious juniors final against an Australian named Ray Kelly—we beat Florenta

Mihai of Romania and Ivan Molina of Brazil in straight sets. I had to shake my head in disbelief: I was a Grand Slam winner at the age of eighteen.

I had to shake my head about something else, too. On that last day at the French, I learned another brutal lesson, about tennis as show business. I played my juniors final in front of about three people—the organizers had helpfully scheduled it at the same time as the men's final, in which Vilas destroyed Brian Gottfried. Then, a little while after most of the Parisians had filed out of Roland Garros, Mary and I won our mixed final in front of a similar-sized gallery.

I would always have mixed feelings about performing in front of an audience, but I knew exactly how I felt about performing in front of nobody: rotten.

I wouldn't have to endure much more of it.

THAT LEFT TWO WEEKS before Wimbledon, so I went to England, practiced for a week on grass, and then played the qualifying matches for the tournament at Queen's Club in West London, the most important of the Wimbledon tune-ups. My opponent in the first round was Pat DuPre, from Stanford. We actually played indoors, on wood, because it was raining. Taking the ball early on the boards, I won the first set handily, 6–1. I thought, "This is pretty easy."

Then, all of a sudden, a woman in the crowd started yelling at me, riding me, really heckling me. I thought, "What's going on here?" It turned out to be DuPre's wife. She was all over me during the last couple of sets, and I lost the match, 7–5, 7–6.

It turned out that she had been doing it to other players as well—I'm not going to say it's the reason I lost, but it definitely threw me off. Here was another lesson: As you play better people in different circumstances, more and more things will start to happen that you have never experienced before. You learn to adjust. At the time, I was just flabbergasted.

My little run at the French had given me enough points to get into the Wimbledon qualifiers, so I figured, *What the hell.* My loss to DuPre had actually turned out to be a great thing—had I made it in, I don't think I would have had enough time both to play the tournament and to try to qualify for Wimbledon. So thank you, Mrs. DuPre!

LONDON WASN'T as intimidating as Paris—at least the language seemed roughly similar to mine. Once again, I managed to find myself more . . . economical accomodations: a dilapidated flat in Earl's Court, four tennis hopefuls to a room, for a couple of pounds a night. I have to say my choice was more out of frugality than necessity—I still had a little bit of my $500 left, and Wimbledon gave players $60 a day in expense money just for being in the qualifiers. So I was loaded!

The qualies were held at a pleasant but unremarkable club called Roehampton, about a half-hour from Wimbledon—whose organizers, I guess, wanted to keep the riffraff at a safe distance from the hallowed lawns of the All England Lawn Tennis and Croquet Club!

I actually came up against some pretty well-known players in the qualifiers, but they all seemed allergic to grass. For my part, I had a little experience under my belt, having played the National Grass Courts in Tuscaloosa, Alabama, a couple of times. The Roehampton courts were in horrible shape, but the organizers threw you out there anyway.

After beating Christophe Roger-Vasselin handily, and a rugged German named Uli Marten in three very tight sets, in the third round I played Gilles Moretton, my doubles opponent at the Orange Bowl. It was raining hard, but it was sink or swim as far as the organizers were concerned. I swam, winning in three routine sets, and I had qualified for Wimbledon.

I remember celebrating with a beer afterward, which came out of a wooden cask and was incredibly bad. It tasted like wood, and it was warm. I thought, *How in the hell do these people drink this? Where's my Ballantine? Who are these people?*

NOW THAT I WAS in the main draw, I felt I deserved a proper hotel room, so I moved into the Cunard International, which was so fancy that it had an ice-cube machine—which, in London, at the time, was nothing short of amazing!

There were still roommates, of course—only now the roommates were better players: Eliot Teltscher, my Orange Bowl finals opponent, who was on his way to UCLA and would eventually become a top-ten pro; and Robert Van't Hof, who was headed to USC and would win the NCAA singles championship in a couple of years (and who now coaches Lindsay Davenport).

There was a rigid hierarchy of players at Wimbledon: From the stars down to the qualifiers, guys tended to mix with their own kind. But when I ran into a guy named Jim Delaney—he was seven or eight years older than I was, and around 100 in the world to my 233—he was surprisingly friendly.

Jim had graduated from Stanford a couple of years before, and, unbeknownst to me, Dick Gould, the Stanford tennis coach, had asked him to do anything he could for me while I was at Wimbledon. I didn't find out about this until years later—thank you, Dick. At the time, Jim just seemed like a terrifically nice fellow, which he genuinely was.

He showed me the ropes around London. For a young player, one of the most important things to know is where to get good, cheap food—which, in London in those days, basically meant pizza and pasta. I had a blast. I enjoyed the city so much—more than I've ever enjoyed it since, even though I still love going there now—because it was the last time I was totally anonymous. I was also slightly clueless. There was a custom there: If the restaurant was crowded, someone you didn't know could just sit down at your table. One night, a strange guy sat down in our booth, and I said, "Who the hell are *you*?"

Delaney also did something else for me, something that really made a difference. Since he'd been on the tour a couple of years already, he knew the players—he could tell me about the strengths and weaknesses of the guys I'd be coming up against in the opening rounds. It was like having a coach for free.

But I still had to play the matches.

It was strange. As I rose through the juniors, I'd always had the idea that the main tour was something special—that those guys were the best of the best. But now here I was at Wimbledon, the main tournament, my first time, winning in the first round (Ismail El Shafei), the second (Colin Dowdeswell), and the third (Karl Meiler). And then in the round of 16, I beat Sandy Mayer, whose game Jim Delaney knew well from their time together at Stanford. That's when I started to believe that I really could be a professional tennis player. I remember thinking, "Either these guys are a lot worse than I thought, or I'm a whole lot better." The level that I'd thought existed between the juniors and pros—the Triple–A League of tennis—was simply not there for me.

COURT ONE, WIMBLEDON. There's nothing remotely like it in the world, and until you actually stand on it, it's impossible to imagine. The smell of the grass, the close-up electricity of the crowd, and the look of the place: how much more intimate it is than TV can ever convey; how vivid the colors are in person—the greens and purples of the backdrops and stands and emblems and uniforms, the whites and pinks and dusty blues of the hydrangeas.

It was June 28, 1977, I was eighteen, and I had done the seemingly impossible (at least till Boris Becker came along): Having arrived at Wimbledon to play the junior tournament, I had won three rounds of qualifying matches to gain entry to the main draw. And having made it into the main draw, I had—as an unheralded amateur with chubby cheeks, thick thighs, and Snickers bars in my equipment bag; a high-school senior who'd skipped graduation to come over and try his luck in Europe—proceeded to win four rounds against top professionals and made it into the quarterfinals of the world's greatest tennis tournament.

Up to that point, as an official nobody at Wimbledon, I had played in total obscurity, both at Roehampton and on the outside courts of the All England Club itself, where you have some of the world's diciest grass and maybe twelve people (four of them asleep, including the linespeople) to watch you. I had been consigned to the "B" locker room with all the other stiffs who were going to be eliminated after a round or two.

Court One, though, was the real deal. Now that I had made it through the merciless gauntlet of seven rounds, the Wimbledon powers-that-be, always condescending to anyone they felt was unimportant (which meant nearly everybody), had finally seen fit to sit up and take notice of John Patrick McEnroe, Jr., of Douglaston, Queens. I was worthy of atten-tion—not Centre Court attention yet, but Court One isn't chopped liver. And I was also worthy of the toughest opponent I'd faced so far in the tournament.

His name was Phil Dent, and he had an unblemished record against me.

YES, IT WAS the same Phil Dent who had beaten me in the second round at the French just three weeks before (and had gone on to the semifinals, where he'd lost to Brian Gottfried). This was not the second round at the French, however; it was the quarterfinals at Wimbledon, an entirely different proposition. The stakes were now immeasurably higher. Dent was the first seeded player I'd faced in the tournament, and even though he was only seeded thirteenth, he *was* seeded, I was nobody, and he was going to defend his position with every ounce of strength in his body and every bit of experience in his brain.

Strangely enough, though, I wasn't overwhelmingly nervous, despite my sudden elevation to such august surroundings. I was riding a wave of confidence: I knew I could play with the big boys, and I thought I could beat Dent. Our match in Paris had been close, after all, and from an early age, one of my strengths had been the ability to figure out an opponent's game after I'd played him once.

I thought I had Dent figured out. I won the first set fairly handily, 6–4, but in the second set, he dug in, and I lost a tiebreaker. I was mad at myself—and, if the truth be told, I was starting to feel a little nervous, deep down. Even when you're playing best-of-five-sets, you want to establish momentum, and I've never been a great come-from-behind player. When I get behind is when the doubts start to seep in.

So as we were about to change sides after the tiebreaker, I put my Wilson Pro Staff racket under my sneaker and tried to bend it until it broke.

And that big, close-in, well-mannered English crowd booed me. Who was this curly-headed upstart, this petulant boy, this *nobody,* to disturb the decorum of Court One?

It was the first time I'd ever been booed. I thought, "That's funny." So instead of picking my racket up, I kicked it along the grass as I walked toward my chair.

The boos got louder.

The English were quite upset with me, but I have to tell you, at that moment I mostly felt amused. As impressed as I may have been with Wimbledon and its tremendous history—and unlike a lot of young players then (and almost all young players now), I really did have respect for tennis history—I found England to be strange and stodgy and quaint.

When I saw those dozing linesmen, I thought, "This isn't what Wimbledon should look like." The club and the tournament were beautiful, but the whole atmosphere was totally set in its ways and self-important beyond belief. I couldn't help resenting how badly the organizers treated the lesser players and how they genuflected to the stars. I was incredulous at all that bowing and curtsying to royalty and lesser royalty. It felt like the class system at its worst. I was a kid from Queens, a subway rider. How could anybody expect me to take all this strawberries-and-cream malarkey seriously?

I'd better get to the top, I thought, so I could be treated well, too.

I STARTED TO GET a few bad line calls in the third set. And so, with Dent's parting words to me at the French Open still ringing in my ears, I took my complaints straight to the umpire, who was about as receptive as you'd expect. I, in turn, started to get a little hot under the collar (just a little, still, at that early point in my career).

Now the crowd was really getting worked up. Callow kid that I was, I found the crowd's extreme investment in the match and its decorum strange and rather comical. In retrospect, though, I must say that my bemusement had a lot to do with the fact that I'd simply never played in front of so many fans before. I should also say that today, after so many years of going to Wimbledon, I've come to cherish the Brits' passion about this great national institution. The English may be reserved, but not when it comes to their games!

Between the line calls and Dent's tenacity, I lost my way a little bit, and I soon found myself down two sets to one, and two games to love in the fourth. It was definitely a tight spot, but then I took a deep breath and gathered my thoughts. It had been a magical ride for me so far at Wimbledon, and I just didn't think it should end here, against this opponent.

I remembered how the shoe had been on the other foot at the French: I'd been up two sets to one and a break against Dent when he'd turned it around and won the match. What had happened then? I'd thought about the stakes of being in my first Grand Slam singles tournament; I had gotten tight and I'd folded.

The same thing could happen to Dent here, I reasoned. Moving on to his first Wimbledon semifinal at twenty-seven would be a huge deal for him: He, too, could get tight. If I just stuck with it, I might be able to turn this match around.

There was another reason I wanted to win. This was a crossroads: If I lost, I would still be able to enter the Wimbledon juniors; if I won and went on to the semis of the main draw, I wouldn't have time to enter the juniors. This was my mind-set: If I lost to Dent, I'd lost in the quarterfinals of Wimbledon—a great result for an eighteen-year-old qualifier. But if then I went over and lost to somebody in the third round of the *juniors*—that result was stained.

Meanwhile, it had turned into a really exciting match. The crowd seemed to get more vocal with each passing minute. They went from their second-set bemusement—"Who the hell is this guy?"—to a kind of incredulous, "This bloke is actually intending to win!" They were more against me than ever, but that day, in that match, it felt just fine.

And I think Dent got peeved. Suddenly, I was a different human being than the one he had seen just three weeks before at the French. What monster had he created? Suddenly the punk kid was questioning calls, kicking his racket. By the fifth set, it was edgy out there between us.

One service break was all it took. I won the last set, 6–4, and when I went to the net to shake hands, Dent barely looked me in the eye.

I was eighteen years old, in the semifinals of Wimbledon.

It felt, at the same time, both totally unbelievable and like the most natural thing in the world.


THE SEMIFINAL MATCHUPS that year were Bjorn Borg against Vitas Gerulaitis, and Jimmy Connors against . . . me. Me! I remember walking into the Gloucester Hotel, the big players' hotel at the time, and seeing the odds posted on a chalkboard (everyone bets in London): "Borg, 2–to–1; Connors, 3–to–1; Gerulaitis, 7–to–1; McEnroe, 250–to–1." Two hundred and fifty–to–one didn't faze me. Just being in that group felt like, "Man, this is the big time."

From that point on, my life would be totally different. (Just for starters, I would never play another junior tournament.)

But it wasn't just that this was the pros. Suddenly, I was in a whole new level of the game. Borg, Connors—these guys were the gods of tennis to me, guys I'd watched on TV! Connors had won Wimbledon in '74 and been in the finals against Ashe in '75. Borg had won in '76. These were two Wimbledon champions. The real deal.

Vitas, at number four in the world, was no slouch, either. He would go on to win the Australian Open later that year.

Going into a match against Jimmy Connors wasn't like going up against any of the pros I'd played before. This man was a legitimately great player. I had sat in the crowd when he'd played Rosewall—himself one of the greats—on the grass at Forest Hills in '74, and it had been a total massacre: Connors had won 6–1, 6–0, 6–1. It was unbelievable how hard he'd hit the ball with that steel Wilson T2000 racket, and how well he'd returned serve. I didn't want to get massacred.

His intensity was also unbelievable. And the fact that I didn't *know* him—had never played him, never even exchanged a word with him— made him all the more intimidating.

Our first meeting (if you want to call it that), in the locker room before our semifinal match, didn't make me feel any better.

Once you're into the quarterfinals at Wimbledon, they move you into the "A" Locker Room, next to Centre Court. That's the main locker room, reserved exclusively for the top 80 players. The big time. I guess I already felt a bit overawed just being there. Then I walked up and tried to say hi to Connors.

He wouldn't look at me. He wouldn't even acknowledge my existence. It was a very short moment.

Like a boxer, I guess, he felt he had to build up a certain level of anger and hatred even before we walked onto the court. And intimidation. I certainly felt intimidated. It was an effort for me just to lift my head, to look him in the eye. I thought, "Do I even belong here with this guy?"

And so, at that moment, I pretty much decided I did not want to win this match. *Don't want to win,* I thought. *Can't handle it.* (Not that I could've won if I *had* wanted it.) He had won the initial battle of wills.

The possibility that I could go from being the best junior in the world to one step away from the Wimbledon championship felt too overwhelming. If I had beaten Connors, I would have played Borg or Vitas, but presumably Borg. Borg was a poster on my bedroom door (right next to Farrah Fawcett). I just wasn't emotionally capable of thinking about beating any of these guys yet.

I had planned my career in my mind. I'd told my dad, "Don't bug me about being number one 'til I'm eighteen; that's when I'll be able to handle it." I had just made a jump almost too great for me to handle. I wasn't prepared to make the next jump. I still wanted to go to college, to have that experience; obviously, if I beat Connors, I wasn't going to go.

In my mind, I had gone as far as I could go—for the moment. It had been an amazing run. As it was, just by getting to the semis I had moved my ranking from number 233 in the world to number 71. Had I won the semi, I would probably have jumped to around 50. Had I won the whole thing, I could have been something like number 30—after two events. It was just too much. . . .

I WAS MORE NERVOUS for that match than I'd ever been in my life. Way more. This wasn't Court One at Wimbledon; this was *Centre* Court at Wimbledon. This was history—not to mention that my dad and Tony Palafox, who had flown over after I'd won the quarters, were in the stands. My legs were shaking. I played an abysmal first game: I was having trouble lifting, moving. My arm and legs were heavy. I was in a freeze for the first two sets, and Connors won them handily, 6–3, 6–3.

But I won the third set, 6–4—and something dawned on me: I started to realize that Jimmy simply wasn't playing very well. I don't know if he would ever talk about it or acknowledge it, even after all these years, but my guess is that he was feeling pressure from playing an eighteen-year-old kid.

I've had the same problem—it's difficult to play younger guys. You have nothing to gain but the victory; they have nothing to lose. At all. Some of Jimmy's problem was that my style was somewhat awkward for him—I didn't give him the pace that he liked to play off of; and, unlike most of the guys he destroyed, I was left-handed. The bottom line, though, was: He wasn't having a particularly good day.

Still, at the end it didn't matter: that one set was all I got. I just wasn't ready to beat Jimmy. Yet.

PEOPLE HAVE SAID that the other semifinal, Borg against Gerulaitis, was one of the greatest matches ever (Borg won in five close sets, and he went on to take his second Wimbledon championship). I never saw it. I was forced to play my quarterfinal of the mixed doubles at the same time, on an outside court, with something like four people watching us. All I could do was listen to the crowd roaring from Centre Court.

Mary and I were playing Martina Navratilova and Dennis Ralston. We were undefeated so far: We'd won the French and we were in the quarters at Wimbledon. Astounding. But then it got to 8–8 in the third set, and Mary was at net and I was returning, and Navratilova was serving, and I made the mistake of trying to hit a lob over Ralston's head. It was a bad lob, and Ralston just nailed Mary—popped her big time. I was really steamed: It's an unspoken code in mixed doubles that the guys don't whale away at the women. This was totally unnecessary. To this day, I don't forgive Ralston, because I'm sure he did it on purpose, and he could have put that overhead anywhere.

Mary totally lost it. I remember changing sides at 9–8 and saying, "Hey, Mary, are you okay?" and her saying, "Yeah, I'm okay"—with tears streaming down her face. I felt like killing the guy.

And we lost. Mary was so shaken that she could barely serve the next game, and that was that. It was sickening to me that Ralston had done such a thing: That was the beginning of the end for me and mixed doubles, right there. Thank you, Dennis!


MY FRIEND Doug Saputo met me when I got back from Wimbledon. We went back to my house, sneaked a beer from the fridge, went up to my room, and listened to Joan Jett. . . . It was the same thing Doug and I had done dozens of times, but now it felt completely different. Maybe Doug was different, maybe I was: I couldn't tell.

It was strange—at first, after my return, I felt like the same person I'd always been. I could still shoot hoops in the driveway or play Ping-Pong in the garage with my buddies, could still hang out with them in my parents' kitchen, drinking milk and eating Mister Salty pretzels. But from the moment I got back, the people I had grown up with wouldn't let me feel the same, or so I thought. Suddenly I was Somebody, while they were still nobodies, just the way I'd always been. Part of me had enjoyed being anonymous, but part of me had wanted—badly—to go on and become a star. Now there was no turning back.

My friends weren't quite sure how to handle it, and neither was I.

.   .   .

I COULDN'T WAIT to call Stacy. I'd just experienced the greatest moment of my life, and I wanted to share it with her. I phoned and said,
"Stacy, I got to the semifinals at Wimbledon" . . . and then she said, "My
father died a couple of days ago."

I felt numb. She had kept from me how sick he was—maybe she'd still
held out hope that her pop would pull through. Now I understood why
she'd had to leave Paris early. I felt so bad—here I was on an incredible
high, and her life was a total disaster. There's no way to really share anything at a moment like that. There's nothing to say, except "I'm really
sorry." It put things in perspective in a hurry.

4

THAT SUMMER after my first Wimbledon, I played twelve out of thirteen weeks—all professional tournaments, even though I was still an amateur. Including my trip to Europe, that meant more than four solid months of playing. I'd never done that before. I did fairly well—I didn't knock 'em dead, but I won a few rounds here and there against stiff competition, and by the time I entered college, I had gotten my ranking up to 21. I lost 7–5 in the third to Connors at a tournament in Boston, the week before the U.S. Open—I was starting to feel that maybe, just maybe, he was conquerable.

One of the best things about that summer was that I got to spend a lot of time with Peter Fleming. Back at Port Washington, when we'd played two-hour chess matches in between tennis, Peter had been like the big brother I'd never had. Now that I was eighteen and he was twenty-two, though, the age difference seemed negligible: Our similarities were more striking. We were both big sports fans, we both liked the same kind of music and a lot of the same bands: Pink Floyd, Foreigner, the Stones. We'd both had strict suburban upbringings, with parents who were deeply ambitious for us. And—I remembered this from Port Washington—we had very similar senses of humor. He'd called me "Junior" then, and that was what he called me now. It had a slightly different spin, now that I had come up in the world, but it still felt affectionate.

Peter and I played three of the same tournaments that summer, in Newport, Rhode Island; Cincinnati; and Boston; and during those three separate weeks, we hung out together almost every night, just drinking beers and talking. Having a real friend took away the loneliness of the tour. The idea of doubles hadn't come up yet. We were each partnering with other guys then: I was trying things out with the South African Bernie Mitton, among others, and Peter seemed to be pretty much paired up with Gene Mayer.

Talking about what makes a good doubles team is like trying to talk about what makes a good marriage: There's a lot that seems obvious, but the intangibles play a big role. In both cases, chemistry is every-thing. In doubles, if the chemistry's not there, the mistakes your part-ner is bound to make (just because everybody makes mistakes in tennis, even at the top level) get on your nerves more and more. And vice versa. As partners on a tennis court, you both have to be able to roll with the punches.

The highlight of my first U.S. Open was my third-round match against fourth-seeded Eddie Dibbs. During the first game, we heard a commotion in the stands, and a couple of minutes later, the umpire informed us that a spectator had been shot. Shot! Eddie jumped up. "I'm out of here," he said. I wasn't far behind. We waited on the side for a while, and eventu-ally someone told us that the message had been garbled and, in reality, the spectator was in *shock*.

We went back out to play, and I won a tight match, 6–4 in the third— only to find out later that the original message had been right. Someone had, indeed, been shot: a stray bullet had come from outside the stadium and hit a spectator's leg!

In the round of 16, Manuel Orantes, the 1975 champion and a brilliant clay-court player, beat me in straight sets. In fact, he gave me an absolute clay-court lesson. *Maybe,* I thought, *those hard courts at Stanford would be good for me.*

In the doubles, Bernie Mitton and I lost a tough match in the second round. Meanwhile, Peter and Gene Mayer had decided that despite a lot of good results, their doubles chemistry just wasn't there and so, having established over the summer that we were very much on the same wavelength, Peter and I decided to give doubles a go.

We didn't get off to a blazing start. In our first tournament together, in September at the Los Angeles Open, we lost early to Marty Riessen and Roscoe Tanner. I felt pretty let down. After the match, though, Peter said to me, "Were you feeling OK out there? I was really tired for some reason."

"I can't believe you said that," I told him. "I felt tired, too, but I was so embarrassed to be tired in a doubles match." And we figured out then and there what had been the problem: the L.A. smog.

It may sound like a small thing, but the point is that in doubles, small things are what make or break you. Communication doesn't just happen on the court—you really have to be able to open up to each other (or wear a gas mask!).

The following week, in San Francisco, we did a little better—and learned another lesson. In a semifinal match against Fred McNair and Sherwood Stewart, we got a bad call on a crucial point in the final set. It was one of those points that matches can hang on, and it had wrongfully gone against us; Peter and I went to the umpire and proceeded to have a joint meltdown. We got so upset that that was effectively the end of the match—we just couldn't play worth a damn afterward.

Peter had always had a temper, especially when he played singles, and mine was just starting to come out of the bottle at that point. However, what Peter learned that day, he later told me, was that he couldn't let it go anymore, not in doubles. You can't have two loose cannons out there at the same time: Someone has to be the emotional anchor, and that day Peter realized that it was going to have to be him.

THERE WAS ANOTHER instructive incident in San Francisco that September: I was playing Cliff Richey, one of the circuit's great characters of the '60s and '70s, a former Davis Cup stalwart. Cliff was a truly fine tennis player, and he was also never the least bit shy about telling anyone, anytime, exactly what was on his mind. Because an earlier match had run long, we didn't begin playing until about eleven-thirty P.M., and by the time we got to the third set, at around one-thirty A.M., there were maybe fifty fans left in the 10,000-seat Cow Palace.

I won't lie to you—I was doing a lot of bitching and moaning about line calls during the match. I know that won't come as a huge shock, but the fact is, I'd really never done much of it before, especially during my junior career. There was just something about the incessant grind of the summer that was starting to wear me down. I also think I was feeling the pressure of performing, solo, on the pro circuit.

Now, there was a rule in the pros that said you could question calls, and I was beginning to feel out the possibilities of that a little bit, but frankly, I was probably over the edge that night. Cliff Richey certainly thought so. After I'd gone off one more time, he stopped play, put his hands on his hips, and proceeded to address the fifty people in the stands.

"I've been a professional tennis player for ten years, I've been the number-one player in the United States, and I refuse to sit back and not say anything about what this kid is doing out here," he said—and then went on for five minutes more about what a disgrace I was, to the game.

I ended up winning the match, but I was incredibly embarrassed— as I should have been. I was totally spent, and showing the strain: I needed to go to college and take a break from the tour. I had learned a lesson that night, but it was a lesson I would periodically forget over the coming years, whenever fatigue got to me.

FROM SAN FRANCISCO, it was just down the pike to Stanford, the next and last stop on my summer-of-'77 tour. It had been a long ride, and a successful one; the paradox of that summer, though, was that I'd been playing enough to make inroads into the big time, but it also felt like just too much. By the time I got to Stanford at the end of September, I didn't even want to look at a tennis court.

Coach Gould was great, though. At the first team meeting, he said, "I know some of you guys have played a lot, and you just come back when you're ready." And so I didn't go to practice from October 1 to December 13, and Dick never said a word about it. The only reason I even went to that December practice was to get ready for a tournament in the Bahamas that my friend Gene Scott was running!

I only spent one year at Stanford, but going there was one of the greatest decisions I ever made. It allowed me to be around intelligent people, and it forced me to be responsible. Now I really was a team player, exactly the way I'd always wanted to be: I had to try to blend in, not just be a star. At the same time, since I was number one on the team, the pressure was on me to win all my matches.

The atmosphere couldn't have been more supportive, however. My close friend from Port Washington, Peter Rennert, was there, and the other members of the squad—Jim Hodges, Bill Maze, Matt Mitchell, John Rast, and Perry Wright, among others—were great guys, too. Bill, a senior and the number-two player, was my doubles partner at Stanford that year, and he also became a friend.

I'll freely admit that academics weren't my forte. My first mistake was in taking the guidance of my advisor, who recommended such courses as anthropology, economics, and calculus. By the time the first semester was well under way, I was already struggling. I said to myself, "I've got to find out what the athletes take," so I asked a couple of football players, and a few of the veterans on the tennis team, and second semester was a big improvement. I tried to take "Parapsychology and Psychic Phenomena" seriously, but I couldn't. In "Sleep, Narcolepsy, and Politics," I was actually able to get an A by playing a charity tennis exhibition. The most memorable was my exposition course: The teacher walked in, stared at us wordlessly for fifteen minutes—it felt like an eternity—and finally said, "I'll bet you're wondering what the requirements for this course are. There's no midterm, no final exam, and there are no papers. Now we're ready to begin the class."

This was more like it!

Meanwhile, there were recreational activities—another important part of college life. There were parties; there were road trips. One of them was with my new friend Doug Simon, to his grandfather's house in Carbon Beach in Malibu—just three houses north of the beach house I would buy seven years later. Doug's grandfather was Norton Simon, the great art collector, and his place was magnificent—full of Picassos and Matisses, among others; and the view of the Pacific was just as impressive. It was my second look at great art, and at Malibu, and both began to get their hooks in me. I'll never forget my first trip with the Stanford tennis team, to Madison, Wisconsin, in February of '78. Bill Maze's birthday came on that trip, and a bunch of us drove out to a bar to try to find Bill, so we could all celebrate. It was like a scene from a movie—we drove up, and suddenly Bill was being thrown out of the bar because he'd thrown a beer in the bouncer's face, and everybody from the bar was running after him. We shouted, "Hey, Willie!" and he dove into the car. . . .

We all stayed up pretty late that first night. There were sleds in the dorm where we were staying, and an incredible sledding hill outside, and a big party going on. We were drinking and doing a few other things, both outdoors and indoors, and not being especially quiet about it! Finally, Dick Gould came in—it had to have been three or four in the morning, and our match was set for eleven A.M.—and said, "Hey, guys, can you keep it down?" And walked out. That was it.

Could Dick possibly not have not noticed that the room was—shall we say—pungent? Maybe he'd noticed, maybe he hadn't. I just remember thinking, "I've got to play my heart out for this guy." This was my kind of coach.

We won that match in Madison, as we won all the rest of our meets in that undefeated year for Stanford. The most thrilling of all was a weekend away match in April, against an extremely tough UCLA team. The stands were packed; people were literally standing in the trees to get a good view. All the matches during that meet, including my victory over Eliot Teltscher (after being down match point), were well-played and close: It was just an exciting event to be part of, one that made me glad to be a member of the team, and that reaffirmed my decision to spend a year in college.

While the team was undefeated, however, Mr. Number One was not: I lost two singles matches, one of them an embarrassing rout by Eddie Edwards of Pepperdine, who completely outplayed me in front of a home crowd. Coach Gould had called me up at the last minute. The other came when I played with a high fever against Larry Gottfried, now of Trinity, but—excuses, excuses! In fact, the pressure of expectations for me as the number-one player provided great preparation for the pros.

* * *

IT WASN'T UNTIL WIMBLEDON in '77 that I felt strong enough to serve-and-volley. I had grown in height (maybe I was starting to stand up straighter) and weight; my leg strength was becoming an asset. My serve didn't get me a lot of aces, but I could place the ball well enough to finish up with one volley, or two or three—as many as it took.

That was when it all came together for the first time. My style of play was very high-percentage—short backswings, no wasted energy, no unnecessary chances. I believed that my quickness and anticipation and hand-eye coordination were better than any baseline player's—that, playing my style against theirs, I could win.

My serve-and-volley game developed even further when I went to Stanford, because, for the first time in my life, I was playing nothing but hard-court tennis. Suddenly I just saw that serve-and-volley was the better way to play. A few of you may still recall tennis as it used to be during the clay-court mid-'70s: Remember Vilas, during his incredible run in '77, playing those withering, interminable rallies? I thought that just wasn't particularly interesting. As soon as I found I had the capability to move right in and end those points, I thought, "Clay-court tennis is for the birds—this is a better way to make a living."

The fact that I was a good volleyer had often been wasted on clay. Wimbledon was something different. Borg wasn't a great volleyer, yet he won Wimbledon five times in a row. On grass, a mis-hit off the frame or the edge of the strings could turn into a surprisingly effective drop-volley, so my theory became: Get close to the net!

But I really could volley, which was good for me at Wimbledon and very good for me on those fast hard courts at Stanford. A solid, good volley on a hard court is even more critical than on a grass court. The problem was, those hard courts weren't especially good for my body: Freshman year at college was when I started to get some back problems.

It was in the lower part of my back. Maybe it was just stiffness from not stretching enough; maybe there was some emotional tension, too—most of the time, I've found, that has something to do with back pain. I know I was putting a lot of pressure on myself, because, well before school ended, I was certain that I was going to turn pro (I also played four pro tournaments that year—still as an amateur—and raised my ranking from 21 to 18), and I felt in my gut that the only way to go out on a positive note was to win the NCAA's, in Athens, Georgia, in May.

Winning that tournament meant a lot to me. To my knowledge, few people had done poorly in their big matches in the juniors or college and then turned around and had fabulous pro careers. Eliot Teltscher was an exception—he lost in the second round of the NCAA tournament, and later reached the top ten—but I didn't want to go out that way. I was the number-one college player and our team was undefeated. I wanted to win this thing and go out with a bang. Anything else would have been lame.

I played a lot of tennis during that tournament. It was a nine-day event, four days for team competition, then five days for individual matches. Over the first four days, I played four singles and four doubles matches, and then over the next five days, six singles and four more doubles matches.

My semifinal in the individual competition, against my friend and doubles partner Bill Maze, stirred up some mixed feelings—and foreshadowed issues that would later crop up between Peter Fleming and me. I wanted this one very badly, and despite my friendship with Bill, I went into the match in a take-no-prisoners, win-at-any-costs state of mind. There were several close calls against me, and I'd give Bill a look: Tennis players know that look, the guilt-inducing stare, that says to the other player, in effect, "You're really going to take that?" Afterward, I was mad at myself: I felt I'd stepped on our friendship a bit. But I couldn't help feeling delighted that I'd won.

I'll never forget the scene at the NCAA finals that year. My opponent,

John Sadri of North Carolina State (not exactly a tennis hotbed), walked onto the court wearing a blue blazer, white tennis shorts and shirt, and a ten-gallon hat! The Southern crowd went wild.

The fans—citizens of Athens and N.C. State supporters who'd been brought down for the event—were overwhelmingly behind Sadri, whereas I only had Coach Gould and Peter Rennert there to support me. But it didn't matter: The frenzy in the stands only fueled and inspired me. I was simply determined not to lose this final.

It was a good thing I was determined. Sadri had one of the biggest serves I'd ever seen, and the match was just about as close as it could be: 7–6, 7–6, 5–7, 7–6. When I won that final point, I felt as if I could fly.

The only downside was that during changeovers in that final—partly because I'd been playing so many matches, and partly because of stress—I had to receive treatment for my back: The trainer made me lie flat and pull my knees to my chest. When the euphoria of the victory wore off, my back was really hurting.

I TURNED PROFESSIONAL at the Queen's Club tournament the next month, June of 1978. Ironically, my first pro match was against Peter Fleming. I almost lost it, too, but then I came back and won in a close three sets. Peter was gracious when we shook hands at net: We were buddies. I got all the way to the final, which I lost to Tony Roche—I think it was the last tournament the great Aussie ever won, toward the end of his career.

Then I lost in the first round at Wimbledon—just like that. I'd gone from the semifinals in '77 to the first round in '78. I think there's no doubt it had to do with my back problem—though, to be fair, Eric Van Dillen played a great match. (There, I said it.) I wore a wrap to keep my back warm—I'd put it on and feel too hot, then I'd take it off and feel too cold. Peter and I did get to the finals in doubles, however (we lost to Bob Hewitt and Frew McMillan), so that salvaged something from Wimbledon.

It was a sign, though. Right from the start that summer, I'd just been getting by, not doing anything extraordinary. In fact, to be honest, I was having mediocre results. I was struggling with just getting to the quarters of tournaments, not really beating any of the top players, losing to the Harold Solomons and Eddie Dibbses of the world on clay. (Nothing against Harold and Eddie—they were tough customers on the dirt. They were known as the Bagel Twins, because they were both short, Jewish-looking guys from Miami, even though Eddie's background was Lebanese, not Jewish.) Anyway, I was winning rounds, but not winning tournaments, solidifying a number-15 ranking, but nothing more. I felt as if I were wilting a little, now that I had truly entered the big time.

I knew I could do better.

TRUE TO MY RANKING, I was seeded number 15 at the 1978 U.S. Open. My lower back still felt tight, and for some reason—to this day, I don't know why—I decided to turn completely sideways when I served. I noticed the difference immediately: It loosened up the tension, relieved the pain. I don't know how it worked; to tell the truth, I didn't really want to know. I just thought, *This feels all right.*

And then I noticed something else: Not only was my back getting significantly better, but people were having a tougher time reading my serve. Because I was so young and flexible in those days, my body weight moved me way into the court. (These days, when I serve, I still do it a little bit—jump, hit, and waltz in. In those days, I was all over it.) Suddenly I found myself up at net faster than ever before, hitting a lot of winning volleys.

The sideways serve was a beautiful double-whammy. People said, "What the hell is this guy doing?" because no one served that way. I felt much better—and, after my results started improving, better still.

To his huge credit, Tony Palafox completely accepted the new serve. This was so Tony: always thoughtful and curious about tennis, and infinitely supportive of me. He never advised me against the change—in fact, he figured it out for himself, so that he could help me do it better! He would stand sideways, or imagine himself in the position, and then I would ask him questions: "How come the serve isn't breaking wide enough in the ad court?" Tony would think for a second, then say, "For that wide serve, it's like throwing a knife—give it that same flick of the wrist."

I wrote that tip down on a card. Ever since I'd started out, and to this day, I've written down tips to myself—"Keep your head up all through the serve"; "Don't open your body too soon on the backhand." I keep the cards in my tennis bag. Sitting during a changeover, I focus myself by looking at those cards. Throughout my career on the tour, I also called Tony whenever part of my game wasn't up to snuff, and he would always tell me what I had to do differently, as calm as Bjorn, while I agonized.

I changed the serve early in the Open, and I got good results right away. I eventually lost in the semis to Connors—Jimmy was still Jimmy, after all; I still hadn't beaten him, and he soundly outplayed me that day. Then, the next night, I traveled down to Chile to play my first Davis Cup match ever.

Tony Trabert, the team captain, had called me a few weeks before and asked me if I would play doubles with Brian Gottfried. I didn't hesitate for a second, and I'll tell you why. Strangely, though it was a boom time for tennis, it was a down time for the Davis Cup in the U.S.A.—the last time we'd been in a Cup final was 1973, when we'd lost to Australia. A big reason for our lack of success was that Jimmy Connors seemed to have no interest at all in the Cup. My guess was that, as one of the most blue-collar guys ever to play the game, he had scrapped his way up from nowhere and didn't want to put himself out unless there was a direct benefit to him. He never said it in so many words, but it was always my feeling that if it didn't put money in his pocket, Jimmy wasn't interested in it. And, at $2,000 per week for singles (the money came, and still comes, from U.S. Open proceeds), Davis Cup wasn't going to cut it for him.

Jimmy was just the most egregious example of this attitude. There were other name players who felt the same way: The money flowing around pro tennis was simply too big to risk losing time and energy (and even injury) playing in what was basically an amateur event, a relic of the good, or bad, old days of tennis.

That was never the way anyone in my family felt about it, though. My parents, influenced by Harry Hopman, always talked about what a great honor it would be to play for one's country: It meant more to them, I think, than Wimbledon or the U.S. Open. They made me promise that I would play if I was asked, so when Tony called—and I don't kid myself, I know it was because the top players were all turning him down—I said, "Where do I show up?"

The answer was Santiago, and down I flew to join Trabert's little band: Harold Solomon, Brian Gottfried, Larry Gottfried, and yours truly, with Van Winitsky as a practice partner. Bill Norris, the great trainer, was also along, as was the wonderful team physician, Dr. Omar Fareed, and the lovely Joe Carrico, then president of the USTA. It was a very small group in those underappreciated days for the Cup—these days, as many as twenty people will travel with the U.S. Davis Cup team. And we were young: Three of the five of us (Van, Larry, and I) were nineteen!

This tie was not going to be any cinch: Chile, which had made it to the finals two years before, had a top-20 player in Hans Gildemeister, and a legitimate chance on its home courts. The South Americans came on pretty strong, and the score stood at one match all when Brian and I stepped onto the red clay for our crucial doubles match against Patrick Cornejo and Belus Prajoux.

Brian and I had barely practiced together. About all we said to each other beforehand was, "You [Brian] play the deuce court, I'll play the ad court." I almost never played the deuce—right-hand—court in doubles. One reason was that if I put my forehand on the left when we were receiving, it diminished the effectiveness of a wide serve on that side.

On paper, we were clear favorites against Cornejo and Prajoux, but paper doesn't mean much in Davis Cup, where an emotional home crowd can become a crucial part of the action. That was certainly the case in this match. What should've been a straight-sets win for us turned into a tough four-setter, but Brian and I finally walked off the courts as winners, helping to seal a 4–1 U.S. victory.

At nineteen years and seven months, I was one of the youngest Americans ever to play Davis Cup, and after our victorious tie, I could sense some new stirrings of interest in the press, for the first time in what felt like a long while. I was very proud of that trip—almost as proud as my mom and dad.

I should also note that there was a sizable earthquake in Santiago that week, in the middle of the night. I slept right through it. I used to sleep a lot more soundly in those pre-fatherhood days!

AND THEN—I don't know any other way to put this—things just exploded. Suddenly, it was as if I'd found my stride. I won my first two tournaments after returning from Chile; at Hartford (over Johan Kriek in the finals) and in San Francisco (over Dick Stockton, despite my being in a frightening car crash the night before; when tournament director Barry MacKay heard I'd been in a wreck, and the car had been totaled, he said, "But you're gonna play the finals, right?").

I would eventually win four tournaments in the indoor season that year. I still hadn't beaten any of the really big boys, though. Then came Stockholm.

THE FIRST TIME I ever saw Borg, I was a ballboy for him.

It was at Forest Hills, at the 1971 or '72 U.S. Open. He would have been fifteen or sixteen; I was twelve or thirteen. I thought he was incredible-looking—the long hair, the headband, that little bit of scruff on his face that he'd get from not shaving for a couple of weeks. And the Fila outfit—the tight shirts and short shorts . . . I loved that stuff! I would trade anything, back then, to get a Fila striped shirt; a jacket was a really big deal. (As a matter of fact, I did once trade about half the contents of my suitcase for a Fila jacket, and it almost fit!)

I remember Vilas bulging out of his clothes, and sweating . . . and Nastase. Those guys looked incredible. The quality of tennis clothing was so much better in those days. I think the baggy shirts and shoes you see now are horrible; and these sneakers that look like rocket ships . . . don't get me started.

But Borg was the one who impressed me the most. I thought he was magical—like some kind of Viking god who'd landed on the tennis court. I can't explain, exactly. It certainly wasn't his personality, that's for sure: You've seen the interviews. He didn't have much to say, on or off the court—but then, he didn't *have* to say much. The way he looked—long, tan legs, wide shoulders—and the way he played, the vibe he gave off, all that was more than enough. Even before he won Wimbledon, when he was just fifteen, there were hundreds of girls around him: tennis groupies, like the Beatles and the Stones had! That had never happened before in the game; it's never happened since.

Some people compare Sampras to Borg. In my mind, there's no comparison. Even though Pete is one of the greatest players, maybe the greatest player, of all time, Borg, by his presence alone, gave a lot back to the game. His story was incredible, too: Who could ever have imagined such a player coming out of Sweden, a country of only eight million people, with a sub-Arctic climate?

He was the best athlete I've ever seen on a tennis court—I don't think people realize how good an athlete he was. And the fact is, he had to be, because his game was bizarre, in a way: running back and forth, well behind the baseline, hitting ball after ball after ball until an angle opened up or the other guy missed. It was so side-to-side, compared to my forward-forward-forward, but Bjorn was so fast he could make up for it. Even today, at forty-five, he's faster than all but a couple of guys playing tennis!

The first time we played—in the semifinals at the Stockholm Open in November of '78—was a perfect scenario for me, because it was on fast indoor tile—yes, tile!—which wasn't well suited to his game, particularly against me. I also think he felt pressure playing me in his hometown, in front of a Swedish crowd who'd gotten excited about the game because of him.

I actually won the match pretty easily. No matter what happened, though, Bjorn always had a beautiful way about him—he never got mad. I think, too, that he was influenced by his coach, Lennart Bergelin, who was also a beautiful man. He'd walk into the airport carrying fifteen of Borg's rackets and sweating, but wearing a huge grin on his face. He was such a positive personality, and he truly loved Bjorn. (At one stage I actually thought about working with Lennart—and in retrospect, I wish I had—but I didn't, because I thought it might make Bjorn unhappy.)

The win in Stockholm was a huge victory for me—I was the first player younger than Borg to beat him—but it didn't make me think one bit less of Bjorn. I just felt that I was with the big boys now—and this was the official coronation.

The night I beat Borg, I remember going off to one of the incredible discos they used to have in Stockholm: Everywhere you looked, there was a good-looking girl. At four or five in the morning however, it suddenly struck me that while I may have reached the apex of my career so far— I still had one more match to play.

I panicked. I thought, "I can't beat Borg and lose to Tim Gullikson!" The good news, fortunately, was that in Sweden they didn't start matches until five P.M., so I figured (I was young!) that all I had to do was get out there and finish it in one hour, before the fatigue set in. And one hour was all that I needed: I won 6–2, 6–2.

I ended the year blazing hot, number four in the world on the computer, and returned to Davis Cup for the finals against England at Rancho Mirage, California. I played singles this time, and lost only ten games in six sets against Buster Mottram and John Lloyd. I was thrilled to be able to help take the U.S. to a 4–1 victory in the tie, and to our first championship since 1972.

It was there that I was asked once again, not about the Davis Cup victory, but about Jimmy Connors's absence and our growing rivalry. My reply, which came to be one of my most famous quotes, appeared on the cover of the *New York Times* magazine a couple of weeks later: "I'll follow him to the ends of the earth."

I wasn't kidding, but I wouldn't have to go that far. In January of 1979, I went to the Masters, at Madison Square Garden, and beat Connors for the first time, although he didn't finish the match. I was up 7–5, 3–0, and he retired, claiming a bleeding callus on his foot. He *did* have a blister, but I still felt gypped: I knew he simply didn't want to give me the satisfaction of beating him. (I also noted that, though Jimmy cited doctor's orders that he take off two weeks for the blister, he played in Philadelphia the following week—and won!)

I'm sure Jimmy didn't like the fact that I was coming on. In retrospect, I can't say I blame him. My beating him was a big deal, and in those days, the Masters was a huge event: Only the top eight singles players in the world, and the top four doubles teams, could play. The crowds in the Garden were amazing—there was all the electricity of a championship boxing match. I was really excited to have beaten Connors in front of my hometown crowd, in Madison Square Garden: On my way off the court after the match, I raised my arms in victory, and the crowd went wild.

In the finals, it was the nineteen-year-old upstart McEnroe against the wily thirty-five-year-old veteran Arthur Ashe. Since the Masters had a round-robin format, I had already played Arthur once, drubbing him 6–3, 6–1 in the first round. However, he was ready for the finals, and to tell the truth, I was a bit overconfident after that first round. Arthur came out very determined, and he started giving me a lot of off-speed stuff, the same kind of slicing and dicing he'd used in his big upset victory over Connors in the 1975 Wimbledon final. That kind of slow pace didn't bother me the way it did Jimmy, but suddenly, in this round, the equation was just different. After we had split the first two sets, Arthur took a 4–1 lead in the third. I battled back to 4–all, but he held his serve to go to 5–4, and then he started finding the range on my serve.

It didn't matter what I did, he rifled it back. The score went to 15–30, then 15–40—double match point against me. I jammed him on the backhand side, and he netted the return—30–40, still match point. Then I remembered Tony Palafox's image of throwing a knife, and snapped a wide-breaking serve to Arthur's backhand. Arthur leaped at it and blasted an unplayable return past me . . .

And then the linesman called my serve out.

Arthur dropped his shoulders—for him, the equivalent of a ten-minute tirade. He walked up to the umpire and asked if he was sure the serve had been out. The umpire nodded. I know Arthur disagreed with that call until the end of his days, but it stood. On my second serve, he went for a forehand winner, and hit the ball just long. Deuce. I held on to win the third set 7–5, and I had my first major title.

To make things even sweeter, Peter Fleming and I won the doubles, against the legendary team of Stan Smith and Bob Lutz.

It was one of those historic moments that become clear only later: What had happened, in a very short span of time, was nothing less than the changing of the guard.

I ARRIVED ON THE SCENE at a combustible moment for professional tennis. The Open era had brought personalities into the game, and personality was generating media exposure, which was generating more money, which in turn guaranteed more media exposure—which in turn drove in even more money. Where money and publicity meet, there's always excitement, but good behavior is rarely a part of the mix. Manners are the operating rules of more stable systems.

I got caught up in the rising excitement of pro tennis—in some ways, I was the personification of that excitement—and yes, my behavior got away from me. That's a big subject. At the beginning, though, it often felt as simple as this: Week by week, I was rising to new heights, and when you ascend that quickly, and at such an early age, the oxygen doesn't always flow to your brain.

At the same time, I must say, I did have an idea in mind: I thought tennis had had enough of manners.

To me, "manners" meant sleeping linesmen at Wimbledon, and bowing and curtsying to rich people with hereditary titles who didn't pay any taxes. Manners meant tennis clubs that demanded you wear white clothes, and cost too much money to join, and excluded blacks and Jews and God knows who else. Manners meant the hush-hush atmosphere at tennis matches, where excitement of any kind was frowned upon.

At my first Davis Cup match in Chile, I'd seen the stands filled with the kind of fans who might attend a World Cup soccer match. There was rhythmic cheering, free expression of emotion: If the crowd didn't like what was happening, they threw coins and seat cushions. I thought that was a step in the right direction. Nobody in South America seemed to feel that tennis was a sissy sport.

Why shouldn't North America (and England) be the same way? Why couldn't the game be more accessible to the average person? Why shouldn't tennis get the same kind of treatment—and interest—as baseball, basketball, or football?

In the late '70s, it was starting to feel as if we could actually get there. The characters who dominated tennis then weren't country-club types: There was Connors, who'd been taught by his mom; Borg, an incredible story, a man with rock-star charisma who'd exploded out of a small Scandinavian country; Vilas, who wore P.O.W. bracelets and wrote poetry; Gerulaitis, a brash guy who *also* looked like a rock star and talked with a New York accent.

At the same time, there weren't many inner-city kids playing tennis at the beginning of 1979. The major events were getting pretty good TV ratings, but the sport wasn't exactly threatening football or baseball. Call me presumptuous, call me egotistical (and believe me, you wouldn't be the first), but I thought that maybe I could do something about all that.

MY FATHER HAS ALWAYS told me, "Look, you don't need to yell—in fact, you'd be a better player if you didn't. Just go out and play, and you'll win."

I've never been totally convinced of that, I suppose, or else I would have worked harder at it. And I admit, there have been many times when I've answered Dad, in my head: *Yeah, sure, what do you know? You're not out there playing.*

But ultimately, I think that he was right—that I probably would have done better had I been able not to lose my temper: *Been able* being the key words here.

People tend to forget the genuinely lousy level of officiating that was prevalent in professional tennis when I came along. That's why, with my parents' words echoing in my ears—*tell the truth; be honest at any cost*—I felt I was (don't laugh) on a kind of quest to get things to improve. There's another thing, too. It's important to point out that my playing career had two distinct periods: For the first few years, I almost never spoke an obscenity to an umpire or a linesman. I said plenty of other things, but in what I like to think was almost a lawyerly way, I avoided dirty words.

Then, at a certain point, I went over the line. There were reasons for it—reasons, not excuses—and I'll talk more about them later. But here's the thing: Once I began to go over the line, I should have been defaulted. In fact, I was only defaulted twice in my career—and once was for being late for a doubles match.

It's not putting the blame on anyone else, but on the way up, I noticed that the better I got, and the more money I made (for myself and for the events that were selling tickets and television rights), the more that linesmen, umpires, referees, and tournament organizers had to put up with from me. The more that professional tennis's money depended on me, the more that things seemed to be under my control when I got on that court.

Except when they were out of control.

People have always said that I was the one person who could actually lift his game by getting angry. That's true—to an extent. Sometimes when I was mad, I could serve aces. Sometimes it threw me off, as it would anybody else. A lot of times, it meant that I was starting to choke.

I've heard people say it was deliberate—that I blew up on purpose to throw off my opponent. That isn't true. I always felt, "Look, if you can't handle my having an outburst, then you shouldn't be in the profession." First of all, I was mainly hurting myself by stopping a match. Second, if by questioning a call for whatever period of time an umpire allowed, it threw off my opponent's game, I simply felt, "That's too bad. That's not winning or losing points. That's what goes on between the points. If you decide you're going to sit there and get hot and bothered because I'm doing this, then you're allowing yourself to be psychologically affected. It's your job not to be."

Some people on the tour decided I was just crazy—they would look at me in a certain way, and I knew that was what they were thinking. Other guys, though, would get annoyed. One time, playing doubles, I rubbed Hank Pfister and Victor Amaya the wrong way, and Pfister said, "I'm gonna kick your ass after the match." Now, Hank Pfister was six-four, and Victor Amaya was six-seven! I said to myself, "I picked the wrong guys."

But cooler heads usually prevail in tennis. It's rare that you ever hear of an actual fight between players, on the court or in the locker room. I've seen a push or a shove once or twice, but I can't recall a single actual fist-fight, with punches thrown and landed. It's not like hockey, where that's par for the course.

In tennis, what you have to worry about is the fans.

You may not remember Bob Hewitt, the South African doubles player, but—before I came along—he used to be known as the guy with the worst temper in tennis. He was also one of the best doubles players in the world for a while.

After Hewitt and Frew McMillan beat Peter Fleming and me in that '78 Wimbledon doubles final, Peter and I weren't able to hook up for a few weeks. He had just met, and was falling in love with, Jennifer Hudson, the English girl he would eventually marry. As a result, I was playing with a number of different partners, and when McMillan decided to take a week off, Hewitt asked me to play with him at a tournament at the Longwood Cricket Club, in Boston.

We were in a quarterfinal match against Victor Pecci and Balazs

Taroczy, and Hewitt was in top—or maybe I should say bottom—form. He was going off about every call, yelling and screaming at everyone in sight; there was no way I could have gotten a word in edgewise, even if I'd wanted to. I was getting more and more worked up—at the time Hewitt was the number-one doubles player, and I was the young buck, so I'd wanted to make a good showing. I began to choke.

We lost the match 7–9 in the third, and after the match, one woman in the stands kept clapping, slowly—clapping and clapping. I was really distraught. But she wouldn't stop clapping, for what felt like hours.

All during this match, the whole time Hewitt was going bananas, I'd simply stood there. Now, though, I lost it. I went over to the woman, spat in front of her, and told her in no uncertain terms what I thought of what she was doing. She said, "You can't do that to me." Then her husband— a middle-aged man (probably around the age I am now)—stood up to defend his wife.

The guy sucker-punched me, right in the stomach. I was so agitated that I barely felt it. I grabbed him by the neck—I was ready to nail him! People were starting to gather around and say, "Break it up, break it up." And I hesitated—because suddenly it occurred to me that if I hit this character I'd get suspended.

Our match had been on an outside court. A TV crew had been covering the singles match on the main court, so after they heard about this commotion, they went and interviewed Hewitt. And the first thing he said was, "McEnroe was in a fight, and I had nothing to do with it." As if! And of course my parents were watching.

They called: "John, are you okay?" I said, "Look, I'm fine; some old jerk threw a punch at me." Of course, I had to worm my way out of the whole thing, and—I guess because I hadn't really done anything other than spitting in front of this woman—I was off the hook. But it was ugly.

So maybe that was the passing of the torch from Hewitt to me.

I'm half-joking.

Connors always had the ability to turn his anger on and off, which amazed me. I was a one-way street—mad, madder, and maddest. There must have been thousands of times, in tense situations, when a joke was on the tip of my tongue, and instead of saying something funny, I'd just let loose.

Then I'd think, "What the hell did I do that for?" To this day I don't know. It had something to do with the fear that I'd lose my edge if I joked around in a match. But there was no *proof* that that would happen, and Connors was living proof that you could defuse a situation with humor.

The way I was brought up, you were supposed to be very serious, totally concentrated. To put humor into a big tennis match felt like being a phony, I guess. It would mean I wasn't a true competitor, a real athlete. It smacked of professional wrestling.

Meanwhile, the irony is that you *can* joke in tight competitive situations (not to mention the fact that pro wrestling is *huge*—those guys are laughing all the way to the bank).

I'm deeply envious of that. In fact, my biggest regret, by far—even more than losing the '84 French Open—is never having been able to turn the other cheek, throw a one-liner, to keep things loose. I should have had more fun doing what I was doing. Ultimately, I think it harks back to my not enjoying competitive tennis that much. To being afraid to lose.

It's an amazing feeling to get to the Wimbledon final and walk out on the court to play Bjorn Borg. That's the ultimate. But the buildup to get there was never pleasant. First round, second round; playing guys you should beat. The pressure of everyone's expectations—especially my own—was enormous.

Maybe that's why Borg and I never had a problem, on or off the court: He understood. He thought I was a little crazy, but it didn't seem to bother him. The way I saw it, he even went out of his way to show me respect.

The second or third time we ever played, in New Orleans in early

1979, it was 5–all in the third set, and I was getting all worked up and nutty, and Bjorn motioned me to the net. I thought, "Oh, God, what's he going to do? Is he going to tell me I'm the biggest jerk of all time?" And he just put his arm around my shoulder and said, "It's okay. Just relax." This was at 5–all in the third set! But he was amused by the whole thing. "It's okay," he told me. "It's a great match."

It made me feel really special. He didn't look at what I was doing as something I'd done to affect him. It was just my own nuttiness.

Plus—and maybe this was the main point—he was still number one.

# 5

WHAT I ALWAYS REMEMBER FIRST about Vitas is his hair—long and blond like Borg's, only Vitas never wore a headband. He was clearly imitating Borg, but I never thought any less of him for that, because, first, it was a cool look if you could bring it off (and Vitas could really bring it off), and second, Vitas was a much stronger personality. It was funny—people mistook him for Borg all the time, but he kind of got a kick out of it. It certainly never hurt his social life.

I first became aware of Vitas soon after I first started playing at Port Washington: I would stand in the lounge and gaze down at the courts, watching him run around with those little bunny steps of his. Harry Hopman always spoke admiringly about Vitas's work ethic, and it was true: He was always practicing, and he could run all day. There were a lot of strong players at Port Washington, but in terms of drive, talent, and charisma, Vitas was clearly the star. Even early on, when people used to joke, "Vitas Gerulaitis—what is that, a disease?" it looked as though he was going to be tremendously famous.

I admired him like crazy, but he wouldn't give me the time of day when I was fourteen or fifteen, and why should he? He was already Broadway Vitas, going out with the likes of Cheryl Tiegs! Why should he pay attention to some boring fifteen-year-old? He brushed me off, which naturally only made him seem more magnetic.

Even when he was a junior, you'd hear the myths: He had been with this woman, had played that tournament under the influence of such-and-such a drug. I wondered how the hell he thought he could get away with burning his candle at both ends. At the same time, though, you didn't see him dogging it on the court. He had incredible amounts of energy.

I first made it onto Vitas's radar screen when I was seventeen, and we played a charity match at the Felt Forum, in Madison Square Garden. A man named Richard Weisman helped put the match together: It was the first time I met Richard, who was to become an important figure in my life. The match was one of those bouts between the up-and-comer and the established superstar. There were no upsets that night—the superstar won—but at least Vitas would speak to me now.

In the next couple of years, as I started to build my own career, I watched with continuing admiration as he rose to number three in the world. I had few doubts about my tennis abilities, but in lifestyle we were worlds apart. He had a mansion in King's Point and a glamorous life in Manhattan; I would come back from my travels with bags of dirty tennis clothes for my mom to wash, then settle back into my old room in Douglaston. Vitas drove a creamy-yellow Rolls-Royce that matched his hair, with a license plate that said VITAS G. I was still driving my trusty flame-orange Pinto. Some evenings, my old friend Doug Saputo and I would get into the Pinto, or Doug's blue Mercury Comet, and follow

Vitas's Rolls into town, to Studio 54 or Xenon or Heartbreak—wherever he was going. We'd promise our parents we'd be home by one-thirty.

For Doug and me, it was like a field trip. It was the height of disco, an incredible scene—blasting music and blazing lights; designer jeans and designer drugs. (That *music,* though—it was awful! Even as I gaped around, with the Bee Gees, Gloria Gaynor, and Donna Summer blasting in my ears, I missed my favorites: Black Sabbath, Led Zeppelin, the Stones). Superstars were everywhere, and a strange man in a white wig, named Andy Warhol, took pictures of everybody. I remember his handshake—it felt like a dead fish. He was always around, and at some point—even at parties!—he'd take out his camera. It felt like an incredible invasion of privacy to me.

But Vitas loved it. He was always in the center of it all, with beautiful women draped all over him. He was funny, he was charming, he was the life of the party—he just couldn't sit still—he could talk with anybody about anything; he had an incredibly positive vibe about him. At the same time, to really get to know Vitas was extremely difficult. Women were crazy about him, and he was always just a little cool with them, which seemed to get them even more excited.

It was a slightly different story with me and women. As I mentioned, I had some hiccups getting started with girls. My shyness tended to get misinterpreted, the way shyness always does. My growing confidence in the tennis world sometimes came across as cockiness, and the tricky thing about cockiness is that, while it's an absolute survival mechanism for a tournament tennis player, it can backfire once you get off the court. It can also impress other people—women among them—for the wrong reasons. So, between my shyness and my audacity, most people tended to overlook my real self. My serious girlfriends knew me (there were really only a few of them, and never more than one at a time). But I didn't always want that kind of intimacy.

.   .   .

BY EARLY 1979, quite a bit had changed. I'd won the Masters; I was number four in the world to Vitas's number three (behind Borg and Connors, two players he would never surpass). I was no longer a blip on his screen; I was the jet coming up fast behind him.

Women were starting to look at me in a different way, and I'll confess: I didn't mind it a bit. This wasn't like Junior Davis Cup, when I'd had to carry around six rackets to try to get people to notice me. Suddenly I was on TV, in newspapers and magazines. I was beginning to make real money for the first time in my life—one of the first things I did with my tournament earnings, and the proceeds from an endorsement deal my dad had hammered out with Sergio Tacchini just as I was about to turn pro in the summer of 1978, was to trade in the orange Pinto for a snappy blue two-seat Mercedes convertible.

Now at least I wouldn't have to look like a jerk when I followed Vitas to Xenon.

In fact, though, following Vitas—in any sense—was less and less what I had in mind.

It was getting increasingly more complicated living at home. I was twenty and becoming financially independent; it was time to jump out of the nest and fly. In mid-1979, I bought my first apartment, on the Upper East Side. My new co-op cost $350,000—big money in the late '70s. I was pretty impressed with myself! Now when I came back from my travels, I was living the life of a well-to-do young Manhattan bachelor, hanging around with my friends at restaurants like George Martin's, Oren & Aretzky's, Herlihy's. That stretch of the Upper East Side was a lively scene in those days. There were a lot of women around, and many of them were models (or said they were); most were a couple of years older than I was, and they liked the fact that I was just twenty. My shyness was starting to wear off.

I was the kingpin of my little group: Doug Saputo, Peter Rennert, Peter Fleming, another Jersey tennis player named Fritz Buehning. In a certain way, we were the team I'd always wanted to belong to. At the same time, though, I was clearly the star, which felt good, but complicated, too.

We were all just kids, really. We fancied ourselves rock-'n'-roll, anti-establishment: We'd wear T-shirts and jean jackets everywhere—even into fancy restaurants—and (I wince to remember) act like idiots a lot of the time. I'd settled into a role: the outsider, the kid from Queens. A rebel. When I first started playing at the U.S. Open and the Masters, I was more interested in hanging out with the parking attendants and towel guys than with the big shots in the stands.

But then hanging out began to get a lot more interesting.

I was starting to run into Richard Weisman, the man who'd set up that first charity match between Vitas and myself, more and more. Richard, then in his late thirties, was quite an interesting fellow. He always had a box at Wimbledon, courtside seats at the Garden and the Open. He collected art, and he gave amazing parties at his place at the UN Plaza, at 49th and First.

But what Richard really collected was people, and so, since I was a freshly minted celebrity, I became one of the people he collected. Richard seemed to know absolutely everybody who was anybody in New York. He was a modern-day Gatsby, a guy who knew Steve Rubell and Peter Beard and Cheryl Tiegs and Warhol, who could get any of them to drop everything and come over. He'd call me up and say, "Listen, I'm having this party Saturday, and Mick Jagger is coming, and the governor of New York, and Jacqueline Bisset and Jackie Stewart, the race-car driver"—he'd list seven or eight totally (seemingly) disconnected people. I'd get off the phone and say, "There's no way all these people are coming to this party." And every single one of them would be there.

Richard's art collection was incredible. Initially, I thought a lot of the stuff was ridiculous, especially the Roy Lichtensteins, which simply weren't to my taste—but then I was pretty impressed when Richard wound up selling them for a huge amount of money. As I learned more about art, I learned more about the aesthetic and financial significance of what he had.

Naturally, Vitas was in Richard's circle, and as I began to mingle in, I felt like a poor imitation of Vitas: still pretty inept socially, a little overwhelmed by the whole scene. I enjoyed it on a certain level, but to the people who used to hang out at Richard's, I know my graces must have seemed a little weak. I'd usually stay quietly in a corner, just taking it all in. Then afterward I'd hear, "He's not very friendly." Or, "He's shy." Or, "He doesn't talk."

I met remarkable people at those parties. After a while, if you meet enough famous people, you almost get used to it. Almost. I was always proud afterward for not gushing: "God, I met So-and-So!"—but there were times when I just couldn't help it.

Ultimately, though, I felt it was best to try to show respect to the people I'd meet, and not to turn into some sort of—well, fan. I didn't want to make whoever it was feel as if I were taking something from him or her. I never wanted to be the way I felt (and still feel) toward people when they invade my privacy or ask for my autograph—all googly-eyed. I always tried to treat anyone I met, no matter how famous, as just a human being—which is what anyone famous really is, much more than most people would imagine.


NINETEEN SEVENTY-NINE was an amazing year for me. I would win twenty-seven tournaments that year—admittedly, sixteen of them were in doubles. Now, just barely out of Douglaston, I was part of an incredibly exclusive and high-visibility group, the top five tennis players in the world: Borg, Connors, Gerulaitis, McEnroe, and Vilas.

It's important to try to understand the steepness of the slope when you're at the summit of tennis. Arthur Ashe once said that there was as much difference between number ten in the world and number five as there was between number 100 and number ten. Going from number five to number four, he said, is like going from ten to five. And from three on up is inconceivable.

I agree with him. The very top, like the summit of Everest, is weird territory, impossible to understand unless you've actually been there.

It all felt real and unreal at the same time: There was the hard work of traveling, practicing, and playing; then there were the cameras, the fans, the parties, the money. The girls. The parties . . .

Part of the unreality was that I was now on a nearly equal footing, and actually hanging out, with Bjorn and Vitas. Connors always stayed kind of unto himself, and Guillermo Vilas was supremely disciplined (and had Ion Tiriac around to make sure he mostly behaved), but Borg and Gerulaitis had, shall we say, perfected the art of enjoying the fruits of tennis.

They traveled together, they practiced together—and then they had fun. The first time I ever went out with the two of them was at an exhibition in Milan, in the spring of '79. I marked the occasion by indulging in something I'd never tried before (never mind what)—and the next thing I knew, Vitas and Bjorn were carrying me back into the hotel. I felt sick but wonderful: I had passed the initiation. I was part of the gang.

Broadway Vitas and Bjorn! To me, they were like elder statesmen— it was so exciting to be running with the best tennis players in the world. And that was more or less all I had to do—just go with them. I prided myself—I still pride myself—on being an energetic, even hyperactive, person, but I didn't have the energy that these guys had! They would run me into the ground on a consistent basis. To be honest, I often felt like a party pooper—I'd eventually say, "I've got to get my sleep."

It's funny—in certain ways, Vitas was imitating Borg, but if anything, Borg followed *him*. Bjorn would let Vitas do all the talk and the work, set

everything up—clubs, women, whatever. Everything except their practice schedule—there, Vitas would defer to Lennart Bergelin (who spent
a lot of the non-tennis hours carefully looking the other way).

With off-court pursuits, Bjorn followed Vitas, but even he could go
only so far. Vitas had a remarkable ability to recover quickly from
whatever fun he was having and reenergize, whereas—off the court,
anyway—Bjorn was much more human. Before that exhibition in Milan,
they'd been in South America, for a week or two, playing some nutty
schedule and, I'm sure, staying up late and not getting enough sleep.
When Borg got to Milan, he couldn't get out of bed, even though he had
an iron constitution. The trip had made him sick. Somehow, though,
Vitas could still play.

On the other hand, Vitas never beat Bjorn in a big match. He came
close—maybe closest in their great Wimbledon semifinal in '77, my first
year. Borg won it, though, the same way he won almost twenty other
matches between the two of them.

I think Vitas figured he could live with that—that Borg was just colossally great, and he was near-great. I think that if anyone really frustrated
Vitas, it was me.

TIM GULLIKSON wiped me out in the fourth round at Wimbledon that
year, 6–4, 6–2, 6–4. Tim, rest his soul, played brilliantly that day, and
perhaps with a measure of revenge, since I'd just beaten his twin brother,
Tom, on the same court in the previous round.

For me, it just felt like a bad day at the office. I don't want to take anything away from Tim, but I think I fell victim to the expectations that continued to follow me after my incredible Wimbledon run in '77. (Those
expectations were also my own. I put a lot of pressure on myself that year,
and it showed in my behavior on the court: I threw my racket a few times,
stamped my foot, and let off plenty of steam at visually challenged lines-

men. The British tabloids christened me with a new nickname: "Super-Brat.") Now that I had won the Masters and risen to number four in the world, the natural assumption—the poetic assumption—was that I would return to the hallowed lawns and take on Borg.

Not yet.

Bjorn, of course, won again, beating Roscoe Tanner, at the time the game's biggest server, to take the fourth of his five titles in a row. He was looking just about undefeatable.

One of the reasons I loved doubles was that it always helped me to feel better about tough singles losses. When Peter Fleming and I beat Brian Gottfried and Raul Ramirez to win our first Wimbledon championship that year, it took a lot of the sting out of my loss to Gullikson. It also felt as though we were starting to bring some excitement into an event that had started to lose steam, now that top players like Borg, Connors, Gerulaitas, and Vilas were looking down their noses at it. Doubles takes time, and different skills than singles does, and it doesn't pay as much— three of the reasons it has (sadly) once more fallen into eclipse today.

In the second round at the 1979 U.S. Open, I faced Ilie Nastase. Nasty, who had won the tournament in 1972, was thirty-three and long past his prime, but he hadn't mellowed with age—if anything, he was crazier than ever. And the big New York crowd at the Open always got him going.

Our night match drew a big crowd, eager to see Super-Brat face down the aging *enfant terrible* of tennis. Frank Hammond was officiating the match. Of all the umpires out there, Frank—fat, bald, and dark-mustached, with a deep voice and a no-nonsense manner—was one of the few I liked. I always thought of him as a player's umpire: He knew everyone by name; he treated you like a person. He'd say, "Come on, John, you're over the edge; I'm going to have to penalize you now unless you pull it together." I felt he was trying to get me back on track so I could play my best tennis.

Frank was known as an umpire who could control the crowd and the players in a difficult match, but that night he didn't have a chance. There was a lot of drinking going on in the stands, and Nasty was on his worst behavior—stalling, arguing, cursing the officials (at one point he kicked over the courtside water cooler), and generally trying to provoke me into going off the rails. Remarkably—and all too unusually—I kept it together. By the third set, Frank had had it: He lost his composure and ranted away at Nasty, docking him a penalty point. The crowd decided then and there that Frank couldn't do anything right.

I was rattled myself, but then, at one set all and down a break, I began to pull it together, and I won the third set, 6–3. I was serving at 2–1, 15–love in the fourth set, when Nasty began arguing about another line call. He sat down in a linesman's chair and refused to play. Frank literally begged him to go on, but Nasty wouldn't stand up. I was furious: It was clear that Nastase knew he was going to lose and was simply looking to prolong everyone's agony. "Game penalty, Nastase," Frank said. "McEnroe leads, three games to one."

Nasty stood up from the chair with his hands on his hips, screaming such vile obscenities at Frank that Frank, after further pleading, defaulted him. Now the crowd really went nuts, throwing paper cups and beer cans onto the court.

Mike Blanchard, the tournament referee, then came onto the court and talked with Nasty and me. Figuring I was going to win anyway, and wanting to avoid a riot, I agreed to play on—despite my memories of the Zan Guerry debacle in the qualifying tournament for the 1976 U.S. Open. I knew I could close out this match. Blanchard told the crowd that if things didn't quiet down, the match would be discontinued.

Still, as soon as Frank tried to start play again, the crowd started chanting, "Two to one, two to one"—the score before the game penalty. The chanting got louder and louder. I had never seen such pandemonium in a tennis match, and I never would again, even in our wildest South

American Davis Cup ties. Finally, Bill Talbert, the tournament director, decided to take Frank out of the match and put Blanchard in the chair. I felt terrible for Frank as he climbed down and walked off the court, the crowd pelting him with garbage. He had lost all credibility. What I found out only later was that the match had essentially destroyed his career. When the ATP hired a group of full-time traveling officials, they didn't choose Frank.

Once Frank was off the court, I knew the air had gone out of Nasty, and I ran out the rest of the match easily. Even the crowd seemed spent by now. It was finally all over at twelve-thirty in the morning. After the match, I was somewhat astonished when Nastase came up to me and said, "Hey, let's go to dinner." Here was another lesson: Business and pleasure must always be separated. "Sure," I said.

On the other side of the draw, Vitas was having a great run: He beat Clerc in the round of 16, Kriek in the quarterfinals, and in the semis, Tanner, who had just gotten revenge on Borg for his Wimbledon loss. (It was funny how Vitas could beat guys who had beaten Borg, and yet, when it came down to it, couldn't handle Borg himself. Tennis always works that way.)

But then in the finals, Vitas faced me.

I was coming off a year in which I had won three big victories over Connors: in the Masters, at Dallas (where I'd beaten Borg to win the tournament), and now here at the Open, in straight sets in the semis. There's no other way to say it—I felt it was my time. I was a little un-comfortable about having to play my buddy Vitas in a big match—but not uncomfortable enough to lose.

In the end, it wasn't even a particularly close match—I won in straight sets, 7–5, 6–3, and 6–3. In fact, I think that Vitas was more uncomfort-able than I was. People were booing, because they were angry that Connors and Borg weren't playing. At that moment they were still the *real* stars—here we were, just two guys from Queens! But I thought it was miraculous: two guys from Queens in the final of the U.S. Open! I was convinced it was never going to happen again. (I'm still convinced.)

For a couple of years, I'd been working to hang out with Vitas, wondering if I could keep up with him off the court. I'd been trying to be his friend. I looked up to him. And now that I'd blown by him, the victory felt hollow. I had taken something from him. He was still a legitimate number four in the world, but now he was off the mountaintop. Now it was Borg, Connors, and me.

Things were never quite the same between Vitas and me after that.


FRIENDSHIP IS A FUNNY THING on the men's tennis tour. On the one hand, guys tend to leave their competitiveness on the court—you may be fighting to the death, but once you shake hands after a match, you can go out for a beer afterward.

However, beneath it all, it's still dog-eat-dog out there. You can be friendly off the court, but when you're all chasing the same dollar, you feel you can never totally let down your guard. It's screwed up, but that's the reality of it: You're basically on your own.

In any sport, you have enemies as well as friends. I couldn't stand a number of players, and I don't think it'll come as a surprise that I've generated a few strong feelings myself. A couple of times, guys have refused to shake my hand—once, Vince Van Patten gave me one of those fake-out shakes—where you put out your hand, then jerk it back at the last second.

Sometimes, though, it's easier to have enemies than to have friends—especially if your friends happen to be fellow professional tennis players and you're on your way to being number one in the world. It may be a cliché that it's lonely at the top, but just because it's a cliché doesn't mean it's not true.

Two of my closest friendships growing up were with the two Peters,

Rennert and Fleming, and both friendships eventually ran into trouble—partly, I think, because both guys began to feel as if they were in my shadow.

My friendship with Peter Fleming has been one of the most complicated relationships in my life. From the start, there was an incredible bond between us. We were doubles partners for over ten years, and we did great things—historic things—together: winning Wimbledon four times and the U.S. Open three times; winning fourteen out of fifteen Davis Cup matches; going undefeated in seven finals at the Masters.

As gifted a singles player as Peter was—and he made it as high as number eight in the world in 1980—he always acknowledged my achievements in an especially generous way. Envy just didn't seem to be part of his makeup. We were a great doubles team because of our respective (and complementary) talents, and that indefinable closeness of spirit. However, Peter has one famous quote that, in a way, will always haunt him: When somebody asked him who the greatest doubles team in history was, he said, "John McEnroe and anyone."

I think it's important to understand the context of that remark. It happened at the 1982 Davis Cup final against France, in Grenoble, after Peter and I had beaten Yannick Noah and Henri Leconte to help ice a 4–1 U.S. victory. Peter had injured his foot in 1980, and his confidence and his ranking had been plummeting for a couple of years, but suddenly he was playing amazingly well again. We'd gone out there expecting to rout Yannick and Henri.

Instead, his foot started hurting again, I played pretty well and he was off, and we had a nondescript match, winning 6–2, 6–3, and 9–7. Peter had expected it to be his big breakthrough comeback, but instead it ended up looking as though I was carrying him—which was what people were always wrongfully saying anyway. At the press conference afterward, Peter was feeling pretty down on himself, and that was when that question got asked.

The second he gave that answer, I turned to him and said, "What are you saying? That's not true." And I meant it from the bottom of my heart—I really was shocked at how wrong that was.

I know it was difficult for him always to be mentioned in the same breath with me. With his talent, he might have made it to the top five, or even higher, if he had possessed the kind of merciless focus a champion needs. That was just what Peter didn't possess, however, and so he had trouble finding his own way. In a sense, he was too generous a guy to get to the very top.

Not that the friendship was totally easy on my side, either. Anyone who's close to me and also plays tennis knows that once I'm out on the court in a singles match, it's basically: Take no prisoners. I'm not saying it's the best way to be—I just don't know any other way.

Some of the difficulty between us was probably my fault early on, when we came up against each other in singles. Sometimes it's harder to play against someone you're really close to than someone you dislike. I could never stand the thought of losing to someone I was friendly with— even my brother Patrick.

It's possible to say, "Look, if I'm going to lose to someone, it's better if it's to my brother or a close friend"—but I didn't quite see it that way. I always wanted my family and friends to do well—I just didn't want them to do as well as I did. It was okay for Peter to get to the quarters in Wimbledon—as long as I was in the finals. That is exactly what happened in 1980, when I had to beat him to get to my first historic match with Borg.

Peter had a blistering singles run in 1979: After we won the doubles at the Open in September (for our second Grand Slam title of the year), we went head-to-head in singles for a little while. He beat me in straight sets to win the L.A. Open, then I had to work hard to beat him at the final in San Francisco, then he got to the final in Hawaii after I lost in the semis. His ranking jumped way up. Not coincidentally, he was traveling with Jenny then, and he was in love; I was traveling with nobody, and my relationship with Stacy was starting to hit the skids.

For all the above reasons—maybe there were others, too—things were starting to get weird between Peter and me. Or maybe I was just the one getting weird. During that loss to him in the finals at L.A., at the Forum, I threw my racket. I was angry and I *meant* to throw it, but then it slipped from my hand and really flew out there—I was lucky it didn't clock someone. (I've been lucky that way. A couple of times, I've lost it and tossed my racket—and then the next thing I knew, it was hitting the top of the backdrop, *this* far from nailing someone in the head.)

When we played in San Francisco, Peter served against me for the match, but I came back and won. We could have met again in the final in Hawaii, but I ended up losing in the semis to a guy I really disliked (and an occasional doubles partner of Peter's in the past), Bill Scanlon.

Scanlon and I had been on the same Junior Davis Cup team one year, so I thought we were friends, at least superficially. We even roomed together one year at the National Juniors in Kalamazoo—I remember walking around with him one night after he'd lost a crucial match, listening to him search his soul, talking a bit about myself, too. For a while, I thought I was one of the guys he was closest to.

The next thing I remember, we were playing a match, having one of our many spats, and I said something like, "Hey, we were on the same team; weren't we friends then?" And Scanlon said, "Friends? We weren't friends."

I don't know—maybe he thought he'd do better in tennis. I actually think he did about as well as he could have: He was an excellent tennis player, but not a great athlete. In certain situations, he played very well. Our match in Maui was one of them—I could barely win a point.

I also have to say, though, that the Maui match probably had something to do with my relationship with Peter at the time—it was just getting to be too much for me. He was too happy! He was with Jenny, and it was getting on my nerves that he seemed so happy and that I was kind of out in the cold. To be blunt, I guess I was jealous. Doubly jealous: that he had somebody, and that she had *him.* I had been leaning on Peter emotionally, as my best buddy—now, suddenly, there was nobody for me to lean on.

Anyway, after beating me, Scanlon ended up playing Peter in the finals at Maui, and I discovered something about myself that I didn't like—something I still don't like to this day. As much as I disliked Scanlon, part of me wanted the guy who'd beaten me to win the tournament—instead of hoping that my best friend would go out and kick his ass!

I remember I couldn't watch the final. I just stayed in my room. Peter and I were playing in the doubles final after that, and I didn't know which end was up.

Then Peter came up from the match and I asked, "What was the score?" and he said, "One and one." I said, "Jesus, you kicked his ass!" And Peter said, "No, I got two games."

And in a sick way, I was relieved. Then, of course, I felt bad about myself.

Then I didn't know how to feel.

Things came to a head two months later, when we played a big challenge event in Jamaica and, sure enough, wound up playing each other. That was another pretty close match, and it was unbelievably hot, which is usually when I act my worst—which is just what I did.

Peter had come to the event as a last-minute sub for another player who'd dropped out. He'd been relaxing with Jenny for ten days, and he was as loose as a goose: tan, happy, joking around with the spectators. I was uptight to start with, because of the Peter–Jenny situation; but in addition, one of my all-time hot buttons is when my opponent does what I'm so weak at doing—jokes around with the crowd and gets them on his side.

Toward the end of the first set, I hit a serve that I knew was good—that I still know was good—but the linesman called it out. This was an exhibition, not a tour match, so I looked over at Peter and said, "You saw it; was it in or out?"

Peter said, "I didn't see it."

I shook my head, looked at the tropical sky, and began to yell. And yell. After a couple of minutes, the umpire said, "Point penalty, Mr. McEnroe. Time delay."

I looked at Peter. "Are you going to take that point?" I asked, none too sweetly.

Then Peter, thinking I didn't believe that he hadn't seen the serve, walked over, all six-foot-five of him, and began to get in my face. "Just because we're friends," he shouted, "don't think I'm the Salvation Army!"

At that point, with all that was happening between us, I just couldn't take it anymore—I didn't feel I could walk off the court in the middle of a game, but I didn't feel I could continue, either. So I just zombied out—sleepwalked through the match, didn't try for anything. I don't think I've done that before or since. (In the round-robin format, I did go on to play Nastase in the final, however. I knew I had made the big time when Ilie announced to the crowd, "He's worse than Connors and me put together." What a compliment!)

The next day, Peter and I sat down and had a Talk. It's funny—our unspoken communication was always so strong, but when it came to saying what had to be said, we weren't much good. Nothing changed that day. I tried to explain how our competitiveness in singles had gotten in the way, but I also tried to tell him about my feelings of jealousy. I did a pretty lousy job. And what could Peter say? In essence, he just said: "Hey, I'm in love."

I thought back to Wimbledon, the year before—how one day, out of the blue, Peter had said, "I met this girl!" And my immortal reply had been something like, "Great, man, whatever."

At that juncture, Peter and I were on the road, playing tournaments, trying to meet girls: nothing heavy. But then it got to the point where Peter was going out to dinner with Jenny—instead of with me, by the way—two, three, four nights in a row. One night, he called me up and said, "Listen, I've got to ask your advice. I've gone out with this girl three or four times, she's great, I think she's wonderful." And, always Mr. Sensitive, I said, "Look, have you slept with her or not?" And Peter said, "No."

So I said, "Look, you've gone out with her all these nights in a row. If you want to know my opinion, if you haven't slept with her by tonight, just forget it." So Peter said, "Okay."

There were three weeks off between Wimbledon and the next time we were due to play together, in Toronto. When we rendezvoused in Toronto, Peter had brought Jenny with him again.

I said to him, "So you've obviously slept with her."

"No."

And I replied, "Are you [expletive deleted] crazy?"

Let's just say that I eventually got the feeling that Peter told her what I had said, which—let's just further say—probably put me in a negative light with Jenny.

She was a very shy, very pretty English girl who clearly just wanted to be with Peter. At that point, I suddenly thought, *Oh, God, this is serious!* Never being one to leave well enough alone, I told him, "You're not going to marry some English girl, are you? Are you crazy? No one does that." I can't quite explain the way I thought then: "Look, you marry an American; that's the end of the story." Maybe it was my mother's influence!

In any case, even though I eventually became the best man at Jenny and Peter's wedding, there's always been that little undercurrent. It was not a good start for me. And they're still together, after more than twenty years.

Five or six years ago, Peter called me at seven in the morning on a

Sunday. Sunday at seven! He said, "John, it's Peter." I croaked, "What *time* is it?"

And Peter said, "I'm just calling to say I forgive you for trying to ruin my marriage."

After twenty years, Peter and I are still working it out between us. But what I realized that day in Jamaica was that I would have to find someone—myself.

In the meantime, I was on my own.

# 6

BACK THEN, people always used to ask me, "What are your dreams, your aspirations?" I knew what they were really talking about: number one. However, I avoided the subject, the same way I wouldn't talk to my dad about the junior number-one spot. I refused to put that pressure on myself. *I'll worry about that when the time comes,* I thought—part of me not actually believing that it would come. . . .

THE TWO BEST YEARS of my career were '79 and '80, when I was number three in the world, hunting down Connors and Borg. I was traveling a lot, winning a lot, and I loved it—loved being the lone gunfighter, working my way up the ranks, but still not being *the* guy.

Professional tennis was so much different then, in so many ways, from what it's become. Of course, there's more money in it now—but that's true of all sports. I had (and have) absolutely no complaints about the money I made, at any point. I still remember the first time I got paid for a set of exhibitions, just after I'd turned pro in the fall of 1978: I played Ilie Nastase in six cities in Holland, over six days, for $11,000. It seemed like a fortune!

Not to mention how great it was to drive around Holland with Nastase—it made me feel I was entering the big time, with a kindred spirit. Ilie's energy was something I could really understand.

Now, though, it feels like tennis has become such a business that all the life and personality have been sucked out of it. It was amazing to drive around Holland with Nastase, at what felt like 150 miles an hour—two crazy tennis players in a little car! These days, it seems everyone in the top ten is a traveling consortium, with a coach, and someone else to hold the player's hand—a nutritionist, a guru, a friend, a lover. Almost nobody could afford a coach back in the '70s and '80s.

And I never wanted one, frankly, even though I ended up hiring coaches a few times, after my peak (although I didn't know then that I had peaked!). I never liked unnecessary baggage, and to tell the truth, I've always been my own best coach. Sometimes it got lonely, but a lot of the time I didn't mind being by myself. There was almost always another pro or two traveling on the same plane to a tournament. Peter and I went to a lot of the same events, so—even if our friendship had grown more complicated—he was often around. And then there was Stacy.

We were trying to make a go of a relationship, though since she was playing successfully on the women's tour, it was difficult (all the events but the Grand Slams were separate in those days). We still wrote and talked on the phone; we traveled together a bit around the time of the majors; I even went to some of her events. We also played some mixed doubles.

It was terrible. Talk about putting pressure on a relationship! In 1978, right after I turned pro, we played mixed at Wimbledon, and in our third-round loss, I got fined $500 for throwing my racket and yelling some obscenities. We hadn't made any money—in those days, you had to get to the quarters in the Wimbledon mixed before you won a dime—and so there I was, right out of the gate in my professional career, starting to rack up the fines!

I actually went in and begged the Wimbledon Committee: "Please, don't fine me, I was playing with my girlfriend and I was stressing out." It's hard to believe, after all that happened there over the years, but they let me off the hook. They said, "All right, don't let it happen again."

I didn't—in mixed!

The last mixed-doubles match I ever played (until the '99 Wimbledon) was at the '79 U.S. Open, with Stacy again. We played Stan and Anne Smith, and lost 3–6, 7–6, 3–6. I lost my serve twice, and nobody else lost his or hers the entire match. That was the ultimate embarrassment. I said, "That's it; I'm never playing again. I can't handle this."

It wasn't Stacy's fault; it was mine. I was pretty match-tough, but that kind of pressure was beyond me.

As was the strain of maintaining a (mostly long-distance) relationship, at that age, amid the distractions and temptations of the road. I actually liked having a girlfriend. I also liked the idea of having my cake and eating it, too.

Then, at the 1980 French Open, I made a mistake that I later vowed I would never make again with anyone as long as I lived. I'd been building up a sense of guilt about having slept with a few other women during the time Stacy and I had been together—and I told her about it.

It was just a disaster. Stacy was very upset, of course: She didn't feel we could go on. And I can't say I blame her. It was so bad—so obviously the wrong thing for me to do. I believe now that if you're committed to someone, it's wrong to be with anyone else. Back then, I guess that was beyond my powers, so the lesson I learned for the time being was, if I was going to be jerk enough to cheat, at least don't tell anyone about it. Learning not to cheat would take time.

That was one of the worst weeks of my life. I was seeded number two at the French, but I felt so bad about unloading this bomb on my girlfriend that I bombed on the court. I couldn't think of anything else but what I'd just done, and I wound up losing to Paul McNamee in the round of 16.

I thought I loved Stacy. Was I *in* love? That's a tougher question to answer. I don't know if, at that age, you can really be *in* love, with all that that later entails. And quite frankly, at twenty-one, I had other worlds to conquer.

AFTER PEOPLE TALK about my temper, the main thing everybody always wants to discuss is my first Wimbledon final against Borg in 1980, the one with the fourth-set tiebreaker that went thirty-four points. It's funny: People usually think I won that match, even though I lost it in the fifth. That's OK with me. In fact, in a way it's OK that I *didn't* win that one.

Unfortunately, I almost always feel like a loser after I'm beaten in a tennis match. It's a sad fact about tennis—and probably other sports as well—that when you lose your confidence in your game, you lose a bit of confidence in yourself as a person. It's hard to overcome that feeling. You always have to fight the thought, "I'm a loser; I'm not the same person I was," when, in fact, you may very well be a better person in certain ways.

Of course, there have been a fair number of times in my career when I not only lost a match that I probably shouldn't have, but also acted like a complete jerk.

However, when you lose the final at Wimbledon 8–6 in the fifth set to Bjorn Borg, that's different. I never acted like a jerk when I played Borg: I respected him too much; I respected the *occasion*. Whether I won or lost was always less important than that I got to be a part of history.

It was the first time I'd ever played Bjorn on grass, and I thought my game matched up perfectly against his on that surface. For one thing, I had beaten him in that final at Dallas in May, on a fast indoor carpet not totally dissimilar to grass. He had a habit of standing way back to receive; I knew I could get to net quickly on most of my serves and take command of the angles. Also, while Borg's first serve was stronger than most people realize, he was never known as a volleyer, and his second serve could be a bit dicey.

From the beginning, everything went according to plan. Early on, in fact, I was amazed at how easily I was winning. To tell the truth, I think I actually let up a little bit—which was my first mistake. I'd won the first set 6–1, and I was up 5–4 in the second, very close to taking a two-sets-to-love lead, at which point I could have just kicked his behind—which is what I expected I was going to do. But my plan went off the rails.

Some of it was just bad luck. First, I had had to play Connors the day before—which, because it was the first time I'd played him at Wimbledon since our '77 semifinal, was obviously an emotional match. To make matters worse, though, since I had spent the past year pushing Jimmy out of his number-two spot in the rankings, there was bad blood between us, and now it was showing itself in the form of some serious testiness.

At that point, my relationship with Connors was the exact opposite of my relationship with Borg—there was little respect for the man or the occasion of playing him. Like two club fighters, we trash-talked each other on the changeovers: Jimmy called me a baby, and I told him what he could kiss. It was exciting, in a perverse way, but it also turned out to be a very draining four-set win.

As if that weren't enough, because of a rain delay earlier, I had had to play the doubles semifinal right after my match with Connors!

Borg, however, had played his singles semi on Friday, so he got to spend his Saturday resting.

Borg never played doubles. Connors stopped playing them very early in his career, and Lendl rarely played them—but I loved playing doubles, for two reasons: First, I liked being part of a team. Second, it kept me sharp for singles, and I preferred it to practicing. Most of the time at Wimbledon, the scheduling worked to my advantage—I could play singles one day, doubles the next. But looking back, I do wonder whether pulling out of the doubles semifinal that year at Wimbledon would have given me the extra energy to win that fifth set against Borg. Still, I know now—and knew then—that I could never have done that to Peter, my friend and partner. It just wasn't my style.

That final was when I saw for the first time how Bjorn's incredible athletic ability and physical fitness could cost me.

At 5–4 in that second set, I got a little tight—maybe at the thought of the match coming too easily—and he got his serve going, which let him come back and win the set 7–5. At that point, something in me deflated. I felt I should have been up two sets to love, and the fact that I wasn't opened the gates to mental and physical fatigue, and I lost the third set, 3–6.

Then he broke my serve once in the fourth set, and suddenly I was serving at 3–5. It felt like a nightmare—it had all happened so quickly. Here I'd honestly thought I was going to win 6–1, 6–4, 6–3; now, all of a sudden, I was almost out of the match.

Which was when something magical happened. I held my serve; saved a couple of match points, then on Borg's serve, I got my fight back. By the time we got to the tiebreaker, I was back to feeling I could win the match.

Greatness is a judgment that's bestowed long after the fact, but I can tell you that while I was in that tiebreaker, I knew something special was going on. In those days, there was still a standing-room section at Wimbledon finals (great seats if you're willing to stand on line for three days), and the crowd was very excited: very vociferous, and then dramatically hushed at other moments. Somehow—maybe because I'd saved those match points earlier—I could sense that even the people who didn't want me to win the match wanted me to win the tiebreaker.

They just didn't want this match to *end.*

And the match *itself* didn't seem to want to end. The tiebreaker kept going back and forth, back and forth, both of us hitting a lot of winners, neither of us able to put it away. I had been feeling tired, but now the crowd pumped me up so much that I forgot about it.

I don't know why it stands out in my mind after so many years, but I hit one running forehand—a winner down the line, as it turned out—and ended up practically in the crowd when I stopped, and Centre Court at Wimbledon is pretty wide. I could feel the excitement coming off those people in waves—to the extent that I actually had to make an effort not to get too excited myself. The further we got into that tiebreaker, though, the less I could hold it in.

And then when I finally won it, 18–16, I knew I'd won the match. *Knew* it.

I thought Bjorn would be utterly deflated after losing that tiebreaker— but whatever he had inside him was beyond anything I could imagine. He was not only undiscouraged, but physically, he was still going strong.

I wondered how this could even be possible. I had forgotten my fatigue during the tiebreaker, but now I was beginning to remember it. Borg served the first game of the fifth set, and I hit a couple of good returns to go up 30–love—and then he started coming up with big first serves. As fatigued as I was, I wasn't making him work hard enough on his serve.

I lost that first game, then held, and then we went into a pattern in which he was holding serve at love or 15 every time. I kept saying to myself, *Oh, my God, I've got to break him now.*

It never happened. When I saw how completely unperturbed he seemed about that fourth-set loss, and how he just kept getting stronger in the fifth—something in me wilted. He seemed totally fresh, and I was drained.

I was amazed. He had won four Wimbledons in a row! I kept thinking, *Come on, isn't enough enough?* As the last set wore on, it became a war of attrition, which was exactly what I hadn't wanted to happen: I just didn't have enough gas left in the tank. Finally, I was barely hanging on: I couldn't even win points on his serve.

And then we were shaking hands at the net. I knew I could beat Borg. But Wimbledon still belonged to him.

I HAD WON THE U.S. OPEN the year before, but I had won it without having to play Connors or Borg. In 1980, I would have to play them both (not to mention Ivan Lendl).

I still consider the '80 Open the best physical achievement in my career. In the quarterfinals, on Thursday night, I beat Lendl 7–5 in the fourth set; the next morning, Peter and I played the doubles final against Stan Smith and Bob Lutz, which we lost in a tough five-setter. I really felt we should've won that match—but I couldn't feel too broken up about losing it, since it felt like kind of a last hurrah for the great doubles team of Smith and Lutz (whom we'd beaten in the final the previous year). I had particular respect for Stan, because of his dedication to Davis Cup.

On Saturday, I played Connors in a wild semifinal. After I'd won the first set 6–4 and gone up 5–3 in the second, I got a little tight and Jimmy went on an unbelievable tear, working up the crowd in his inimitable fashion, boosting his own energy in the process, and winning the next eleven games in a row. After taking the second set 7–5 and the third, 6–0, he was now up 2–0 in the fourth, and I was, frankly, feeling a bit embarrassed.

At that point, I received a gift from a crowd that had been on Jimmy's side: Now, since they wanted to see more tennis, they started to cheer me on. And suddenly the strange chemistry of tennis matches altered—now Jimmy got tight, I raised my game, won the fourth, 6–3, and went up 5–3 in the final set.

Then Jimmy got the crowd back.

Our seesaw battle sawed once more, and we wound up in a fifth-set tiebreaker, both of us (I'm sure) feeling that this match was going to be horrendous for whoever lost. I know I felt I was going to tear my hair out if I didn't win.

I should mention that I've always liked the tiebreak rule: It makes for more drama, because the crowd knows the match is going to end, and so do the players. And in the final set, that knowledge—that the end was in sight—helped me. In a tiebreaker, the rule of thumb is that the stronger server has the edge, and I knew that was me. I knew that if I could just get a couple of good serves in, I could win.

Which was just what I did.

Then on Sunday, still depleted, I got into another one of my classic battles against Borg (who hadn't had to play doubles, or Connors). The fast court favored me, but after I'd gone up 7–6, 6–1, Bjorn, once again capitalizing on my fatigue and his superior conditioning, started inching his way back into the match. I'm positive he had our Wimbledon match in mind—I know I did. He must have been thinking that I would wilt again, and the king of five-setters would once more prevail. (Bjorn did much better in five-setters, overall, than he did in three-setters, simply because he was so much fitter than almost anyone else.)

Not so fast.

I'm sure that after I lost the third and fourth sets, the crowd thought Borg would ride his momentum to take the fifth set and his first U.S. Open title. Strangely enough, though, that very expectation (the crowd is always a critical component in a big match) helped me relax, and pump myself up. I had lost a match I should have won at Wimbledon; I didn't want to do that again.

I had come this far, I thought; I *could* stick with it and win this match. I had a surprise in store for my hometown crowd. Getting off to a good start in the fifth set helped me to grab a second wind, a last shot of adrenaline. In the end, one break of Bjorn's serve was all I needed.

When we shook hands, I could see that he was devastated. He had started out the year by winning the Masters, his first-ever major title in New York: This was supposed to have been the other bookend. I sensed he felt I had finally gotten the upper hand on him.

AFTER THE OPEN that year, it was clear that the rivalry between Borg and me had become a hot sports story, like those boxing matchups that promoters are always fanning into flames. The story seemed to have plenty of dramatic elements: the champion versus the young contender. The Swede versus the American. The cool, withdrawn one against the hot and stormy one. That fourth-set tiebreaker we'd played at Wimbledon had begun to take on mythic overtones, and as great as it had been, in my private moments I sometimes wondered if the sportswriters and commentators weren't being a little . . . poetic about it. That's the funny thing about tennis points, and games: They may be awe-inspiring at the moment, but then—except for the videotape, which really tells only a little bit of the story—the moment is gone. They're like poetry written on water.

Still, I didn't mind the attention! Or the money. Money in professional tennis builds exponentially, on that old the-rich-get-richer model: The better you do, the more tickets (and everything else) you can sell, and the more money people throw at you.

Even by those standards, though, the offer that came into my father's office in September of 1980 looked almost like an optical illusion: A South African businessman named Sol Kerzner, who had built a huge casino in the middle of a desert in a place called Bophuthatswana, wanted to pay Borg and me $750,000 apiece to play a one-day exhibition in December at his casino, which was called Sun City. The winner of the exhibition would also get $250,000, making it a potential million-dollar payday.

A million dollars for a *day!* Even today, that seems like an unbeliev-able amount. In 1980, when the dollar was worth more than twice what it is now, the figure was even more incredible. After my eyeballs stopped twirling in their sockets, however, I said to my father, "This kind of money has to be about more than tennis."

And indeed it was. When we looked into it, we found out that Kerzner wanted us to play the match on Bophutatswana's "independence" day, but that the state, which the South African government had established in the 1960s (and which the outside world didn't recognize politically), was very far from independent—it was, in fact, a desperately poor tribal enclave.

Kerzner's idea—to create some kind of neo-Vegas in the South African desert—was brilliant in its way, but the more I talked to trusted friends and advisers, the more I felt I should stay away. There were some persuasive arguments on the other side (besides the money), but Arthur Ashe was the one who ultimately convinced me that I was right. Arthur himself had gone to South Africa several times to play tournaments and to try, through his words and presence, to bring anti-apartheid pressure to bear on the government. He felt that my taking a huge sum of money to play the exhibition would be a very different matter—that it would both tacitly endorse apartheid and look bad for me.

After weeks of talking to dozens of people, my dad and I decided to walk away from the offer (something Frank Sinatra did not do when he signed to perform for a week at Sun City's opening in early 1981). I thought I had better ways to make a million bucks. I was proud to look at myself in the mirror after that: For one of the first times in my life, I had actually taken a stand.

NINETEEN-EIGHTY HAD BEEN a tremendous year for me; I was en-joying the life of a touring tennis pro very much, and now I was a solid number two on the computer. I came into the Masters, at the beginning of January, full of confidence—and also a wee bit chunky.

Shades of Junior Davis Cup! The holidays were the culprit, I think. When I stepped on a scale at home just after New Year's, right before the Masters started, I weighed 182—at least ten pounds over my ideal weight. For the first time in a long while, I felt a little bit of panic. The Masters had always been one of my big events: I liked to make a good showing at my favorite venue, in front of the hometown crowds.

Which was exactly what I failed to do that year. The crowds were electric, but I lost to Gene Mayer, to Borg (in a match that drew the biggest crowd ever to attend an indoor tennis tournament), and then to José-Luis Clerc, and was only able to salvage the week by winning the doubles with Peter for the third straight time (fortunately, in doubles you don't have to cover as much court!).

I went straight home and came down with the flu, and spent a week in bed. Afterward, I made a New Year's resolution to get in better shape, and I cut out beer and dessert completely. It worked—a bit too well. By April, when I was on the West Coast for the hard-court tournament at the Los Angeles Tennis Club, I stepped on the scale at Stacy's house (we were having one last try at getting our relationship back together) and was mildly shocked to see that I weighed 154.

Apparently, it was a good fighting weight: I beat Sandy Mayer in the final at L.A. Also, at the end of March, I'd defeated Borg on indoor carpet in Milan, and Tomas Smid on the same surface in Frankfurt; and later in April I won the big indoor tournament in Dallas (which was on a par with the Australian and French Opens in those days).

HOWEVER, the big story of my spring that year was Davis Cup. I had played three years for Tony Trabert, and had helped us to win in 1978 and 1979. After we lost the Cup in 1980, though, Tony felt he'd had it as captain.

I don't think my behavior helped. When it came to Davis Cup, I was kind of a one-man show, and Tony was getting tired of the act. I wasn't one iota less temperamental and argumentative when I played for my country than I was when I played for my living, and I know that didn't always sit well with Tony (it also doesn't sit well with me, at this distance, that I failed to give respect to a fine former player like Nicky Pietrangeli, who refereed at our tie against Argentina, and whom I burdened with my usual nonsense).

Tony had been a fine player himself—he was the last American before Michael Chang to win the French Open—but he was old-school: You let your racket do the talking.

I was definitely new-school.

The proverbial back-breaking straw was probably our 1980 tie against Mexico, in Mexico City. The Latin American Davis Cup crowds were always pretty out-there—lots of rhythmic chanting, flag-waving, and drum-beating—and this crowd did all that and more. If the Mexico City crowd didn't like the way things were going, they threw coins and seat cushions onto the court. They were pretty wild.

So was I. In fact, Peter Fleming and I were partners in crime that year—we were pretty much on our worst behavior during our doubles match. I didn't help matters any when I cursed at Mexico's captain, who didn't need a translator to understand.

Arthur Ashe replaced Tony in 1981, and what a difference he made: not that he was a better or worse captain, just very, very different. Tony was a talker: Before a match he'd ask if there was anything you wanted a reminder on during play—to keep moving forward, keep the service toss high, whatever. I liked that.

Arthur was a statue. Don't get me wrong: Off the court, I thought

Arthur was a great guy. We could have dinner together, talk, laugh. On the court, though, he said next to nothing. If I was going nuts about a call, he might come over and ask me, in a soft syllable or two, to try and take it easy—but that was it. Mostly, he just sat in his chair by the net and watched.

Our first tie that year was against Mexico again, at home this time (thank God!), at La Costa, down near San Diego. Arthur's big thing, for his Davis Cup debut, was to try to get both Connors and me to play for him. As I've said, Jimmy wasn't precisely a Davis Cup stalwart—"hold-out" would be putting it more accurately.

This year wasn't any different. Connors hemmed and hawed, he said he had scheduling conflicts, his toe was hurting—whatever. What else was new? For Jimmy, tennis meant money, and Davis Cup wasn't money.

Then, however, when we got to La Costa, who should appear but James Scott Connors—to practice with us! Arthur's usual sphinx-like expression turned almost puzzled on that one. It felt like a big tease—who knows what Jimmy had in mind. Who ever knows what Jimmy has in mind?

As it turned out, we could have used him on the court. Even without their drum-beating and seat-cushion-throwing hometown crowd, Mexico almost stunned us after Roscoe Tanner lost his first match to Raul Ramirez, and then Ramirez and a seventeen-year-old Los Angeles high-school student named Jorge Lozano beat Sherwood Stewart and Marty Riessen in doubles. I had to beat Ramirez in the final match to pull out the victory: It was the first time the U.S. had come back from 2–1 down since 1961.

Arthur almost smiled.

MY DRAW AT THE FRENCH wasn't too difficult that spring—until the quarterfinals, when I went up against Lendl. However, despite having been on a bit of a losing streak against him lately, I actually felt quite confident about beating Ivan. My confidence was up in general, and I was trim, fast, and strong. I felt like a world-beater.

That just goes to show you how unpredictable a game tennis is. Paris was cold and misty that spring: the air was heavy, *Court Centrale* was damp and slow. The conditions did not favor a serve-and-volleyer—it was just too hard to finish off points. It felt as if no matter what I did, Lendl had an answer. He ended up beating me in straight sets.

I sucked it up. I firmly believe that one of the hallmarks of a champion—any champion—is the ability to absorb losses and regain confidence immediately. The loss in Paris hurt, but in the larger scheme of things, I knew it was just a momentary stumble in a strong year. And I had my eyes on a bigger prize.

My next win, at Queen's, the big grass-court tune-up for Wimbledon, convinced me I was ready. In a strange way, though—it's hard to explain this—my confidence itself made me nervous, deep down, in places nobody but I knew about. One of the hardest things for me has always been the pressure to live up to my potential—to beat the guys I shouldn't lose to in the early rounds, and get to the finals, where I was supposed to be.

I wouldn't have told this to a soul back then, but as early as my first Wimbledon in '77, I realized I had the potential to be the very best: the best tennis player in the world. I confirmed it for myself as I rose through the rankings—but then, more and more, the problem became that almost everybody was somebody I shouldn't lose to.

The pressure became incomprehensible. I countered it by building defenses that almost nothing, and nobody, could get through.

Almost.

You see it with the great players in any sport, but particularly in tennis, because you're out there by yourself: Disasters can happen even when things are going well. The reverse is also true—you're never out of it. But at the same time, you can never totally relax.

For me, the disasters have almost always occurred inside my own head.

You try to get yourself to the point where you're as fit and match-tough as possible. Once you've put in the work, though, the game becomes extremely mental. I had enough inner strength to know I could beat anyone at all, anytime, on any surface. But behind my defenses were some very dark places. There was always a devil inside me whom I had to fight. And the devil was fear of failure.

For me, the relief of not failing has always been just as strong as, if not stronger than, the joy of winning. They say that when things are going really well, you should just let it happen, but that's exactly when I always started to get nervous. And that's often when my outbursts began.

I could be dominating a guy, up 6–2, 6–2, 2–0 and 40–love on his serve—but if he somehow got out of that game, the negative thoughts would start to creep in. Then, since I couldn't joke around to ease the tension, the tension built up until it started to come out of my ears.

And then my mouth.

I was unbelievably tense at Wimbledon in 1981 because I knew, after beating Borg at the Open, that I could win it, should win it, *would* win it—unless disaster struck.

Well, disaster did strike, and kept on striking, round after round, and somehow I kept getting through—endearing myself to nobody in the process.

I had been famous for a few years now, but Wimbledon in '81 is where I became infamous.

IT BEGAN AT THE BEGINNING. Although this was to become one of my most famous matches, I'm positive almost nobody remembers who I played, and when I played it: Tom Gullikson, first round, Wimbledon 1981. Court One. I was often extra-nervous in the early rounds of tournaments, but this year, at this tournament, I was as tight as a piano wire.

The umpire, a pleasant-enough middle-aged gentleman named Edward James, came up to me when I first walked onto Court One and said something that seemed totally off the wall: "I'm Scottish, so we're not going to have any problems, are we?"

I guess since my name started with "Mc," he thought we were soul brothers! "I'm Irish," I told him, curtly. Nervously.

Things went downhill from there.

I had behaved badly at Wimbledon before. I was already "Super-Brat." Now I upped the ante. Tom could be a pretty tough opponent on grass, but I had a much tougher adversary out there that day. Even though I would eventually win in straight sets, 7–6, 7–5, 6–3, I just couldn't rest easy when I got ahead: The devils were crawling all over my brain that afternoon. When Gullikson went ahead 4–3 in the second set on a miserable line call, I smashed my Wilson Pro Staff racket, and James issued me a warning. And later, when a linesman called a serve deep that I had clearly seen throw up a spray of chalk, I threw my *new* racket and gave a scream that came straight from Queens—but that has traveled very far in the years since.

"Man, you cannot be serious!"

I stopped play, walked up to Mr. James, and asked him if he'd seen the chalk fly.

"There was chalk," James said. "But it was chalk which had spread beyond the line."

I rolled my eyes, shook my head, and walked back to the baseline to play. But then, at 1–1 in the third set, Gullikson hit a serve that was long, and nobody called it out. After we'd played the point, my disbelief mounting with each shot, I asked James if he'd happened to notice that the serve was out.

"The serve was good, Mr. McEnroe," he said.

"You guys are the absolute pits of the world, you know that?" I screamed. Another colorful bit of Queens-ese.

James scribbled something on his notepad, then looked up. "I am going to award a point against you, Mr. McEnroe," he said.

Mr. Edward James had never been to Queens. It later turned out that what he had written down on his pad was, "You guys are the absolute *piss* of the world." Hence the point penalty, for "obscenity." I didn't know that at the time, of course, and I saw red. I demanded to see the referee. Out came the referee, Fred Hoyles, a farmer from Lincolnshire. Appropriately (or not), I used a barnyard epithet to describe my opinion of the situation. Then I pointed at James and yelled—loud enough for the TV microphones, and most of Court One, to hear—"We're not going to have a point taken away because this guy is an incompetent fool!"

After the match, I was fined $750 for the obscenity, and the same amount for an unsportsmanlike comment about the umpire, and I was threatened with an additional $10,000 fine, and possible suspension from the tournament, if I engaged in any further "aggravated behavior." And I want you to understand: I felt terrible. I've felt awful virtually every time I've had one of my on-court meltdowns, with the exception of a few occasions when I really believed I needed to let someone have it. But those really are the exceptions. I've apologized a number of times afterward to umpires and players.

And to anyone out there who felt they deserved an apology but didn't get one: I apologize now.

The London tabloids went wild after that match: THE SHAME OF JOHN MCENROE; DISGRACE OF SUPER BRAT, read the huge black headlines. One paper quoted a psychologist at a local hospital, who called me a classic example of a "hysterical extrovert."

A hysterical extrovert! I'll take the former—with an asterisk—but I'm not so sure about the latter.

Stacy, who was playing in the women's draw, was rattled, and rattled even further when a crowd of reporters and photographers followed her to her practice session the next morning. (It didn't help that, while she had been my girlfriend publicly, and the press was treating her as such now, our relationship was sputtering to a close.) She lost her match that afternoon, and flew back to the States.

I bit my tongue—more or less—for the next four rounds. I told my dad, though, that if I won this year, and if the tournament officials and English press continued to fire away at me like this, I wasn't coming back.

IT SEEMS TO HAPPEN pretty regularly at Wimbledon that some un-seeded phenom will streak through the tournament, knocking off a big name or two, and reach the final rounds. Sometimes it's even a young qualifier! Besides me, there was the even more amazing example of Boris Becker in 1985.

It happened in 1981, too, not with a qualifier or a young up-and-comer, but with a twenty-eight-year-old Aussie named Rod Frawley. He was a good grass-court player, but when I met him in the semifinals, he was also unseeded in the tournament (and number 110 in the world). The whole scenario drove me nuts.

I was champing at the bit to get to Borg, who I felt certain was going to beat Connors in the other semi. I was also incredibly anxious—never my finest state. Here, in the person of one Rod Frawley, was the kind of match I most dreaded: one I had to win, or I'd look like the world's worst choker.

Frawley had a big mane of wavy hair, like a rock star, and an edgy at-titude: He had nothing to lose, he had come this far, and he was going to pull out all the stops. Besides, Aussies, as a rule, don't tend to be espe-cially reverent.

I was beyond irreverence: I was contemptuous. From the moment play began, I was muttering to myself about this upstart who felt he de-served to be on the same court with me. It was pure bravado, of course, born of sheer anxiety—the prospect of being stopped just short of my date with destiny was unthinkable, and yet, to the demons that always lurked on the edge of my mind, all too thinkable.

If Frawley didn't hear my mutterings, he certainly picked up the message, and he didn't like it a bit. Whenever I would complain about a call—and my complaint rate was starting to pick up fast in this match—he would complain to the umpire, R.A.F. Wing Commander George Grime. We played a tight first set (a lot tighter than I would have liked), and after one "out" call, my needle went into the red. "You're a disgrace to mankind!" I screamed. (Not every line can be immortal.)

"Warning, Mr. McEnroe," said Wing Commander Grime.

"But I was saying it to myself, umpire," I tried—not really knowing, to tell the truth, whom I had said it to.

I won the match in a jittery three sets, and the other shoe dropped: I was fined $10,000 for my aggravated behavior. (I later appealed the fine and won.)


HOW CAN I DESCRIBE my feelings going into that final? Happy but tense, or tense but happy? I was thrilled to be in the rematch I'd wanted so badly, but Borg had won here an unbelievable five times in a row. On the other hand, this time I had actually experienced a Wimbledon final, a final I had almost won. I had my U.S. Open victory against Bjorn under my belt. As confident as I felt about my chances, however, I knew that anything could always happen in a big match, especially on Centre Court.

One thing was for certain, though: There would be no more misbehavior from me in this tournament. Thanks to my action-packed lead-up, I knew the crowd and the officials would jump all over me the second I opened my mouth. And I knew I'd need every ounce of my energy.

I got off to a sluggish start. I was tight, nervous, over-impressed with the occasion. I could feel the crowd was against me (I was beginning to get used to it). At the same time, it was hard *not* to be over-impressed:

This was the apex of tennis, the rematch I'd dreamed of, against the player I'd idolized since my early teens.

Borg won the first set, 6–4.

As I loosened up, the match turned into a dogfight. I won a tight tiebreaker to take the second set, and the third set was going in that direction, too. Underneath my nerves, and my certainty that I had to play every point to my utmost, a strange idea was starting to materialize: *He's not quite as hungry as last year. This is my match to take, if I can take it.*

Borg had a set point in the third-set tiebreaker. Then a bad call against me gave him double set point. I summoned everything I had, and negated one set point. Then the other. Then I won the set.

I never relaxed until the last point, but after I took the third set, I knew in my bones that I was going to win.

When we shook hands, Bjorn looked oddly relieved. (And what about me? Was I more relieved at not losing than thrilled at winning? I'm not sure I could tell you even now.)

But the minute I picked up that trophy, I'll tell you this: No matter what I had said to my father, I wanted to win it again. I knew then that I was coming back.


SHORTLY AFTER THE MATCH, Alan Mills, the tournament's assistant referee, called my father and asked if I planned to attend that night's Wimbledon victors' dinner. My father said that he'd ask—but I pleaded exhaustion. I just wanted to relax (at last!), and celebrate with my friends, including some new buddies from the Pretenders (whose lead singer, Chrissie Hynde, would soon incorporate my now-famous phrase "You are the pits of the world!" into her song, "Pack It Up"). Frankly, the Wimbledon dinner sounded like a snooze. Maybe I could just stop by for coffee and dessert, we suggested, and say a few words?

That sounded all right to both of us—but when Mills relayed the word to Sir Brian Burnett, the head of the tournament, the answer came back like a rocket: "If John does not attend the entire banquet, his invitation is withdrawn."

Withdrawn! We simply found that unreasonable. It felt like Wimbledon high-handedness at its worst, so I gave the banquet a miss. I wanted to be with my friends.

The London tabloids had another field day. The news came later that, for the first time in a hundred years, Wimbledon had decided not to give the men's champion an automatic membership in the All England Club, "due to Mr. McEnroe's poor behavior and antics in the fortnight."

My initial response in New York was an eye-rolling shrug. The next time they would see me was when I would defend my title.


NUMBER ONE.

It happened at the '81 U.S. Open, and it happened in the most bizarre way possible.

I finally seemed to have Bjorn Borg's number. I'd now beaten him the last three times I'd played him: at the last year's Open, in Milan, and at Wimbledon. Now, if I got through to the finals at Flushing Meadows, I would play him for a championship he had never won and that I'd won the last two years in a row.

I played Vitas in the semis. It was a tremendous five-setter, the antithesis of our 1979 final, which had ultimately felt hollow to me because of his lackluster play. This time he was hitting the ball with a fury I had never seen before. His serve let him down a little bit in the fifth, and that made the difference.

The next day, in the finals, Borg and I split the first two sets, and he was ahead 4–2 in the third. He had broken me twice, and was serving to go up 5–2, but I hit two great topspin-lob winners over his head in that game, and after the second one, I could've sworn I saw the air go out of him.

From there on in, it looked as if Bjorn was doing something I had never seen from him before: throwing in the towel. After having been down 2–4 in the third, I wound up winning that set 6–4 and cruising through the fourth, 6–2. In the last set, it looked to me as though he was barely trying.

There are times—usually in exhibitions, but sometimes even in big tournaments—when you feel so bad physically or mentally that you're simply not able to go all-out. It's a tricky situation. You don't want to lose by just missing every ball, so you hit a shot and leave a part of the court open.

At that point, your body language clearly says, "I'm not going to cover that—just hit it there, it'll be a winner, and the people will think, 'Look, he was too good.' " That's what happened with Sampras when he played Lleyton Hewitt in the finals of last year's Open: Pete had just run out of gas—he looked as if he had glue on his feet.

And that's what happened with Borg in '81—except that it didn't look physical to me. He came to the net and shook my hand. Then he went over to his bag, picked it up, walked off the court, walked out of the stadium, got into a car that apparently was ready to go, and—within minutes of the last point—left the facility.

No ceremony. No press conference. Nothing. The only other time I've ever seen that happen was at the '77 U.S. Open, when there was a bad call on match point between Vilas and Connors, and even though Vilas had beaten him 6–0 in the last set anyway, Jimmy walked off the court without shaking Guillermo's hand, and left the stadium.

It was later revealed that apparently Bjorn had received some type of death threat. Obviously, that would put a strain on you, so maybe that explains it. Or maybe it doesn't.

Whatever the reason, I had now officially replaced Borg as number one in the world.

THE YEAR ENDED with a bang, at the Davis Cup finals in Cincinnati. We had lost to Argentina the year before, in Buenos Aires, and now it was payback time—except that facing a team led by Clerc and Vilas wasn't going to make payback very easy.

Both of them were brilliant singles players, numbers five and six in the world at that point, and while I felt reasonably confident I could win my singles, Roscoe Tanner was iffier against Vilas.

Doubles was going to be crucial.

On paper at that point, Peter and I were the number-one doubles team in the world, but paper and reality are sometimes very different matters in pressure-cooker situations—and no situation is more pressured than a Davis Cup final.

Then throw into the mix the fact that José-Luis and Guillermo weren't speaking to each other.

Argentina is a lot smaller than the U.S.A., and Clerc and Vilas cast proportionately bigger shadows there than any tennis player could here, even in the game's boom days. They were both national heroes, each of them vain about his looks and reputation and standing. Vilas was a god in Argentina, a national legend: No one in tennis, let alone from Latin America, had ever had a year like his 1977. Clerc was just a notch below him, and coming on strong. He was also just twenty-three, while Guillermo was approaching thirty—a little long in the tooth for a tennis player. All that made them naturally competitive to start with, and there had been disagreements—about who should captain their Davis Cup team, about how the money for the tie should be divided.

Peter and I may have had our disagreements, but nothing like that.

Still, I'm of the opinion that when you take two great singles players and put them together, they can make a highly effective doubles team—whether they're talking to each other or not. And that's exactly what happened in Cincinnati.

That, and a lot more.

From the beginning, it was a wild afternoon: It seemed anything that could happen in a tennis match *did* happen: bad blood (Clerc and I also happened not to be crazy about each other), bad calls, bad behavior.

Peter and I went out swinging, and we won the first set easily. The crowd was shouting, stamping their feet, waving American flags. But then the Argentineans did something odd in the second set: they switched sides. Perfectly legal. Vilas, a left-hander, had been playing on the left to start out, but now he was on the right, and their forehands were in the middle. Suddenly they were playing much, much better than they had been earlier.

We didn't quite notice it at first. Then, however, in the middle of the second set, something truly weird happened.

One of your advantages as home country in Davis Cup is that you get to select the surface on which you feel you can win. Naturally, in South America, we always had to play on red clay, and I had to adjust my strategy a bit to longer rallies. At home this year, we'd picked a fast indoor carpet, to suit my serve-and-volley game. In the middle of the second set, Vilas walked over and pointed his racket at a split seam in the surface. "*Rota,*" he said. "Broken. It's coming apart."

Now the two of them went to the umpire, Bob Jenkins of Britain, and told him they wanted the court fixed. Right away. "We'll fix it later," Jenkins said.

"No, no, we want it fixed now," Vilas said. "We're afraid we're going to fall on it."

From our perspective, these guys were just trying to throw us off—

break our rhythm. They were starting to gather a little steam; they wanted to take a break, marshal their strength (and maybe mend a fence or two), and come out smoking. We shook our heads.

The umpire was still hesitant. Then Vilas walked over to the split seam, reached down, and grabbed it. He's a very strong guy. He picked up the edge of the carpet and pulled, until about thirty feet of it had come unglued. "Oh, look," he called to the umpire. "The court is not playable. Come look at it now."

They got their delay, and we were just steaming. We went to the locker room and sat for twenty-five minutes, with images in our heads of the two of them laughing about the whole thing.

Sure enough, when they came out again, they were a *team*—and not just any team, but a super-team, like Batman and Robin. The momentum of the match shifted completely, and they won the second set. The quality of the tennis throughout was amazing: Both teams were playing very sharply and aggressively, and every rally seemed to go five or six shots longer than anybody would have imagined.

Meanwhile, their captain, Carlos Junquet, kept jumping to his feet and questioning every call that went against Argentina. After a while, I couldn't take it anymore. I went over to him and told him what I thought of his coaching style.

Clerc, by far the more hotheaded of the team, called over to say what he thought of me. I gave him some back.

"Be quiet, John," Arthur called.

The crowd stamped harder, shouted louder, waved faster. We won the third set. We needed one more.

I was serving in the first game of the fourth set. Every time I went to the line to serve, Clerc or Vilas, whichever one was receiving, would walk off to the side, wipe off his racket, talk to the other guy for a moment. It was a delaying tactic, pure and simple, designed to throw off my rhythm. It didn't work, though: I won my serve anyway.

As we were changing sides, Clerc was standing and talking to the umpire, complaining about something, and—I admit it; I was just sick of his gamesmanship—I trash-talked him. It happens more than you'd think in professional tennis (with the women, too, by the way): If you're not passing each other in icy silence when you change sides, you're muttering things at each other, sometimes even giving each other a little bump as you pass. You're gladiators out there, after all. Even in Davis Cup.

This was a little louder than a mutter, though. And Clerc turned to me and lisped, in a mincing, effeminate voice, "You're so nice, John."

I went ballistic. I threw down my racket, got right up into his face, and started screaming at him. He was screaming at me. Everybody ran over to try and break it up: Peter, Vilas, Arthur, their captain, and the referee, a Dane named Kurt Nielsen. Arthur was really steamed at me now, so much so that—believe it or not—Peter literally had to hold him back as Arthur tried to push me away from Clerc. The crowd was on its feet, going crazy.

Finally, after a few minutes, we actually went back to playing tennis. At one point, when I made a loud remark, Arthur pointed at me and said, "You stop it. Just stop it and play." I was impressed enough to shut up: I had never seen him like this before. However, on the next changeover, Arthur started to lecture us anyway. Peter interrupted him. "Come on—we're all on the same *team*," Peter said, impatiently. "Let's just go back and beat these guys."

Clerc and Vilas kept alternating their big ground strokes with topspin lobs—mixing it up, throwing us off. They took the fourth set, 6–4, and then the final set seesawed until they got a bead on my serve and broke me (Peter and I were always more vulnerable when he was at net). And then Vilas was serving at 7–6.

If he held, that would be the match, and probably the tie. Argentina would be ahead 2–1, with Tanner to play Vilas after I played Clerc the next day. I knew I could beat Clerc, but Roscoe over Vilas would've been an upset.

We broke Vilas at love.

Clerc was serving at 9–10, the twentieth game of the fifth set—the crowd was hoarse by this time—to try to even the score. His serve had been huge for the entire match: He had held twelve straight times. This was his thirteenth service game, though, and since there's always something weird about big Davis Cup matches, it made a strange kind of sense that this game would be bad luck for him. When my lob over their heads at our ad kissed the corner lines and bounced out of reach, Peter and I threw up our arms, and the crowd jumped to its feet. The twenty-game set had been the longest fifth set in a Cup final since 1907.

The weirdness settled in even further after the match was over, when we remembered what Victor Amaya, our practice player, had said at the warmup that morning. All the rest of us had been convinced that Peter and I would just roll over Vilas and Clerc. But Vic had said, "I think you'll win it 11–9 in the fifth."

THE NEXT DAY, against Clerc, I was—practically—a perfect gentleman. Whatever nonsense we had had to air, we'd already aired it in the doubles: Our singles match was just tennis. Really good tennis. After we split the first two sets, I got down 1–3 in the third, then won five games in a row to take the set before going into the locker room for the break. I was determined to jump right on Clerc after the break and close out the match, but instead he jumped on me, surprising me with his aggressiveness and grabbing the fourth set, 6–3.

So once again, it all came down to the fifth.

I must say that even if my fitness has occasionally been suspect, I think my overall record in five-set matches is up there with practically anybody's. The fifth set is for all the marbles, and while I've been known to choke under certain conditions, I would never have accomplished what I did if I hadn't been able to lift my game for the big points, the big games, the big sets. What changed for me in the fifth set that day was my serve. It had been good for the first four sets, but now I felt I could win service points at will. When I broke Clerc at love in the fourth game of the fifth, I knew the match was mine. I was running on fumes and adrenaline, but I knew the match was mine. When Clerc hit that last volley in the fourth game long, I jumped a foot in the air and pumped my fist; the crowd jumped to its feet, yelling, "U–S–A! U–S–A!"

That gave me goosebumps. I couldn't squander the rare opportunity of having an entire arena full of people all on my side, and I knew I wouldn't let my country down. Every time you change sides at a Davis Cup final, the cup itself is sitting there on a table, staring you in the face. I wanted it.

I served five rockets in the last game. On the first, I butchered an easy volley, but I didn't make that mistake again. Clerc barely got his racket on my last serve. I leaped in the air, let out a victory cry, then jumped the net to shake Clerc's hand. I threw myself into Arthur's arms, and then Bill Norris's. I turned to the crowd and stuck both my index fingers into the air. It was impossible to hear. Then I hugged every guy on the team.

I was a hero: a very strange sensation for me, let me tell you.

It was Sunday, December 13, 1981. It had been a long year, and an amazing one. I had won Wimbledon, the U.S. Open, and three points in the Davis Cup final. The last American to do that was Don Budge, in 1937.

I was on top of the mountain. Where would I go now?

# 7

TRUE STORY: in late 1980, I played an exhibition with Borg, Connors, and Vitas in a beautiful hall in Frankfurt. In the semifinals, Vitas was playing Borg, Bjorn missed a passing shot, and—thinking the crowd would be making a lot of noise—he said, "Shit!" At the instant he said it, though, it happened that the hall was relatively quiet, and everybody in the place heard him! Vitas's mouth dropped open, and then he fell down on his knees and started bowing to Borg, as the crowd gave Bjorn a standing ovation.

It was so conspicuous when Borg reacted that once; I felt just as conspicuous whenever I made a sound in a match against him. The contrast was glaring when I played him, much more so than with the other players, most of whom reacted on some level. Later on, even Sampras questioned calls! *Wilander,* for God's sake, questioned calls and occasionally got angry. Lendl was never considered a bad actor, and he got peeved plenty.

How could a guy not change his facial expression more than three or four times over the twelve years of his career?

I think what was happening at that Frankfurt exhibition was that Bjorn was finally starting to relax. It could also be that he had already made a very important decision.

In the fall after the '81 U.S. Open, several of us played a set of exhibitions in Australia. Vitas, Bjorn, and I were in a room, having a beer before a press conference, and Bjorn said to us, "I'm quitting tennis."

We barely even responded to it. In fact, Vitas and I laughed. "Are you joking?" I said. "What the hell are you going to do? You're twenty-five!" But Bjorn was dead serious. All he would say was, "No, no, no, I'm not playing anymore." Vitas and I just sat there, dumbfounded. Then we walked down to the press conference, and Borg promptly told the reporters how excited he was to be playing next year! I remember thinking, he would've made a great politician. He certainly had me confused.

There was some speculation about Borg at the time, because he hadn't signed the ATP commitment for the coming year—each year, at the U.S. Open, we had to make a schedule for the entire next year and sign a form saying what tournaments we were going to play. Borg didn't want to sign his commitment form in September of '81. He felt that, emotionally, he wasn't in a position to do it.

He was told that if he didn't sign the form, he would have to play the qualifiers for every event in the coming year. Along with everyone at the top of the game, I felt that this was a slap in the face to one of our greatest champions, but the ATP said, "We've got to go by the rules."

It felt obvious to me that this organization wasn't looking out for the best interests of the game. It was like something you'd find in a Communist country. I thought it was scandalous that they would do this to their number-one person. If anything, I felt their attitude should have been: "Look, this guy is burnt out; he needs a break. Let's give him the time he needs—let him take two, three, four months away from the game, and whenever he's ready to come back, let him do what he wants."

As a result of all this, everyone was asking Bjorn, "What are you going to do next year?" I just assumed that his saying he was quitting was a negotiating ploy, or that he needed some time off, or that he was mad he had lost his number-one ranking and hadn't won the Open—any number of things. I didn't think he really meant it.

Then I realized he was serious.

That was when people started saying to me, "You drove him out of the game." People said Borg realized he couldn't beat me in the U.S. Open or Wimbledon, that my style of play was too much for him. And so that was it, he quit.

Here's the thing, though: At that point, he had defeated Connors something like ten times in a row; he had beaten him in the semis of the Open that year. At the very worst, he was a clear number two. You never knew what could happen in major events. I could lose, and Bjorn wind up playing someone besides me in the finals, maybe Jimmy. I could get injured. A lot of things could happen. To walk away so quickly when he was still so close to number one seemed crazy.

I do think I had something to do with it—he might have thought, *I can't be number one, so forget it.* But, amazingly enough, I also think that he had other things on his mind besides me.

Here's what I speculate: Borg was on the verge of being overwhelmed. He was also the first guy who could afford to quit. He'd started so young; at age twenty-five, he'd already traveled the circuit extensively for ten years. His life had become so regimented, and the superstitions so ingrained, that for the five years he won Wimbledon, he'd stay at the same hotel, practice at the same time and place—all day. Every day, he'd eat the same meals, get a massage at the same time.

So when he saw what Vitas was doing, which was the other extreme—

the staying up all night, the partying, the women—when Bjorn experienced it on a small scale at the exhibitions, just enough to give him a taste of what he had been missing . . . well, that was that.

Bjorn is like Jekyll and Hyde. A couple of years ago, when I was playing an exhibition with him in Stockholm, he said to me, "I'm two people." And he is. He's the world's greatest guy, and then he's completely out of his mind. I'm crazy to begin with—somewhat crazy and somewhat normal. Bjorn goes *way* to the extremes.

After he made the rash decision to say, "Forget it, I don't need this anymore," I think he found he'd dug himself into a hole and he couldn't get out of it. He's got so much pride, it would simply have been too hard for him to admit he was wrong and come back.

The only thing I can even begin to compare the impact of his decision to is the NBA, when Magic Johnson and Larry Bird came in to the league in the early '80s and sparked a renaissance. Eventually, the Lakers and the Celtics were the two best teams. Magic had great players around him, Kareem and James Worthy and Michael Cooper; Bird had Kevin McHale and Robert Parrish.

Now, imagine, right at the peak of this renaissance, if the entire Laker team had retired!

Borg's leaving tennis was like that: a huge blow for the sport, and for me personally. It was unbelievable: The matches between us had become really exciting, and even though Jimmy had slipped a bit (or so I thought), he was still certainly a major threat—and now, suddenly, Borg was gone. It took the wind out of my sails: I had a very tough time motivating myself and getting back on track. It took me a couple of years to start improving again.

As I've said, I'd always felt that I would deal with being number one when I got there—I wasn't going to worry about it before it happened. I hadn't realized what it entailed, however; it was far more than I'd imagined. The weight of people's expectations felt huge. It was very difficult to get comfortable.

First of all, I was amazed at how differently people treated me now. I'd thought number two was a pretty big deal! But number one was a very strange place indeed—the peak of the mountain, those icy winds blowing around my head. I was alienated from my competitors, and I had an even tougher time with my friends. I was less trusting in all relationships, because I felt, more than ever before, that everybody was out to get something from me. The sheer volume of attention was unbelievable—nobody who hasn't been there can begin to understand it. I was unable to relax into it, unable simply to focus on the work of playing tennis. A line from a letter sent to me by my old high-school friend Melissa Franklin kept ringing in my ears: "You always seem slightly distressed." I knew she was right, and I kept wondering why.

B O R G  H A D  W O N the last two Masters; now that he was gone, there was a slight power vacuum at the top of the tour. I was officially number one, but the shock of Bjorn's departure, combined with a huge playing schedule in 1981, had left me feeling tired and flat by the end of the year. Factor in a rough autumn for Connors—he and his wife, Patti, were in the process of separating (temporarily, as it would turn out)—and the conditions were ideal for the rise of Ivan Lendl.

Lendl had come a long way since my easy dismissal of him from the '77 French juniors. Back then, he had just turned seventeen, still had a little baby fat on him, and wasn't nearly as powerful and agile as he would later become.

Over the past four and a half years, though, he had lost the fat and turned into six feet two inches of sinew and muscle, the best-conditioned athlete on the tour (and he would become even fitter in years to come), with ferociously powerful serve and groundstrokes. With his size, fitness, and power, he was really an early prototype for the players on today's men's tour. Lendl rarely came to net on his serve, but—like most of the current guys—he had such a powerful serve that he could usually put himself into position to hit a big forehand and control the point. He was so strong and fit that he could beat almost anybody from the backcourt.

He was also a very strange guy, to put it charitably. His parents had both been top players in Czechoslovakia, his mother much higher-ranked than his father—she'd actually been number two there at one point. Legend had it that when Ivan was little, his mother used to leash him to a fence while she played.

It couldn't have helped his personality. Whatever had happened to him as a kid, it had left him with an odd, harsh demeanor—kind of bullying and babyish at the same time—and a mean sense of humor: He would make merciless fun of lower-ranked players, who, because of tennis's pecking order, often had to pretend they thought he was funny, even when the joke was at their expense.

Not me. For a long time, I was the one guy who seemed to have the solution to Lendl's game. I beat him the first few times we played as professionals, and I never took any nonsense from him, on or off the court—quite the opposite: I almost enjoyed getting on his case at every available opportunity.

In November of '79, for example, I played him in the finals of an exhibition in Milan—they used to have amazing exhibitions there: big crowds, big money (at least for the time). The house was packed for the final, the crowd was excited, and I wiped Lendl out in the first set, 6–1. Halfway through that set, I could see his shoulders slump—I could tell he'd given up, and now he was dogging it. He was just standing there, barely even trying.

That's not good if you're playing in an exhibition, especially one with a sizable crowd, so I got a little hot under the collar. I felt we were being

With my brother
Mark (on the right),
in Douglaston, Queens.
*(McEnroe family photo)*

Mark, me, Patrick (in front),
and our mom, Kay.
*(McEnroe family photo)*

With Dad and Mom
at the Orange Bowl
tournament, 1972.
*(McEnroe family
photo)*

The Stanford collegiate championship team, 1978. I'm second from the right in the front row. *(Stanford University)*

My first Grand Slam singles title, at the 1979 U.S. Open, in which I beat Vitas Gerulaitis. *(AP/Wide World Photos)*

The Queen's Cup, 1979. Already earning the name "Superbrat." *(Photofest)*

The rewards of fame. On the set of *Players,* 1979. Left to right: me, Robert Evans, Pancho Gonzales, star (the late) Dean-Paul Martin, and actor Tommy Cook. *(Photofest)*

The 1980 Wimbledon final against
Borg: an amazing five–set match.
*(Tony Duffy / GettyImages)*

Borg falls to his knees after winning.
It was his fifth straight Wimbledon title.
*(Tony Duffy / GettyImages)*

Jimmy Connors and I exchanging
trash talk at Wimbledon, 1980.
*(Hulton / Archive)*

The infamous 1981
Wimbledon. Kicking
my racket against
Tom Gullikson in
the first round.
*(AP/Wide World Photos)*

Making the choke sign against
Rod Farley in the semifinals.
They didn't understand that
I was referring to *myself*.
*(©UPI/CORBIS)*

Victory! Borg's streak
was snapped and I had
my first Wimbledon
singles championship.
*(Tony Duffy/GettyImages)*

The 1981 U.S. Open. Borg walked off the court, out of the stadium and—for a while—out of tennis. I was now officially number one. (©Bettmann/CORBIS)

With my doubles partner, Peter Fleming, at the U.S. Open, 1981. (Peter L. Gould/Woodfin Camp & Associates)

Sweet victory over Ivan Lendl at the 1984 U.S. Open, after an excruciating loss to him at the French Open. This would be my last Grand Slam singles championship. (AP/Wide World Photos)

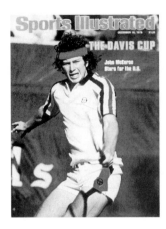

My *Sports Illustrated* covers
(*From top left:* JOHN G. ZIMMERMAN, *Sports Illustrated*;
*next three*, WALTER IOOSS, JR., *Sports Illustrated*; *next two*,
STEVE POWELL, *Sports Illustrated*; MANNY MILAN,
*Sports Illustrated*)

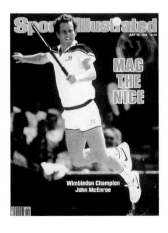

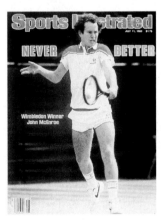

Kicking a camera at the 1985 U.S. Professional Indoor Championship. *(AP/Wide World Photos)*

Patrick and me at the 1991 Volvo championship—the first time we ever met in a championship final. *(AP/Wide World Photos)*

A new career as a commentator, here at the 1994 French Open. *(Photofest)*

The 1997 unveiling of the new Court 1 at Wimbledon. (Boris Becker is behind me to the left.) *(EMPICS Sports Photo Agency/Steve Mitchell)*

Greg Gumbel and I entertain the troops between matches, Wimbledon 1997. *(AP/Wide World Photos)*

On the 1999 Seniors Tour, celebrating a point against Mats Wilander. *(AP/Wide World Photos)*

In the 2000 Davis Cup, as captain, here next to Pete Sampras and Andre Agassi. *(©AFP/CORBIS)*

Surrounded by schoolchildren while in Zimbabwe for the opening round of the 2000 Davis Cup. *(AP/Wide World Photos)*

With Nelson Mandela.
*(AP/Wide World Photos)*

Celebrating a victory over the Czech Republic in the Davis Cup quarterfinals, 2000. *(AP/Wide World Photos)*

With Borg at a charity match at Buckingham Palace, 2000. My four-year-old daughter, Anna, has the trophy. *(©Reuters NewMedia Inc./CORBIS)*

A stunt for the David Letterman show, 2001—I hit a ball from the roof of the Broadway Theater into the lighted window of the Ed Sullivan Theater across the street. *(CBS Worldwide Inc.)*

My family—the picture was Patty's birthday present to me, February 16, 2000. Anna is on my lap. Behind us, from the left, are baby Ava, Emily, Ruby, Sean, Patty, and Kevin. *(Frank Schram)*

Rock and roll! With David Bowie, Keith Richards, and Tina Turner in 1983.
*(Bob Gruen/Star File)*

With Eddie Van
Halen and Vitas
Gerulaitis.
*(Glen LaFerman)*

Sting, beware!
*(AP/Wide World Photos)*

I still can't believe it myself. With Ronald and Nancy Reagan in 1981 as part of a joint Davis Cup/U.S. Ski Team celebration. I'd just won the U.S. Open. Arthur Ashe is in the background.
*(White House)*

With George H. W. Bush
at Wimbledon in 1997.
*(AP/Wide World Photos)*

With Bill Clinton at the U.S. Open in 2000 *(©Reuters NewMedia Inc./CORBIS)*

well paid, and so the crowd should get its money's worth. I said, "Listen, Ivan, you're acting like a pussy. Get out there and start playing. You wimp!" He started whining: "You can't talk like that to me! You can't talk like that!" But I wouldn't let up.

In the second set, he again played an abysmal game, putting virtually no effort into it. I gave it to him again, totally roasted him: "You're a quitter, man."

"Sergio!" he called—Sergio Palmieri, later my agent, used to be the tournament director there—"Sergio, you tell him to stop that! He can't talk to me like that!" And I still wouldn't let up.

I often wonder why I didn't just let him make a complete ass of himself in that match. Because then, all of a sudden, Lendl started playing harder than I'd ever seen him play before. I'd gotten him so worked up that he wound up beating me!

Another example: A while later, we were at an indoor-clay exhibition in Barcelona: America versus Europe. The American team was Vince Van Patten, who was having a hot year; Andrés Gomez, who, as an Ecuadoran, somehow counted as American; and me. Lendl was one of the guys on the European team. It was basically just a fun occasion: You never had to take exhibitions as seriously as you did tournaments.

Predictably enough, I wound up facing Lendl in the final, and—this is how high I was riding at the time—I was sitting with Gomez and Van Patten before the match, and I said, "What score do you want me to beat him by?" We decided it was going to be 6–2, 6–2.

I went out on the court and everything was just perfect: I won the first set, 6–2. Meanwhile, Lendl was whining: "My arm hurts. I can't play." I told him, "Don't play, then. Either play with some effort, or don't play at all." He kept saying, "One more game, one more game; if I don't hold serve this time, I quit."

This was at 6–2, 1–0. I broke him. He said, "I'll play *two* more games." Now it was 3–0. I said, "Yeah? Now what?" People were starting to boo him, because he was basically dogging it. Then it got to 5–0: It was 6–2, 5–0, and Gomez and Van Patten thought I was Superman, because I was doing exactly what I'd claimed I would do, right on the money. I was winking at them.

But then it got tricky, because Lendl held his serve—still trying his song-and-dance about his arm—to make it 5–1. Now *I* was serving. if I won my serve, it'd be 6–2, 6–1—not the right score! I got to 40–30 in the game—it was 6–2, 5–1, match point. What should I do?

Unfortunately, I decided to throw the game, so I could win the match as predicted, 6–2, 6–2.

It was not a good decision. I lost my serve, then I blew the next game, with Lendl serving at 2–5. I thought, "Damn! I screwed it up," but at least I was still serving at 5–3. I made the effort—then I lost *that* game. I had another match point at 5–4, and blew that, too. Suddenly, Lendl's arm wasn't hurting him anymore.

He won the second set, 7–5.

I lost it. Totally snapped. By the third set, the crowd was booing *me*, and throwing things, and I was putting first serves into the stands, making rude gestures. Of course I wound up losing the match—I didn't win another game. When I walked off the court, Van Patten and Gomez didn't know what to say.

The cat was now officially out of the bag. Lendl could beat me.

Maybe because of his background, Ivan was always going into strange sulks and weird head trips. Sometimes the victim was his opponent; for a long time, it was just as often himself. For quite a while, he had a reputation for choking away big matches.

Once he decided to work on his mind, body, and game, however, he started cutting a wide swath through professional tennis. As much as I may have disliked him, I have to give Lendl credit: Nobody in the sport has ever worked as hard as he did. Some people have natural talent, which in our sport, I divide into two categories, athletic ability and tennis skill. Ivan wasn't the most talented player, but his dedication—physical and mental—was incredible, second to none.

He was very stiff—almost robotic—but he learned how to hit a reasonable crosscourt backhand return and a really reasonable volley, based largely on his ability to physically intimidate the other guy by getting into position and then swinging away. And he did it all through sheer rehearsal.

Some people don't want to rehearse; they just want to perform. Other people want to practice a hundred times first. I'm in the former group: I've always felt that if I practiced too much, I'd get stale, that the thrill of hitting tennis shots would go flat. Practice has always felt like a chore to me. Sometimes I'll say, "God, I'm looking forward to practicing"—and then within a couple of minutes, I'm bored. Then I want to play games or sets, to make it more interesting.

I did spend a lot more time practicing than most people thought I did, however, and a lot more time *thinking* about tennis. That may sound like a cop-out, but it's not. I've always thought constantly about the game, almost the way chess players think about chess. Tony Palafox drilled it into me: *Be ready for the next shot. Know what you're going to do next.*

As a result, because of my talent, my mental preparation, and a reasonable state of conditioning, I always figured that for two hours it was going to be a real pain in the behind to play me—and that 90 to 95 percent of the time, my matches weren't going to last more than two hours. When they went longer, I became much more vulnerable, because I wasn't in the amazing physical condition of a Borg or a Lendl; even then, my ability, my intensity, and my desire would always take me a long way. I'm a fighter. I'm going to hang in there and win a lot of my matches.

I call tennis "the lazy man's game" now. Guys rely on giant serves and huge groundstrokes, but little thought, strategy, or passion goes into it—or so it seems. That's largely why no one truly dominates the sport now. There's loads of talent out there—just look at players such as Lleyton

Hewitt, Gustavo Kuerten, Yevgeny Kafelnikov, and Marat Safin. But does anybody have the fire of Connors, the dedication of Lendl, or the physical presence of Borg? Not that I'm aware of, at least not yet.

Through some difficult times, Lendl turned himself into an incredibly tough player, mentally as well as physically. He just said, "I'm going to do it until I get it right, and I'm going to keep doing it and doing it, for hours and hours and years and years." You have to credit that type of perseverance: Very few people can stick with it that long. And very few people have great natural ability. Everyone else—and this is true of most players these days—is in the middle: On a given day, a guy is a world-beater, then the next day he's just not there.

As much as I hate to give Lendl credit, he became a great champion. And in a way, he has me to thank for it, I think. I goaded him into it.

BETWEEN OCTOBER of 1981 and February of 1982, Lendl won forty-four matches in a row, mowing down everyone in his path, including me. He was running, bicycling, doing calisthenics, and practicing, practicing, practicing. I was doing what I'd always done—playing tennis, period. That was enough to allow me to compete at the highest levels, and to win almost all the time, but it wasn't enough to push me through to a new peak.

I kept thinking that maybe Bjorn would change his mind and come back. Meanwhile, I was drifting a little bit. . . .

In February of 1982, Stacy and I finally broke up definitively. She told me that we were either going to get married or stop seeing each other. I was just turning twenty-three, however, and I certainly didn't feel old enough to get married. I'm not sure she did, either, or could ever trust me again, so we both went on to lead our lives—with some regrets on both sides, I'm sure, but probably a little bit of relief, too.

Spring brought a new relationship. Stella Hall was a model in New

York, a dark-haired, willowy North Carolinian, and both Doug Saputo and Peter Rennert had been very interested in her for a while. I'd been interested, too, but had always felt funny about even seeming to move in on a close friend's girlfriend.

When it became clear, though, that nothing was developing between either Doug or Peter and Stella, I let her know about my interest. And Stella said she felt the same about me.

Stacy and I had broken up, not out of a lack of affection or physical attraction, but because of distance and my need to sow my oats. There were a lot of pluses to being involved with a tennis player—another player understood perfectly that you had to practice and rest, and that you didn't always want someone around when you were doing either—but there were minuses, too. A natural competitiveness can crop up between any couple, for instance, and it's only aggravated when you're both playing the same sport.

However, distance was most of it. There were only so many occasions when Stacy and I could play in the same event, or in the same city at the same time. More and more, we had to rely on phone calls and letters, which didn't work for either of us. If I was going to be committed to just one girl, I wanted her to be with me, and since my job required a lot of travel, that meant she had to travel with me. If it ran counter to her needs . . . well, I wasn't thinking about anyone else's needs at that point.

Nobody will be surprised to hear that number one in the world requires major-league ego. You need ego to get there, and ego to stay there. I had never been short on that quality, but when I was a kid, I'd never felt that there was a lot to be cocky about. I wasn't particularly successful with girls, and the sport I was most successful in wasn't one that generated a lot of attention in high school.

As I moved to the top of pro tennis, though, cockiness became a survival mechanism. I don't care who you are, Borg or Sampras or Michael Chang—you can't exist at the top without it. Self-confidence is a must, and so is selfishness. Tennis is an individual sport, and athletes in individual sports—whether they're figure skaters, boxers, gymnasts, or sprinters—are self-involved by nature. Star tennis players all like to think they're much more well-rounded than they are. We're not well-rounded. Nothing in the game asks you to be, or helps you to be.

In addition, because of the success of tennis in the '80s, the star system was like nothing anybody has seen since. Everything was about *you*, about whether or not you won, and for four years, I was the biggest winner in the game. People around me were constantly saying, "Did you eat at the right time? Did you get everything you need? Is everything okay? We'll pay you this, we'll do that, we'll kiss your behind." You only have to do what you want; your reaction to anything else is, "Get the hell out of here."

For a long time, I'll admit I didn't mind it a bit. Would you?

After I beat Borg at Wimbledon, I went to see the rock musician Joe Walsh at the Forum in L.A. Backstage before the show, Joe said, "I hear you play guitar. Do you want to come out and play?" I'm not a good guitar player now, but at that point I could play just a couple of chords—I mean, I was *bad*. I told him, "No, no thanks, I'll just enjoy the show," and I sat on the side of the stage.

For his encore, Joe sang his classic, "Rocky Mountain Way," and in the part where the song says, "Bases are loaded and Casey's at bat . . . time to change the batter," he changed it to, "Bases are loaded, Borg's at bat . . ." It was a subtle little thing, but I felt like a million bucks.

That kind of thing was starting to happen more and more. Eventually, it almost seemed normal, even though it was nothing like normal. The challenge (when I thought about it) was to enjoy it for what it was worth, because I never knew if it would happen tomorrow. . . .

But when you're number one, you're not thinking that much about tomorrow.

As for the outside world—what outside world? I was vaguely aware that the American hostages in Iran had been freed, that a woman had been appointed to the Supreme Court. When the air-traffic controllers went out on strike, that was kind of a big deal: It disrupted my travel a bit. After I won the '81 U.S. Open, I was invited to the White House— and I didn't want to go! It was on a day's notice, the meeting was set for early in the morning; it all just felt too inconvenient.

My mother said, "You've been invited to meet the President and you're thinking of not going? You're going." I went. It was the story of my life—I always had to be pushed. I was glad I did go, too: I had never met a President before, and I felt something very special about Ronald Reagan. He was funny; he seemed to have a way with people; he had a real presence about him. And—having said all that—he had absolutely no clue who I was!

Just after the 1981 U.S. Open, I started my own exhibition tour, "John McEnroe Tennis Over America"—on the same model as a rock show, or so we hoped. It had always been my fantasy to be a rock musician, and this was the closest I could get at that point! The plan was for me to play twenty cities a year, during off-weeks from the tour; every match would be an event—loud music, light show, break dancers, the works. And, oh yeah, there was tennis, too. Vilas was my main playing partner, but Vitas, Yannick Noah, and Mats Wilander came along from time to time.

One of the people who came up with the tour concept was Gary Swain, who eventually moved to the International Management Group (IMG) and became my tennis agent. Gary used to travel with me on this tour and took care of everything, from the venue to the accommodations. It was big-time show business: Lear jets and limos, the best hotel suites.

Prior to the tour, Gary asked me what kinds of things I wanted before, during, and after each match. One of the things I asked for was sawdust. I used to keep sawdust in the pocket of my tennis shorts during a match, to absorb the perspiration on my hand.

When we arrived at one of our first venues, Cobo Hall in Detroit, there was a can of sawdust at courtside. The match began, and Vilas held his serve. When we changed ends, I went over to the can of sawdust, looked at it, and knocked it over with my racket.

Gary came running over. "What's wrong?" he asked.

"You call that sawdust?" I said. I was actually screaming at him: The sawdust was ground too fine! "This looks like rat poison! Can't you get anything right?"

So Gary ran out and, twenty minutes later, came back with a fresh can of coarser sawdust . . . and twenty dollars less in his pocket: He'd had to pay a union employee to grind up a two-by-four.

This is what it was like to be number one.

Around that time, I went to Japan to play a couple of exhibitions in Osaka and Tokyo. On the bullet train to Tokyo with a few of the other players, I started drinking shots of Suntory whiskey. It was the fastest train in the world, the whiskey was potent, and I was twenty-two years old. When we pulled in to the station, I started to feel woozy. I turned to the dignified Japanese lady by my side—and immediately threw up all over her.

I was so sick that I had to be helped off the train by the tournament officials and taken to the hotel, where I slept it off. The next day, after my match (I was a lot more resilient in those days), I was astonished to see the lady of the previous day coming up to me. Before I could begin to stammer an apology, she bowed and apologized to *me,* presenting me with a gift! (Needless to say, it wasn't a bottle of whiskey.)

This is also what it was like to be number one—and in Japan, where the niceties could make a Westerner's head spin.

Number one.

I had agents to set up opportunities for me. I had people around who'd been hired to do this and that. My girlfriend was there to be a complement to me. I surrounded myself—the old story—with people I'd known before I was famous. I tried to find people who were sincere. I went by my gut; I felt I was a reasonably intelligent person who had gone to Stanford. I'd made some friends there whom I'd kept—Bill Maze, Matt Mitchell, Ken Margerum, and Renée Richards (no, not *that* one). Peter Rennert was still around, though that relationship grew increasingly complicated as Peter struggled on the pro tour. Peter Fleming and I were still winning doubles matches, but that friendship wasn't getting any easier, either. I still had a few old friends from high school and earlier, like Doug Saputo and Andy Broderick. I also began spending a lot of time with my brother Mark. Now that he was at Stanford, the three-year age difference between us seemed negligible, and our closeness was strengthened by the fact that he didn't have a jealous bone in his body. He was one of the very few people I could trust absolutely.

However, I always had to fight to find my best self, to be aware of other people's feelings—and the devil's bargain of it is, the players who are more aware of others struggle more. Boris Becker was like that, too. We would have brilliant moments on the court, and total meltdowns. There was just too much going on inside.

I even had to struggle to act human with my mother. Every now and then, she would break down: "You treat me so badly! Why can't you treat me the way you treat your friends?" And I'd say, "Because you're my mother!" Then she'd start crying and I'd realize how asinine I was being. "Because you're my mother, I can treat you like dirt"—that's basically what I was saying.

You come full circle when you have kids yourself. When my kids give it to me, I realize, *God almighty, what an ass I was.* It's embarrassing. I really was pretty much of a jerk. Believe it or not, I'm a lot better now.


IN MARCH OF '82, I sprained my ankle badly at a tournament in Brussels. It happened on the last shot of a practice session—I ran wide for a forehand I probably shouldn't have run for, and there was a chair there I hadn't seen, and that was that.

I had to default in the quarterfinals, and my ankle wasn't really right for a long time. Inevitably, when you're young and macho and you have a place in the rankings to hold on to, you come back sooner than you should from an injury, and you play slightly hurt, and so you have one more excuse to offer when things don't go right.

Not much went right that spring. Five weeks after the injury, I lost to Lendl in the finals of the WCT, in Dallas; in May, I lost to Eddie Dibbs in the semis of a clay-court tournament at Forest Hills; and then the next month (after skipping the French), I lost to Connors in the final on the grass at Queen's. It wasn't a good sign. . . .

I was determined to behave myself at Wimbledon that year, and I did, in my fashion. There were a few disputed calls, a couple of balls whacked in anger, and a stupid locker-room shouting match with a player named Steve Denton, but compared with the previous year, Wimbledon '82 was a cakewalk. It was all tennis. I had a feeling the London tabloid reporters were chewing their cheeks in frustration—I didn't give them anything!

My ankle, though, still wasn't 100 percent, and I was in a strange state of mind, a kind of continued mourning for Borg. There was something especially pointed about his absence here, of all places—it felt almost eerie. However, I was fortunate enough to have a relatively easy draw: I didn't lose a single set until the quarterfinals, against Johan Kriek, and even then it was only one. Tim Mayotte, fresh out of my alma mater, Stanford, had a great tournament to get to the semis, but he essentially conceded the match to me (sometimes the intimidation factor really does work in your favor) before he stepped on the court.

Then came Jimmy.

Connors was never intimidated by anyone—at least he never looked that way—and he was in the midst of an amazing year. From the jump, we played a very aggressive final, nothing like either of my last two against Borg, where the play had been more consistently fine, but also more subdued. Every match I ever played against Jimmy was like a prizefight. At Wimbledon that day, I was ahead two sets to one, we went to a tiebreaker in the fourth, and then I was three points from winning the match. Yet somehow, I just couldn't dig deep enough to pull it out— maybe Jimmy was just hungrier. In retrospect, I should've said to myself, "Don't let it get to a fifth set—stop him here or you're finished."

But I didn't stop him, and when we went to the fifth, I think my body language showed what I was really feeling: Between my ankle and my state of mind, I had done well just getting this far in the tournament. And that was as far as I went in the longest final in Wimbledon history. Connors pulled off an amazing feat—he won his second Wimbledon championship eight years after his first—and I would have to wait an-other twelve months before I could prove I wasn't a flash in the pan.

To top off my lousy Wimbledon, Peter and I lost the doubles final to Peter McNamara and Paul McNamee.

I saved my greatest tennis in '82 for the Davis Cup. Just a week after that heartbreaking final against Connors, in our quarterfinal tie against Sweden in St. Louis, I achieved one of my proudest wins, in a six-hour-and-thirty-two-minute marathon with Mats Wilander. It's still the longest men's tennis match in history. Then, over Thanksgiving week in Grenoble, on a slow indoor red-clay court the French had built specifically to try to thwart me, I beat Yannick Noah in an epic five-setter that helped us clinch a 4–1 victory and our second Cup championship in a row.

Playing for my country, and with a team, helped raise my spirits, and my game, to the optimum. When I was on my own, it was another story.

WHEN YOU'RE OUT THERE all by yourself, you tend to place a lot of blame on a lot of other people. If you play a poor match, you're busy trying to come up with excuses. Even when I was younger, I never felt the guys were just too good for me: If I lost, there was always a reason. I wasn't tall enough yet, I wasn't strong enough, I didn't play enough. There are always any number of things. . . . The bottom line is, it's very difficult to be out there by yourself.

It's also difficult to look in the mirror and say, "You know something? It was me."

I wasn't handling number one very well; it felt sort of empty. Whose fault was that? In fact, in some ways, you could argue that Connors was really number one in '82. He won Wimbledon, and he broke my three-year streak at the Open, where Lendl beat me in the semis and Jimmy beat Lendl in the final. (And all that time, Jimmy was separated from his wife—which, somehow, actually seemed to fuel him. Incredible!)

At the Open that year, instead of feeling I could win for the fourth time in a row, I actually remember thinking, "Wow, three in a row is amazing." Deep down—on a level I never would have discussed with anyone at the time—it felt alienating to have to go in for the kill at each and every tournament. Tennis really is single combat, and it's exhausting to be a gladiator. You pay a heavy price to be on top, and just at that moment, it wasn't one I was willing to pay.

And when that's the case, someone who is willing to do just a little bit more will always slip by.

The fact is that the moment I reached the top—the place for which I'd theoretically been aiming since the moment I turned pro—everything started spiraling slowly but surely downward, and kept going that way for the next couple of years. I held on to number one, but just barely, without really winning the big matches as often as I should have.

After the '82 Open, I went on the kind of streak that number-ones are supposed to have, winning twenty-six straight matches going into the finals of the Masters in January—where Lendl cleaned my clock once more, beating me for the seventh straight time and winning his fifty-

ninth (!) straight indoor match in the process. I couldn't even come close
to breaking his serve at that point.

The one light moment of the tournament came during my semifinal
match against Guillermo Vilas: During a changeover, someone tapped me
on the shoulder and said, "Hey, John." I ignored him, and ignored him
again when he tapped me once more. Finally, extremely annoyed, I
turned to find myself face to face with Ronnie Wood of the Rolling Stones,
who had come specifically to see me. My excitement helped me cruise
through to an easy 6–3, 6–3 victory.

Later that month, I went to Philadelphia to play in the big indoor
tournament they used to have there (one of a number of major American
events that went by the boards after tennis's boom years). I was seeded
first, and Lendl was seeded second, in a pretty strong field. One night,
during the early rounds, I got a phone call from Don Budge.

Budge, of course, was one of tennis's all-time greats, and the last
American to have won the Grand Slam, in 1938. He was also a hell of a
nice guy, and a number of times over the course of my career, he made
it a point to call me with advice or congratulations. He loved to give advice if you were willing to listen, and I was always more than willing. I
knew the suggestions would be good, and it gave me a warm feeling to
have this connection with the history of tennis, and to sense how much
my respect for Don's great achievements pleased him.

An important aside: I think one of the big problems with tennis today
is the failure of its current stars to acknowledge the game's history. If you
think I'm going to single out the Williams sisters, you're right—but only
because they've done so much, and come so tantalizingly close to trans-
forming the entire game. What's held them back from making that final
step is their us-against-the-world mentality: Look at the difference between the Williamses and Tiger Woods, who really has transformed golf,
not just through his athletic genius but by his embrace of the game's tradition; how gracefully he gravitates to great old champions like Jack

Nicklaus and Arnold Palmer. (Don't worry, Venus and Serena: I'm not saying you should be nicer to me!)

Don Budge was calling that night to tell me how to beat Lendl.

"You've got to attack him right up the middle," he said. "Stop giving him the angles—he's killing you on those angles."

It was simple advice, but the more I thought about it, the more sense it made. Lendl loved to run, he could go all day, and his groundstrokes were tremendous. He *liked* being stretched out in the corners. If I approached up the middle, he'd be forced to lob or hit to my volley—my strengths. I'd be taking back the angles.

Suddenly, I had a game plan against Lendl that I hadn't had before—and it worked: I won the final in four sets. Putting Don's counsel to work in that tournament gave me back my confidence that, despite Ivan's tremendous power and conditioning, my game—going quickly from defense to offense, using my speed to get to net, and using the angles—could ultimately beat his game. I would win my next eight matches against him.

Meanwhile, though, little things happened that kept me off my game for weeks at a time and prevented me from dominating the tour. Ironically, during the final with Lendl, I had tweaked my shoulder, but my adrenaline was so high that I barely felt it. The next day, though, I could hardly lift my arm. It was still hurting when we went down to Buenos Aires to play our first-round Davis Cup tie against Argentina, and I lost both my singles matches. After Clerc beat me in five tough sets in the first, I went flat as a pancake against Vilas, who came from 2–4 in the first set to win the next fifteen games in a row against me! I'd literally never been steamrolled like that before—maybe it was why I was able to crack one of my first jokes ever in a tight situation, a rarity that produced an even greater rarity—an on-court laugh from Captain Arthur Ashe! Down 4–6, 0–6, 0–5, I walked over to Arthur and asked, "What should I do?" He cracked up.

P.S.—I saved my honor by pulling out that game and avoiding the double-bagel. But Argentina beat us, 3–2, and we wouldn't defend the Cup that year.

One day in May, I was practicing with my seventeen-year-old brother, Patrick (who, while I wasn't looking, had become the number-three junior in the country!), at Tony Palafox's indoor club in Glen Cove, Long Island. I was playing with my trusty old Dunlop Maxply, and Patrick—at a point when most of the top players were shifting away from wood rackets—was using one of the new models, the composite Dunlop Max 200G.

About halfway through the practice, he cracked a couple of nice backhand returns by me. I motioned to his racket. "Let me try that," I commanded, in the tone of voice that comes so easily to older brothers. He handed it to me. It felt comfortable right away, and I noticed an immediate improvement in my game: more oomph on my serve, more pop on the groundstrokes.

I took both of Patrick's Max 200Gs with me down to Dallas to play the WCT Championships, where I beat Lendl in the final, continuing my roll against him and matching his power with a little of my own!

I beat him again in the semis at Wimbledon, in straight sets: a more one-sided victory than at Philadelphia or Dallas, but Ivan always did say he was allergic to grass. The semi on the other side of the draw was Kevin Curren against a young guy from New Zealand named Chris Lewis, who was having the tournament of his life. I actually worried about Curren—he was the Mark Philippoussis of the '80s, with an unbelievable serve, very dangerous on grass.

However, Curren wasn't the only thing I was worried about. Here's where my head was then: I remember watching Kevin play Lewis, and thinking, "I've got to play Curren in the final, because he's the tougher, more legitimate opponent, so if I lose to him it would be understandable." Then I thought, "What are you, crazy? If you can play Chris Lewis, you've got an unbelievable chance to win this." *Then* I thought, "Why was I even thinking about losing?" My self-doubts were still hanging around.

Somehow Lewis managed to beat Curren, and I took care of him handily in the final. It wasn't one of my most glorious victories, but it was my second Wimbledon—and the All England Lawn Tennis and Croquet Club finally gave me that coveted honorary membership!

Then I managed to lose to my nemesis (or one of them), Bill Scanlon, in the round of 16 at the U.S. Open. Yes, he played a great match, and yes, I was off that day, but that didn't stop me from being extremely disappointed in myself.

IN DECEMBER I played the Australian Open for the first time. The tournament was still on grass in those days, in Melbourne's venerable Kooyong Stadium, Harry Hopman's old stomping grounds. In the past, traveling all that way for a comparatively minor major (if you will) had always felt like too much to me. However, the fact that guys like Vilas and Kriek had won it (twice apiece! On grass!) in the last few years goaded me. The field that year was strong—Lendl, Teltscher, Kriek; the up-and-coming Swedes Jarryd, Nystrom, and Wilander; and a hot young Aussie prospect named Pat Cash—but I felt I had a good chance to win the tournament. In fact, I felt I should win it.

The courts at Kooyong were a little odd: There was a slight uphill grade from baseline to net on each side, to facilitate drainage, and that tiny hill changed the usual grass-court equation ever so slightly, which allowed players like Kriek and Vilas to triumph over serve-and-volleyers.

And it was *hot:* December is the beginning of the Australian summer. Those are my excuses.

I made it through to the semis without much difficulty. The day before my match against Wilander, I was practicing with Peter McNamara, who had had a horrific knee injury earlier in the year—the week after he had beaten Lendl in the finals at Brussels and going to number seven in the world. Peter was just starting to come back, but he was still limping pretty badly. I thought about how my ankle and shoulder had healed, and I had one of those there-but-for-the-grace-of-God moments: I thought, "Man, I am so lucky I've got my health—I'm going to win this thing!" I really thought my chances against Wilander on grass were excellent.

And then that night, somehow—it had to be psychosomatic—my knee went out on me! I wonder to this day: Was it really too much for me to relax and smell the roses for just that one moment? Did it feel like too big a deal to win the Australian my first time out?

In any case, the next morning I was panicking. I went to the trainer, who taped me up, but after splitting the first two sets with Wilander, I felt I wasn't moving right, and I ripped all the tape off. It didn't help. I lost in four sets, and Wilander killed Lendl in the final.

I had learned my lesson: Don't relax. Not while you're trying to stay on top of the world. Something changed for me at the end of that year—maybe the losses to Scanlon and Wilander woke me up; maybe I'd finally accepted that Borg wasn't coming back. Maybe it was the fact that, after my mystery knee problem quickly cleared up, I was completely healthy for the first time in months. Whatever the reason, I realized that the months were slipping by and I wasn't going to be young forever. I was about to turn twenty-five, middle-aged for a tennis player. It was time to seize the moment. Something in me clicked then, and I went into the new year ready to take on the world.

# 8

SINCE I TRAVELED SO MUCH, my parents always asked me to try to be home at Christmastime. I almost always obliged, and it usually cost me in the Masters, which followed shortly thereafter. The tournament was important to me, but I'd managed to win it only once, in '79. My usual training regimen in mid-to-late December was as follows: I'd sit around and eat and drink and watch TV, and never pick up a racket. Meanwhile, Lendl was riding his bicycle up hills.

For five or six years, the organizers of the Australian Open had been trying to get me to come play, but I had always refused, saying I wouldn't play a tournament that was held at Christmas. This year, though, the organizers had called my bluff and moved the event to earlier in the month, and I'd gone to the Australian instead of staying home and eating ice cream. I was back for Christmas, in far better shape than I had ever been in in December. I was playing great tennis, and I destroyed Lendl to win the '84 Masters.

I noticed it from my first match in the Garden that year: My quickness and my serve-and-volley game were dictating play every time out. I was at the kind of level you dream about, thinking, "God, this is pretty close to the best I can play." I'd finally taken my game to what felt like a notch above all my opponents'. It should have been great. I wish it had been. But it wasn't.

It still felt hollow—I'd thought it would help straighten me out after my long grieving for Borg, but it wasn't doing a thing for me inside. It reminded me of the story of King Midas: My success wasn't translating into happiness.

Stella and I had been living together for close to two years in my co-op at 90th and East End, and because she was a couple of years older than I was, I think she was feeling some pressure from her parents—perfectly nice, very traditional people who still lived in North Carolina—to formalize our relationship or move on. I was very fond of Stella, but—once again—I didn't want to get married yet. I was looking to broaden my life, but I didn't want to lose my tennis, either, and somehow it felt as if the formality of marriage would get in the way.

There was another thing. With all respect to Stella, I probably knew, deep inside, that we weren't meant to be life partners. Maybe she knew that, too.

We decided to go our separate ways. To make it cleaner (and because I was earning a bit more money), I bought an incredible apartment at the top of a building on Central Park West—the very one in which I live today. It was a huge place for just me, but I think I realized in the back of my mind that I'd need a big nest for the family I wanted to have eventually.

Just after I moved across the park, I had a brief, slightly intense relationship with a very famous, very attractive older woman who lived nearby. Out of respect for her, I won't mention her name. I'm bringing this up for a reason: not to boast, but to mention two things about her that made a big impression on me at the time. The first is that she had two children whom I liked very much: I was thinking a lot about children that year, wondering what it would be like to have them, and being around this small family stirred my imagination.

The second thing was her relative ease about her own renown. Maybe it was even a kind of exhibitionism. As the number-one tennis player in the world, I was exponentially more famous than I'd been as number two or three, but that part of the deal wasn't giving me much pleasure. My new lady-friend was always eager to go out to whatever new restaurant happened to be in vogue at the moment, and the second she mentioned it, I would balk. I'd think, *That's crazy! I can't be seen with you.*

I can't tell you why I had a problem with being seen in public with an attractive, well-known woman. I don't really know what I was thinking. At the time, though, it infected my whole being: I just didn't want to be in the gossip columns as a couple, didn't want to be photographed with her. That kind of thing has always bothered me, but it can be handled gracefully—in those days I just wasn't up to it.

It was the same problem I had on the court: I couldn't look at the lighter side. I hadn't learned my lesson yet: If you're going to be with a famous, beautiful woman, you have to pay the price. You can't expect her to stay indoors all the time and make love to you whenever you want! It's a two-way street. As it was, I was so turned off by the fact that she wanted us to be seen together that when I left for Europe that spring, I said, "I'll call you when I get back"—and never did. I thought, "Forget it. She wants something from me."

I guess twenty-five wasn't such a mature age after all.

But I didn't look back. I was on my way to Europe to play the French and go for my third Wimbledon. And this was my year—I knew it. I was playing so amazingly well that I thought no one could beat me, on any surface.

Not even Lendl. Not now.

IT WAS THE WORST LOSS of my life, a devastating defeat: Sometimes it still keeps me up nights. It's even tough for me now to do the commentary at the French—I'll often have one or two days when I literally feel sick to my stomach just at being there and thinking about that match. Thinking of what I threw away, and how different my life would've been if I'd won.

Connors had two Wimbledon titles and five U.S. Opens at that point, but he'd never won the French. Borg had won the French six times, and Wimbledon five—an unbelievable record!—but never the U.S. Open. Besides the Masters—which, because of the limited field, was a different kind of test than a regular tournament—Lendl had never won a major. Lendl choked away majors. Everyone knew that.

I had two Wimbledons and three Opens. A French title, followed by my third Wimbledon, would have given me that final, complete thing that I don't have now—a legitimate claim as possibly the greatest player of all time.

Looking back, I try to see the glass as half-full rather than half-empty—otherwise I'd tear out what little hair I have left and work myself into a tizzy every day of my life, playing that match over and over again in my mind. I try not to do that, because, God knows, I'm an intense enough person as it is.

But I still do it anyway.

I can never escape that gnawing feeling: How badly did I want it? Not badly enough, obviously. Whatever the reason—friends, relationships, having a good time—when push came to shove, I couldn't beat Ivan

Lendl in the final of the French Open in the greatest year I ever had, the greatest year any tennis player had ever had. I blew a two-sets-to-love lead, but I could have sucked it up in the fifth set. Instead, I let it slip away; I just couldn't find a way to muster up anything else.

It was a total disaster.

I get a feeling from time to time, when it seems that things are going too well, that something bad has to happen. Was I feeling that way before the '84 French final? I'm not sure. After I won the first two sets, I could read the expressions of my friends in the stands: Their faces were saying, "This thing is over in a half-hour; there's no way he can lose it." To make a comparison to golf, it was like a gimme. And I blew the gimme. I blew a twelve-inch putt to win the Masters. That's hard to live with.

It was meant to be mine—even though the French is on slow red clay, which favors baseliners like Borg and Lendl, even though I'm a serve-and-volley player, and my best surfaces were always grass and hard-court, where my serve came off the ground fast and I had that extra fraction of a second to get to net and punch the volley. On red clay, the ball bites into the surface, and you lose that fraction, even with the fastest serve: The receiver gets extra milliseconds for a passing shot if you come in.

But I was at the top of my game that spring, and my game plan was this: Don't change a thing. Serve and come in. I knew my volley was the best in the business. I knew I couldn't lose. Peter Fleming was planning a victory party even before the match began.

The day of the match, I saw a caricature in a French newspaper. In the picture, I was on one side of the net, pointing a gun at Lendl, who stood in the corner on the other side, shivering, sweat pouring off him. I loved that picture.

The French fans evidently felt the same way. When I was introduced on Center Court at Stade Roland Garros, I got the greatest hand I'd ever received at the start of a match—a huge roar! And by the end of the match, in my own inimitable way, I had somehow managed to get the entire crowd against me once again. . . .

I HAD NOT ONLY WON the first two sets, I was ready to take over the third. Everything was perfect—it was astonishing how well I was playing—and then it happened. A very loud noise started coming from the side of the court. An NBC cameraman had taken his headset off, and it was sitting there, squawking, while I was trying to play.

Maybe someone else wouldn't have noticed it. Maybe, on another occasion, *I* wouldn't have noticed it. It wasn't as though you could have heard that headset squawking from the top row of the stands. At that moment, though, that's how it sounded to me.

I've told you how the doubts can come storming in, piling one on top of another. I was playing beautifully, but this was also the surface on which I was most uncomfortable. It was hot out. It had been cloudy and unusually cold in Paris—in the fifties, in late May!—for the first eleven days of the event, but then, the day I played Connors in the semis, the sun had come out for the first time.

I ran through Jimmy pretty easily that day, but the heat stuck around for the final, and that worried me. What if I did lose to Lendl? It's not a great excuse to offer at a post-match press conference: "It was just too hot out there today." That's right up there with "Yeah, I had a hangover," and "I didn't sleep well last night"—wink, wink.

It might've been better if I had been up breaking training, because the fact is, I *had* slept terribly the night before. Out of the blue, Stella had decided to phone me.

We hadn't talked for two or three weeks, and I don't know why she was calling. "Bunny!" she said—she used to call me that—"I miss you!" "I miss you, too!" I said. We talked for a while. "But we're not getting back together," I told her.

When I hung up, I thought, "Wow! That's just what I need." (Never mind how it might have affected *her.*) It sent me into a tizzy, completely threw me off, because it made me think, and the last thing you need to do the night before a huge final is think. I spent the night tossing and turning.

That phone call was lodged somewhere in the back of my mind, and then this headset at courtside started blaring, and it was hot, and suddenly what had been in the back of my mind flooded into the front of my mind, and the doubts started creeping in: *I've been playing so amazingly,* I thought. *How can I keep it up?*

I know the squawking headset was an innocent technical glitch—it wasn't as if anybody had said, "Let's screw McEnroe up," but that's how I took it—and, just like that, my concentration was shot.

I got very angry, because nobody was dealing with the situation. On the changeover, I went over to the headset and screamed into the little mike, *"Shut the f*** up!!"* (Whoever was on the other end is probably still deaf to this day.) Then, as I went over to my side, I thought, "What the hell am I doing?" If you start lashing out when things are going well, you may be letting your opponent think that you're not as sure of yourself as you seem.

Usually I didn't mind if my opponent saw me get upset. Some people thought I played better when I got angry—which was sometimes true and sometimes not—but it didn't bother me if others believed it. Even if the guy on the other side of the net didn't buy into the myth, everyone has doubts. If he sees me upset, so what? He gets upset sometimes, too. I can still overcome it and win.

All the big players had their shtick. Connors worked the crowd. Lendl looked like a scary robot: He'd hit a missile at you if you came in on his drop-shot. Borg never changed his expression. Ashe was the same way. You could never read what they were thinking. It can be a weapon.

Becker was a big guy with a huge serve; he was deliberately intimidating. He always walked around with his chest stuck out, like "Oh, you're lucky we didn't win World War Two."

My shtick, of course, was getting upset. Did it help me more than hurt me? I don't think so. Ultimately, my father was right—I probably would have done better if I hadn't ever gotten into that. But I could never rest easily on my talent—or on anything. If I was ahead a service break, I liked to try to make it two—or three. I was always a better front-runner than a comeback player, because I could keep the doubts at bay when I was ahead, but they tended to seep in when I fell behind. I haven't made a lot of amazing comebacks. I've won the great majority of my five-set matches—I'll stack my five-set record up against anyone's—but I didn't win my first match from being down two sets to love until 1990, late in my career.

In a way, that's a good statistic. It means that I didn't get down two sets very often. All told, I won a lot more matches than I lost—my career singles record was 82 percent—but I didn't have a lot of stirring come-from-behind victories.

That was a disappointment to me. I'd always thrilled to the stories about how Laver was down a couple of sets when he won the Slam. *My* story is that I would have won the Slam had I not blown a two-sets-to-love lead against Lendl.

I went from two games to love in the third, to losing the set 4–6. But then I was up 4–2 in the fourth, serving at 40–30.

And that, to me, is where I really lost the match.

Tony Roche had been coaching Lendl for a while, and they had worked on how to play me. They knew my left-handed slice serve in the ad court was a killer for most right-handers—the guy would be in the stands before he got his racket on it. Even Lendl, as good as he was, couldn't drive that serve back.

So he and Roche determined that whenever I served wide to his backhand on the ad side, he was just going to chip it crosscourt. The ball would be sinking, with backspin on it, and I'd have to hit my volley up instead of punching it deep. That let him stay in the point and try to take back the offense with his big groundstrokes.

That was his plan, and I knew it. So I served wide, and sure enough, he chipped crosscourt, and I was right there.

My first inclination was to hit a drop-volley and go for the winner, but then I decided, *no, no, just play it a little safe,* because even though I'm known as someone with pretty good hands, a soft touch, the drop-volley is a low-percentage shot. I decided just to float the volley deep, make him pass me. I went against my gut.

And I missed the volley. I pushed it the tiniest bit, and it floated out.

I don't remember the points after that. It goes by in a blur. It's now eighteen years ago, but I've never watched that match once. I can't bear to. So I can't tell you the exact details of what happened next. It's too sickening to me.

I do remember the crowd started to boo me. Some of it was just the French, because they're bizarre, they switch gears, and some of it was because if I won, the match was going to be over in an hour and forty-five minutes, and they wanted to see more tennis. I can understand that. I was upset, though, that when I really needed them at the end, when I was fatigued and tight and feeling this whole thing slipping away from me, I got nothing. Nothing.

And yet I think I've got to be given credit for my own demise. Good sports fans can always sense when you're giving them something they can respond to. There's a way to win them back to your side when they're all against you—which, as I've said, is a talent Mr. Connors had that I didn't. There are countless other examples of it—the L.A. fans booed Gary Sheffield, Mr. "I want to be traded; I will never play as a Dodger again!" Then he hit a home run, and it was "Yayyy!"

But I wasn't giving that French crowd anything. I wasn't able to let them know that I really needed the help. When people boo, I have a hard time not taking it personally. It's one of my biggest problems. I feel isolated out there in the first place, but if anyone's against me, I find it incredibly difficult. The crowd can be for me 99 percent, but if there are a couple of hecklers, I get bent out of shape. Not my finest trait.

My Dad and others have always said: The great majority of people are on your side. At times, in a semi-serious way, I've wondered about going into politics. In politics, if you win 60 percent of the vote, that's great, even though there's still 40 percent of the people who think, "This guy stinks!" That would toughen me up in a hurry.

Against most other guys, I would have won that French anyway. I have to give Lendl (grudging) credit for being who he was, and for being fit enough to be able to get better as the match progressed. It's the only match in which I ever felt I was playing up to my capabilities and lost.

But he didn't beat me. I beat myself. Lendl got his first major, and I took his title, Choker-in-chief, away from him.

Temporarily.

SOME PEOPLE TALK about my 6–1, 6–1, 6–2 destruction of Connors in the 1984 Wimbledon as my greatest match ever, but the truth is—between you and me—I thought Jimmy was just a little flat that day.

I was also having one of those days when everything seemed to be going almost too right. I got out of bed in the morning feeling great, and in my practice session, the ball looked as big as a cantaloupe. Since I always manage to worry when things are going well, I stopped the session early—I was afraid of leaving my best stuff in practice.

But it just kept getting better.

In fairness, Connors had had a tough semi against Lendl, a four-set slugfest on a very hot afternoon, while I had won in three against that feisty Aussie whippersnapper Pat Cash. Cash was a tough serve-and-volleyer in that great Down-Under tradition, still a little green at nineteen, but a great athlete and a fine tennis player. I thought he was a comer—especially after he shouldered me on a changeover during the second-set tiebreaker! That, I felt, was a very interesting move: Here I was, number one in the world, a two-time Wimbledon champ, one of the game's grand old men at twenty-five . . .

*This kid's got the right attitude,* I thought.

Meanwhile, my attitude had utterly changed. I had wasted too much energy at the French by getting angry, I realized; from the first match at the All England Club that year, I was determined not to do anything that would derail me from avenging Roland Garros—my only loss in fifty-two matches so far in '84—and winning my hat-trick Wimbledon. I was on a five-match winning streak against Jimmy, and I felt confident I could make it six.

I just didn't know it would be so easy.

The heat wave had continued, but I was hotter than the weather that Sunday afternoon. From the start, Connors just couldn't find his rhythm, while I was serving unbelievably well— slicing it wide, popping it up the middle, doing whatever I wanted. I hit 74 percent of my first serves in the match, with ten aces and no double faults. I had three—*three*—unforced errors in the match.

"That's the best I ever played," I said in the press conference afterward. It was also the best I'd ever acted at Wimbledon: The London tabloids dubbed me "Saint John."

Actually, as I look back on it now, I had done just as well, if not better, that past March, in Brussels, where I sustained that kind of play over an entire *tournament.* I had done it all—sliced and diced, basically ate people up: I lost no more than three or four games in any match. It was incredible how good it had felt. Now here I was on the same high plateau. And I didn't want to let it go, didn't ever want it to end.

. . .

NINETEEN EIGHTY-FOUR was also the year that Arthur Ashe decided he was finally going to push hard to get Connors to play Davis Cup. Donald Dell was Jimmy's manager, and he was also Arthur's agent, and that was how it all came together. Dell thought Jimmy should have Davis Cup as that final notch in his belt, as he made his big transition to corporate life—they'd planned it all out. I always thought that was a load of nonsense, by the way: As his career wound down, I remember Connors used to say in interviews, "I'm a businessman." And I'd be thinking, "What business is he in? He's in the business of endorsing products!" I'd think, "Hey, I'm a businessman, too!"

Anyway, Arthur said, "Look, we've got the two best players in the world, Connors and McEnroe; it's a slam-dunk; let's put them together." So Jimmy came on board, for his one and only year while I was on the circuit. It was a big deal; the USTA was very excited. They took a picture of us together: McEnroe and Connors, the Dream Team.

The only problem was that things between Jimmy and me continued to be edgy at best. We'd simply gotten off on the wrong foot in the Wimbledon locker room in '77, and we'd butted heads ever since. It made for some great matches, but the tension was always there.

The year we were thrown together as teammates, the tension was at its peak. Our first tie, in February against Romania, had gone all right, but then I'd beaten him pretty badly at the French Open, and we'd had a series of trash-talking confrontations on the changeovers ("You're acting like my four-year-old son," he told me; I told him what *he* was acting like) and I destroyed him at Wimbledon. By that point, we were no longer speaking to each other.

The week after Wimbledon, we were to play Argentina in Atlanta (it was a big match, because they'd upset us the year before). One night, before the tie, I got a call from Arthur, who said, "Listen, is it okay if you don't come to the team dinner?" There was always a traditional team dinner, the Tuesday or Wednesday before the tournament. I said, "What are you talking about?"

I wasn't wild to go to the team dinner—it was, frankly, a pretty deadly evening: You'd put on your jacket and tie, and the USTA president would make a speech—still, it was a ceremonial occasion, and getting together as a team meant something.

"Why don't you want me to come to the team dinner?" I asked Arthur.

"Jimmy would prefer it," he said

"Jimmy would prefer it?" I repeated, incredulously. "I've played every match for the last six years, and now Jimmy *prefers* that I not come, so you don't want me? Gee, Arthur, that doesn't seem like too cool a thing."

Arthur thought about it for a minute. "You're probably right; that probably isn't too cool a thing." He apologized, and told me to come ahead to the dinner.

So then Jimmy refused to go.

Not only that, he also refused to stay in the team hotel—mainly because of me, I assume. He also showed up for the tie on the Thursday before our Friday match. Lesser mortals sometimes show up as much as five days before a big tie, and practice five hours a day. Jimmy didn't feel he needed to practice. And this went on. We played the whole tie, never practiced together, and didn't talk.

And our team won the match 5–0.


IN MID-AUGUST I went to the Canadian Open, in Toronto. The word around the tournament that week was that Vitas was having problems controlling himself.

This was the '80s, and drugs were at least as prevalent around the

184 | *John McEnroe*

circuit—where there was plenty of money to pay for them—as in the rest of society. (I also suspect that steroids and amphetamines were, even then, beginning to make inroads into the top ranks of tennis.)

In the past, I had known Vitas to get crazy at exhibitions; in between events, he occasionally went off the deep end for a couple of weeks. However, that was considered legitimate—a form of relaxation. Besides, his energy and resilience were always so amazing that nobody really noticed.

Now, though, I think he was pushing the envelope. The custom at the time was to give the tournament some respect. As screwed-up as it might seem now, players actually contemplated: How many days before an event was it cool to get loaded? A week before? The night before? It all depended on the person.

I ran through Vitas, 6–0, 6–3 in that final; I even had to throw him a couple of games to make it look competitive. I could tell by his play that something was off; that he wasn't himself. That was when I really started to worry about him.

But maybe the person I really should have been worrying about was myself.


STILL, the McEnroe juggernaut just kept rumbling on. In the second round at the U.S. Open, I destroyed a young Swedish upstart named Stefan Edberg, 6–1, 6–0, 6–2, then burned a swath through to the semifinals without dropping a set. On what came to be known as Super Saturday, after the three-set men's thirty-five-year-olds division final, after the Lendl–Cash semi (which ran quite long, Lendl winning in a fifth-set tiebreaker), *after* Martina Navratilova beat Chris Evert Lloyd in a three-set women's final—Connors and I finally walked onto the court at close to seven P.M.!

Here was Jimmy's chance for revenge. In the press conference after the Wimbledon final, I'd said that I now felt all I had to do was play well and I should beat everybody out there. Connors had taken grave exception. "That's an awfully big statement to back up for the next four or five years," he said.

Now, at Flushing Meadows, it was put-up-or-shut-up time. Jimmy had won the tournament the last two years in a row; he could work the New York crowd like nobody's business. He was angry, and hungry.

But so was I. I really didn't want Connors to equal my three-Opens-in-a-row record, and I really wanted to get through to the finals and get revenge on Lendl for the French.

The match with Jimmy was a slugfest from the start, an exciting five-setter that wound up running until eleven-fifteen P.M. The Flushing Meadows crowd, exhausted with over twelve hours of tennis, started filing out of the stadium when we went to a fifth set. It killed me that we were playing such a great match, but that the stands were only a quarter full by the time we finished.

But by the time we finished, I was the winner, 6–3 in the fifth—fifty-one games, three hours and forty-five minutes later.

I got home very late, still so jazzed up (yet exhausted) from the match that it was past two A.M. by the time I finally got to sleep. I could barely imagine having to play a final against Lendl—God almighty, that same afternoon! I woke up at noon on Sunday and staggered out of bed. By the time I got to the locker room at Flushing Meadows, I was so stiff I could barely walk. I was very worried—until I looked across the room and saw Lendl (whose match against Cash had gone three hours and thirty-nine minutes) attempting to touch his hands to his toes. He could barely get past his knees!

*He's worse off than I am,* I thought. A jolt of adrenaline shot through my body.

I felt that if I could just get in a good two hours of tennis, I could beat him. My body was saying, "That's enough," but in some weird way, the fatigue worked for me that afternoon. The fact that I was tired made me concentrate better; the more tired I felt, the better I seemed to hit the ball. It was a purely mental thing—*push, push*—and I didn't get angry at anything because I needed every ounce of energy I had.

I won the first set, 6–3. At one juncture, after I double-faulted in the second game of the second set, he had a break point. I came to net on a first serve at 30–40, hit the volley, and Lendl uncorked a huge forehand to try to pass me on my backhand side. The ball hit the tape and caromed up at a weird angle, and I swung around in a full circle and hit the forehand volley for a winner. Sometimes it helps to be unconscious!

Second set, 6–4.

That was when visions of the French final flickered through my head. However, I knew I couldn't—and wouldn't—choke this one away. I gave the third set everything I had: When I broke his serve once, that wasn't enough for me. I wanted to drive a stake through this guy's heart. I got the second break, went to 4–0, and even though Lendl never stopped trying (the way it seemed he had the previous year, in the final against Connors), I had too much momentum. Final set, 6–1.

I had my fourth Open.

It was the last Grand Slam title I would ever win.

AT THE END OF SEPTEMBER, we played Australia in the Davis Cup semifinals, in Portland, Oregon. Connors was there, and we still weren't speaking. Peter and I took our doubles match handily, and we won the tie, 4–1. I should have been on top of the world.

But on October 1, 1984, I was standing in the Portland airport, waiting to board a flight to L.A. for a week off, and suddenly I thought, *I'm the greatest tennis player who ever lived—why am I so empty inside?*

Except for the French, and one tournament just before the Open in which I had been basically over-tennised, I won every tournament I played in 1984: thirteen out of fifteen. Eighty-two out of eighty-five matches. No one had ever had a year like that in tennis before. No one has since.

It wasn't enough.

The feeling had been building up for a while. I'd been number one for four years, and I'd never felt especially happy. I had written it off to the fact that Borg had stopped playing, and that my relationships weren't going well. Now the year was winding down, and it was nearly six months since I'd last lived with Stella.

It was hard for me to pull away from that—from having someone to live with. I was comfortable traveling without a coach, just hooking up with tennis friends on the road and with non-playing friends in New York and L.A. At the same time, both of my two closest friendships, with Peter Fleming and Peter Rennert, had taken turns for the worse. Both guys were trying to make their way on the singles tour, and they were having a tough time. I knew they felt in my shadow, which didn't help matters. Nor did the fact that Peter Fleming had gotten married.

I wasn't comfortable being totally alone. But what were the alternatives?

Stella and I had gotten together again, very briefly, around the time of the Open, but she still wanted a commitment. I'd made an offer to her: "Why don't we just have a baby? That's a commitment, isn't it?" To my twenty-five-year-old mind, that seemed like a good idea: I needed a change. For some odd reason, though, Stella still wanted to get married, and that was that.

I would meet girls on the road: It didn't take a whole lot. Friends of mine would bring them. If I went to a restaurant, they'd be there. I'd go to a nightclub; they'd be there. There were always girls around the tennis matches. Were they out-and-out groupies, the kind they had in rock-

and-roll? I wouldn't go quite that far. However, Borg had certainly opened the floodgates, and I reaped a few of the benefits.

Girl tennis players were also an option. I never had to try too hard, wherever I was. When you're number one, everything comes to you.

But I wasn't very happy.

VITAS HAPPENED TO BE in L.A. that week, too, and one day he told me, "You've got to come to this party!" Richard Perry was a friend of his, a music producer who threw legendary parties at his place in the Hollywood Hills. It sounded too good to pass up, so I went.

It was a warm October night in Los Angeles, one of those L.A. nights when the air smells like orange blossoms and feels like silk on your skin. I walked into the party and almost had to laugh—there wasn't anyone in sight who wasn't famous. However, my eyes went right across the room to an intense, sharp-featured girl with dyed red hair, and then her eyes locked with mine.

I went over and introduced myself, even though no introductions were needed. I knew very well that Tatum O'Neal had been the youngest person ever to win an Oscar, in 1974, for *Paper Moon.* I knew she'd starred with Walter Matthau in *The Bad News Bears,* which I'd thought was an excellent movie as well. I was all too aware that her father was Ryan O'Neal, the Tom Cruise of his day.

Was I overly impressed? A bit starstruck? Maybe.

Maybe Tatum was, too. It's a funny thing when two well-known people meet: There's an immediate magnetism, because you seem to have so many things in common—not the least of which is that you both instantly feel liberated from what the rest of the world usually demands. After all, someone else who's famous would never act like a *fan.*

However, as I'd learned way back when I started going to Richard

Weisman's amazing Manhattan parties, famous people are fans, too. They're just more sophisticated about hiding it—and hiding things and assuming you have a lot in common without looking too far underneath isn't a great way to begin when you're trying to get to know someone.

Of course, Tatum and I didn't know any of that then. Our eyes had locked, we were physically attracted, and we each knew and liked what the other had done. And we were both searching for something. Maybe my fiery spirit reminded her of her father's own famous temper. For my part, I liked her confidence, her total ease in the midst of this star-studded evening. She wasn't even twenty-one yet, but she had the poise of an experienced woman. While the party boomed and buzzed and milled around us, we sat in a corner, talking and talking and talking. From time to time, she leaned over and whispered something funny about this person or that person around the room. The conspiracy was sexy, the whispering was sexy, and the way she smelled when she leaned close was sexy, too.

And so at a certain point it felt quite natural to kiss her. She smiled. I kissed her again.

That was as far as it went that evening. But as I drove back down through the purple hills after the party, Tatum's phone number scribbled on a scrap of paper in my pocket, my heart felt full for the first time in a long while.

THE STOCKHOLM OPEN was where I had won my first giant victory over Borg in 1978. I'd won the tournament that year and the next, and now I was coming back as number one in the world.

I was also coming back as a very unhappy guy.

The last place I wanted to be right then was at a tennis tournament in Sweden. Tennis felt beside the point now. Tatum and I had played phone tag when I'd returned to New York, and the more we kept missing each other, the more urgent it felt to talk. We finally connected while I was in Stockholm, and the more we talked, the more I wanted to go home and get to know her better. The more we talked, the less I felt like being halfway around the world from her. I was lonely, burnt out, and exhausted. Something had to give.

I was almost constantly on edge during that tournament—especially as I got pumped up in tight situations and the anxiety started to creep in. I got into a tough semifinal match against Anders Jarryd: In the third set, he actually had a match point against me. Where was Borg? I thought. Who in God's name was Anders Jarryd, and what was he doing with a match point against *me?* I got out of it, but then when there was a line call that didn't look so great, I went ballistic.

I called the umpire a jerk. He hit me with a $700 fine. I whacked a ball into the stands—another $700. Then I smacked a soda can with my racket. That was another $700, plus, as an added bonus, I got soda all over the king of Sweden, who was sitting in the front row. (I didn't get charged extra for that.)

I somehow managed to win the match—and to beat Wilander in the final the next day—but I realize now that I was begging to be defaulted. And they wouldn't default me.

Why didn't they? The answer is simple, but not so pure: They had a show to put on, and my presence put behinds in the seats. It happened at tournament after tournament: I would freak out, the umpire would hit me with a warning, a point penalty, maybe a measly fine or two (in a year where I was earning a couple of million dollars, seven hundred was pocket change), and life (and the match) would go on. If I went home, they lost money. The tournament directors knew it, the umpires (who got paid by the tournament) knew it, and the linesmen knew it. I knew it. The system let me get away with more and more, and—even though to some it looked as if I was glorying in my bad behavior—I really liked it less and less.

Since the tournament didn't have the nerve to default me, the ATP suspended me from playing tournaments for three weeks. It was originally going to be six weeks, but then they said that if I agreed not to play any exhibitions, they'd cut it to twenty-one days. (If I could play exhibitions whenever I wanted, a suspension wasn't much of a disincentive.) Even the Association of Tennis Professionals wanted to keep the biggest bull in the china shop happy.

However, that suspension was just what I wanted. I badly needed to take a few weeks off from playing tennis.

Here's how distanced I was from real life in those days: Having never voted before, I wanted to cast my ballot in the 1984 presidential election, so I flew from Stockholm to London, then took the Concorde back to New York. (I'd registered to vote in Long Island, where I'd recently bought a house in Oyster Bay. It had been my father's lifelong dream to have a property with a tennis court, and now my parents lived in one of the three houses on the property.) But there was a snowstorm in the city, my flight was diverted to Washington, and I never made it to the polls. In fact, I never made it, period, until the *2000* election.

I HAD THE THREE WEEKS OFF I'd been looking for, so I flew to Los Angeles. Tatum and I had talked—and talked—while I was in D.C., and I realized I had to get back to her.

However, it was also Hollywood that I had to get back to. There had been something about that party at Richard Perry's that night—something so exciting, so seductive. It was Tatum I missed, but it was also Tatum *in her element.*

At the end of 1984, I'd gone from someone who'd had trouble getting into Studio 54 to a celebrity on the Hollywood A-list. At the time, it seemed fantastic. In London, fame was almost a liability. In New York, people tried to act blasé about it. In Los Angeles, though, people were uncynically excited about it: Fame applauded itself constantly. In L.A., fame seemed to be your ticket to all the best things life had to offer, whether it was hanging with Keith Richards and Ronnie Wood before a Rolling Stones show (and feeling, God, there was no place on earth you'd rather be), or being at yet another Hollywood party where the cast of characters was a total Who's Who of the movies, and the stiffs were the big TV stars.

I remember going to Penny Marshall's birthday party. She and Carrie Fisher had the same birthday, and so each threw a party for the other in alternating years at their respective houses. I looked around the room and saw Bette Midler, Debra Winger, Jack Nicholson. I thought Nicholson was the greatest actor of all time—and then he walked up to me, shook my hand with an admiring look in his eyes, and said: "Don't ever change, Johnny Mac."

It was happening more and more. Suddenly, I had such grand notoriety that people I looked up to seemed to be looking up to me—whether it was Jack Nicholson, or Mick Jagger, or Carlos Santana, who told the crowd at a concert, "I'm dedicating this song to John McEnroe," and then went into a soliloquy about what a beautiful person I was.

Part of me thought it was great—and part of me was glancing backward to see if they were talking to the person behind me. I was only a tennis player! But I also was a kind of performer, and my performances—my televised outbursts—broke through the clutter and drone of canned television. I had anger, presence, integrity. I was a rebel.

And I was *famous.*

Still, some deep part of me felt that I was out of my depth in the star-world of Los Angeles. And Tatum knew that world like the back of her hand; she was nonchalant, almost jaded, about it. I thought she could help guide me through it.

Was I looking for the love of my life? I don't know. I was searching for something. In a sense, finding her then was a matter of timing as much as anything else. I was just sick of feeling empty. I wanted something more than money out of all I'd accomplished.

After having played an insane schedule for the past seven and a half years, I felt I was slipping, that something bad was going to happen. I didn't know what, but things were clearly going from bad to worse: I couldn't control my behavior anymore. I just couldn't stay on the merry-go-round.

I thought Tatum could help me, and I thought I could help her. The more I got to know her, the more she seemed like the perfect partner for me. I thought she was a young woman coming into her own. As the daughter of a famous father, and as someone who had had early success and a tough time afterward, she had obviously struggled with her identity. Now she was trying to break out and find herself.

Tatum told me she was planning to leave Los Angeles and move to New York. She wanted to make a clean break from her mother and father, who had been divorced for a long time, but who each continued to have a bad influence on her. She wanted a fresh start.

She seemed like a diamond in the rough. I saw a person who had been through a lot of what I'd been through—dealing with the media, the paparazzi—and done a reasonably good job. I thought, believe it or not, *This is a better version of myself.*

I was more attracted to her all the time. She had grown up a bit of a tomboy, so she did certain things unexpectedly well—she was an excellent pool player, a great Frisbee thrower, a good skier. She was very easy to spend time with: In some ways, it was like being with one of the guys.

I felt we were a good match. We were both shy, but we each also put up a tough front—although as I got to know her, I realized her toughness was more real than mine; she had been through a lot more than I had.

She talked constantly about her father. I began to feel I was in a strange kind of competition with him: that what Tatum was really looking for in me was a better version of her dad. I eventually came to feel that Ryan was a very manipulative guy, but when I first met him, he could be extremely charming. He was the type of guy who could walk into a party or Spago and wow a room—you could practically hear an announcer saying, "Here's Ryan O'Neal!" He would crack jokes and tell great stories and tell you how terrific you were. And you'd say, "Man, this guy is wonderful company."

And then there were moments when it seemed he could tear your head off. I sensed that during one of the first times Tatum took me up to Farrah Fawcett's place in the Hollywood Hills. Her father was living with Farrah, whom Tatum hated. I got the feeling that he and Farrah were so obsessed with their looks that they'd spend the whole day doing fanatical workouts. I remember seeing Ryan running on the beach all the time—the guy would run for five or six miles, but he wouldn't eat the whole day; he'd get the munchies, but still he wouldn't eat, and then he'd take a steam or a sauna and sweat some more. . . .

So by the time they said, "Do you guys want to come up for dinner at six?" Ryan was probably at the point where he'd eat anything! Besides which, if you go through a day like that, you're probably going to end up incredibly angry.

We went to the house, and he said, "Let's play racquetball." Before dinner.

I'd only tried racquetball a couple of times in my life, but never with anyone who really knew how to play. I was in my jeans, he was in his shorts, and I saw right away that he was pretty good. I could see immediately that it was a game of angles—that you could hit the ball in the corner where it wouldn't bounce, and that was how you won points.

Ryan would hit a shot and plant himself right in front of me. Now, if you hit the other guy in racquetball, you're supposed to play the point over, so I was forced to lob the ball to try and keep it away from him—then he'd put it away.

I thought, "God, this is screwed up." But he kept doing it! I could have put welts in his back, but I never laced into him, because I thought, "I'm not going to risk getting into a fight with this guy." And I lost, something like 21–18.

In retrospect, it's lucky that I didn't get into a fight with him—he was crazy about competing in general, and he'd been a Golden Gloves champion as a kid. There were also a few times he put on boxing gloves with me. I'm lucky he didn't punch my lights out. I caught him in good moods. He'd sort of let me hit him, and he'd just bob and weave, and after a minute my arms would get tired. His build was the opposite of mine—he had a big upper body and skinny bird legs, and I have big legs and a small upper body. I didn't think that boded too well if the boxing ever got serious.

BUT NOTHING BODED WELL, now that I look back on it. The first time Tatum and I made love, we were high, and it was terrible.

Shouldn't that have told me something?

Tatum said, "Let's go up to Farrah's place." I don't even know why she wanted to go up there—I think it was just because she knew that Farrah and Ryan weren't at home, and we happened to be close by. It wasn't a particularly romantic occasion. We were jittery, a little paranoid. We both seemed to be feeling, "Let's just do it to do it, so we can say we did it, and then we'll know we mean something to each other, and we'll really get into it when we're in a better frame of mind."

We went up to the house, up to the guest bedroom. It was very cold in that room—it felt like forty degrees! The combination of the cold and that weird buzz . . . It was just awful, not an especially good start. The truth is, though, I was as responsible for it as Tatum.

It wasn't as though she was saying, "Please, let's do drugs." I was the guilty party also. In fact, in retrospect, I believe she was trying to get away from all that: That was part of her reason for wanting to move to New York. Her mother, in particular, was in horrible shape. Tatum was trying to escape from what felt to her like some sort of terrible destiny.

I pulled her back into it, in a way, just because I was burnt out and looking for relaxation. I exacerbated the problem, not recognizing at the time how much of a problem it was. . . .

The next morning, we were down at the beach, and we decided to go to a restaurant I knew for breakfast. I was sitting there eating, when I looked up and saw, a hundred yards away, a guy taking our picture! I thought, "What the hell?!" That had never happened to me before; I had never been in the *National Enquirer* until that picture. I still remember the headline: "McEnroe–O'Neal Love Nest: The Brat and The Brat." It started the whole ball rolling. But Tatum had an incredible ability just to let all of that roll off her back. . . .

My suspension ended, but the end of '84, from Thanksgiving to New Year's, was a strange time for me. I'd committed to play the Davis Cup final in mid-December, in Sweden, but then I pulled out of the Australian Open, which started the week after Davis Cup.

I had had enough; going to the Australian didn't matter to me. In retrospect, since I wound up never winning the Australian, it wouldn't have been a bad idea to go and play the tournament when I was at the top of my game.

But tennis was the last thing on my mind at that moment. I was in love. And when you're in love, of course, you don't always see things too clearly.

It was time for me to leave L.A., to go back to New York to train for Davis Cup. Tatum was still talking about moving, as soon as she could track down some kind of place in Manhattan. And impulsively, I said to her, "Just come stay with me."

We flew east together.

YOU KNOW THAT LINE in the Beach Boys song "Sloop John B."—"This is the worst trip I've ever been on"? That's what it was like to fly to Sweden and play Davis Cup that December. As it would turn out, it was my last Cup match for three years. I really went out with a bang.

My heart sank as the plane took off from Kennedy. Tatum was back at my apartment. Connors and I still weren't speaking. My mind was a million miles from tennis. I sighed and sank into my seat, hoping the week would pass quickly.

I arrived in Gothenburg Tuesday morning to find a debacle already in progress. Jimmy had come over despite the fact that his wife was just about to give birth to their second child, so he was totally on edge, and acting like it. To give just one instance, the car that had been supposed to pick him up for practice on Monday hadn't come, so he was furious, and—if you can believe it—wrote a nasty message to Arthur in the snow.

Things felt frosty between Peter Fleming and me. And Jimmy Arias was our fourth player, and he's always been a personality I don't quite get—I just don't understand his sense of humor. Add to this the fact that I was in love and wishing I wasn't there in the first place. . . .

What's the opposite of team spirit? That's what we had in Gothenburg.

Connors played Wilander the first day, and he completely lost it. He just snapped. I certainly know what it's like to make an ass out of myself on a tennis court, but this was one of the all-time displays. He cursed and lashed out at everyone in sight, to the point where it felt like a miracle they didn't default him. In Sweden! In the Davis Cup final!

The Swedes had done the same thing the French had at Grenoble in '82—built an indoor court of slow red clay, to work against Jimmy and me, and for their baseliners. However, the court was horrific: It hadn't been packed down well enough—they'd wanted it as slow as possible—and it was literally coming apart.

The whole scene was just ugly, and Arthur didn't know what the hell to do. His way of dealing with it was not to deal with it at all. He wouldn't sit us down and talk to us—nothing. It was a terribly uncomfortable situation. Ironically enough, after Jimmy lost it, I played a miserable match and I didn't get mad at all. I lost to Henrik Sundstrom, who at the time was a top-ten pro, a very good clay-court player. It was actually one of the few times that I barely said anything.

At the end of the first day, we were down two matches to zero. That was a very big hole to be in against Sweden, in Sweden, on slow red clay. The next afternoon, Peter and I played doubles against Edberg and Jarryd, and very quickly found ourselves down two sets to one, with the Davis Cup on the line.

We were down 5–6 in the fourth set, and Peter was struggling with his serve. All of a sudden, Connors was on the sidelines clapping and yelling, "Come on, guys!" And I thought, *Who the hell are you kidding?*

I have no idea what was going through his mind. Maybe he'd realized for the first time that we weren't going to win the Davis Cup. My next thought was, *We're not going to win this. We're not going to come back. I'm not coming back. Screw you!*

But then I thought, *How can you think that? You're playing for the United States of America!* Still, I couldn't help myself. I had won four Cups already; this was the seventh year I'd played, so my record was pretty strong. *Four wins and a final isn't bad*, I thought. *The hell with this guy. You want to win? Try again.*

I wasn't terribly proud to be thinking this way. I'm still not proud.

Edberg and Jarryd were a great doubles team, and there was no reason to expect we could come back and win the match. And we didn't. Peter double-faulted on match point. It was the first Davis Cup doubles match we'd ever lost. I felt awful, but at least I could console myself that I hadn't missed a ball on purpose or done anything that caused us not to win, once Connors started clapping.

Half the loss was mine, anyway. My intensity level had been low; I wasn't into the match. It's not much of an excuse. It's just what happens when a team isn't really a team.

Then, that night, suddenly, somehow, all was forgiven between Connors and me. Don't ask me how. We all went out for dinner, and one of Jimmy's cronies (he always had cronies around), a red-headed guy named Billy, said, "Hey, why don't you let bygones be bygones?" We both just shrugged and said, "OK, why not?" Jimmy and I ended up having a drink or two late into the night, feeling like we might even be able to be friendly from then on.

He went back home the next morning to be with his wife. We had two singles matches to play that afternoon, meaningless except to allow us to save our honor. I beat Wilander, and Arias lost, playing a tough match against Sundstrom, and cramping up because he was so uptight. We played hard, but we lost the tie, 4–1.

The final blow for me, and the event that changed my Davis Cup life, was the ceremonial dinner that night. Imagine, in the first place, having to sit through a long ceremony in a foreign country when you've put in a poor showing and functioned horribly as a team. Those dinners are deadly to begin with, and this one felt twice as long as usual. It just went on and on.

We were all bored and miserable and fidgety. At one point, during "The Star Spangled Banner," Jimmy Arias, who was at my table, was talking a little bit, just being his usual self, laughing about something in a smirky way. It wasn't anything mean, but it would become a crucial detail in the case that was later mounted against us.

After what felt like about four hours of speeches and toasts, I leaned over to Ashe and said, "Listen, Arthur, when can we leave this dinner?

Isn't enough enough?" Arthur said, "You can leave after the next speaker." So the next speaker finished, and Arias and Peter Fleming and I all got up and left. What we didn't know—and I don't think Arthur knew, either—was that the *next* speaker was to be Hunter Delatour, the president of the USTA.

Delatour had seen Arthur excuse us, but now he looked to our table, where Arthur was sitting without any of his players, and saw red. He proceeded to give an apologetic oration, saying that the team's behavior during the matches (lumping me in by implication—I guess for past indiscretions—despite the fact that I hadn't uttered a peep) had made him embarrassed for America, and ashamed to be the USTA president.

My father, who had come to Gothenburg to watch the tie, was furious, as was the normally unflappable Arthur, who felt Delatour had no business washing dirty linen in public. Arthur told my dad that he thought Delatour, who was in his last year in office at the USTA, was kissing up to Philippe Chatrier, the head of the International Tennis Federation at the time, in hopes of landing a position there.

However, the upshot of that whole week was that the USTA drafted a new Code of Conduct. From here on, if you didn't sign the Code, you couldn't play Davis Cup.

I wouldn't compete for my country for two years.

TATUM AND I spent Christmas in New York, then flew back to L.A. for New Year's Eve. That night, we and a few friends went out drinking, then later, the two of us were back at Ryan's house, playing pool with Tatum's half-brother Patrick. By now it was three or four in the morning, and I had to fly to Vegas the next day to get ready for an event. Finally, I said, "Look, I've got to go to bed."

Tatum stayed up, drinking and playing pool with Patrick. I don't know when she came to bed, but it probably wasn't until six or seven. At around eleven A.M., I nudged her and said, "Listen, I'm going to Vegas. Do you want to come?" I had had enough of L.A. and partying, for the time being: I was a tennis player, I wanted to go play tennis. I was sure Tatum wouldn't get out of bed, because she'd been up all night partying. But she did. She got in the car and went with me. We were together now, for better or worse.

That was the start of our 1985. It was a hell of a beginning to a hell of a year.

9

Now I knew what Peter Fleming had gone through when he'd had that blazing streak in 1979: It was the rocket surge of first being in love. At the beginning of '85, I was still riding my incredible tennis wave of the previous year, except that now I was reenergized. I was happy—I felt I'd found my other half, my life partner. Tatum was traveling with me, and in the first few months of that year, it seemed as though I couldn't lose a set, let alone a match.

I obliterated Lendl in our third consecutive Masters final, 7–5, 6–0, 6–4—in one stretch I ran off eleven straight games. In Philadelphia, I won the final over a rising Czech star, the deceptively languid-looking Miloslav Mecir, who was shooting up through the rankings (and had made quick work of Connors in the semis). I took the title in Houston by beating the hard-serving (and equally fast-rising) Kevin Curren. And in Milan, I won the final against my near-nemesis Anders Jarryd, who had held another match point against me in the early rounds of the Masters.

In the first round at Milan, I made quick work of a big red-haired German seventeen-year-old named Boris Becker. I have to say, I didn't find him especially impressive that first time out—he actually seemed more annoying than anything else. He spent the entire match complaining and whining about line calls and his own play. I figured that was my turf! I also figured that at that point I had a lot more basis for my attitude than he had for his. I told him he should win something before he started complaining.

I think he heard me.

AS A DIRECT RESULT of our screwed-up Davis Cup final against Sweden in December, the USTA told me I would have to sign a Code of Conduct if I wanted to play for the team in 1985. I said, "I'm not signing anything. You've got to pick me or not pick me. You know what you're getting with me: On a couple of occasions—one of which, by the way, was not Sweden—I've misbehaved. But I'll try to act the best I can and recognize that playing for my country is different than playing for myself."

It was an impasse. Of course, I could have signed and acted exactly the same way I always had. What were they going to do, sue me? Withhold my pay? By that time, it was ten thousand dollars for the entire week. What the hell difference did it make, to sign this piece of paper? Nothing. I refused to sign.

In the first match of 1985, we played Japan. We could have sent our junior players to beat Japan. Eliot Teltscher and Aaron Krickstein went over and won, 5–0. The next match, however, was the quarterfinals, against Becker in Germany. Boris had just come from winning Wimbledon, and Teltscher and Krickstein didn't stand a chance against him and Hans Schwaier. So that was that—there went 1985. I didn't play. Connors wasn't playing anymore. Lendl was claiming to be an American, but his citizenship hadn't come through yet. We were back to struggling with the Davis Cup.

All for a piece of paper.


EVER SINCE the first time I'd gone to California, I'd been crazy about Malibu. Stacy had taken me there when we were together, and I'd loved the peace and beauty of the Pacific, the magnificence of that long stretch of coast.

I first got it into my head to buy a place there soon after I turned pro. I looked at places on the beach, but at the time they started at around a million dollars, and my dad said, "You're not going to buy a place that costs that kind of money." My father had been handling my business affairs since I started on the tour. In a lot of ways, it was a great arrangement—there was nobody I could trust more, and I only had to pay him his hourly rate instead of a percentage of my earnings—but it could also be difficult, as you might imagine.

He was right, though: I didn't have the money to spend a million dollars for a house on the beach in 1979 or '80, not after taxes, so I decided to buy a beautiful little bachelor house, on the bluff, for around $400,000. I ended up changing my mind, though, because my business advisor (Dad) worried about what would happen to a house on a hill if there was an earthquake.

Fast-forward to February of '85, after I'd had another five high-earning years. Now I could afford to buy that beach house! And not just any beach house, but Johnny Carson's, on the Pacific Coast Highway at Carbon Canyon Beach in Malibu, for $1.85 million plus three tennis lessons that Johnny insisted I throw into the deal! I was thinking more and more about making Los Angeles my base of operations: I loved the beach;

sitting and staring at the Pacific surf at sunset made me feel at peace more than almost anything else I knew.

Unfortunately, though, I also wound up bringing Tatum back into the very environment she was trying to leave. She was struggling to get away from her family, and living just down the beach from her father, who exerted a powerful negative magnetism, didn't help matters.

At a tournament in Houston, I was fatigued from traveling and not taking care of myself as well as I could have. In the first round, I took my funk onto the court and got into a bad fight with Wojtek Fibak, the Polish veteran. Fibak was a very smart, skilful player, extremely canny psychologically, and about seven years older than I was. He was playing a great match, but I also felt he was being manipulative, using the John Newcombe kill-you-with-kindness approach to get the crowd against me. Finally, I laced into him, hit him with a barrage of obscenities.

It was stupid and ugly. Where once I'd been lawyerly and careful about what came out of my mouth—even when I was furious—now the floodgates had opened.

I was out of control. It would have done me a world of good to get defaulted from tournaments at that point. Instead, I manipulated the rules by getting suspended on purpose at times when I needed a break.

The rule was that if you went over a certain amount in fines—initially it was $7,500—you'd be suspended. So I'd accumulate some fines, and then I'd think, *Okay, I'm at $6,800, so if I get fined this week, I'm suspended for twenty-one days.*

I'd have exhibitions scheduled, though, so I'd keep playing those. That was when the ATP realized that they'd have to tighten up: They set the initial suspension at twenty-one days, but if you played exhibitions within that period, the suspension was doubled to forty-two days (that's what had happened to me after the '84 Stockholm Open). As a result, I had to be a little more careful, but it was still a game I played, and I wasn't the only one.

Once I began to have bad outbursts, like the one against Fibak, I felt a lot of remorse, but I wasn't able to do much about it. I wasn't able or willing enough to change.

Part of me felt entitled, since I was the best tennis player in the world—a very important guy!—but even that didn't make me feel good. When you can't control yourself, you want someone to do it for you— that's where I acutely missed being part of a team sport. What if I'd been playing for the Knicks? People would have worked with me, coached me. Somebody would have said, "You're hurting the organization, but we want to help you because we want you to stay here."

Instead, I felt more and more alone on the tennis court. Nobody was trying to help me, and I wasn't asking anybody for help. I dug myself deeper and deeper into a hole, and I felt worse and worse about it.

THAT WAS WHEN I had my brilliant idea.

My idea was that Tatum and I should have a baby. It just seemed so *right*—having children was something that had been on my mind for a while. The other thing that crossed my mind, I have to admit, was that maybe if Tatum got pregnant, she would clean up her act. Maybe it would force us both to clean up our act.

THE TABLOIDS had been following us around for six months, and that was also driving me crazy. I had had notoriety in the tennis world; I had been in *People;* but I had never had the distinction of making the *National Enquirer* until they'd photographed Tatum and me in December. Now it felt like open season on me, on her, and especially on the two of us together.

Suddenly, wherever I went, it felt like a spectacle. Even my tennis events were drawing crowds of paparazzi types, people I'd never seen around the sport before. As a result, for the first time in my career, I chose to alter my preparation for Wimbledon, and not play Queen's, where I had been in the final for seven years in a row.

However, I still wanted a French Open title badly. I got through to the semis, where I faced Mats Wilander, who had broken into the top five in the world. It was an extremely windy, cold day when we played. Connors was to play Lendl in the first match, at twelve-thirty P.M.

I was trying to figure out when to eat—it may not sound like a big deal, but it's very important. You try to judge when you're going to play, and back up a couple of hours from there. You really don't want to be too full or too empty: A match can hang on the right timing. It's a little difficult, and the unexpected often happens.

I came back to the hotel at eleven-thirty A.M. from a practice session and ate a good-sized lunch. By now, it was pouring rain. I'd practiced indoors, but I figured that with the rain, the match might not go on anyway. Then I turned on the TV and watched in total horror as Lendl and Connors began to play in the rain. They put them on the court, for whatever reason.

And Lendl was just killing Connors. I don't know what had happened to Jimmy—either he was hurt, pretending to be hurt, or just totally in the doldrums. Lendl wound up destroying him in something like an hour and twenty minutes. At two sets to love, I was still at the hotel. It was 6–2, 6–3, 3–0 when I arrived at the courts. You usually want to give yourself around an hour at the venue before you play, just to get dressed, stretch, settle down. When I went out to play, I was totally unprepared.

It was just one of those days. I lost the first set, 1–6. I had set points in the second set at 5–4 to level the match, but I lost it, 7–5. I was up 5–1 in the third set, then lost that, 7–5. I should have been up two sets to one, and instead, I lost the match.

The tabloids were all over us again in Paris, so I was in a pretty ragged mood when I came back to New York. I was glad not to be playing Queen's. I decided to give myself a break, just train for a week or ten days on the grass courts at Piping Rock (a club in Nassau County) or Forest Hills, and then go back and try to win another Wimbledon. I had been in five straight Wimbledon finals, so skipping the tune-up was a big move for me, but I just needed the peace and quiet.

Then Boris Becker won Queen's, and Johan Kriek, whom he had beaten in the final, said: "I predict that if Boris is still playing this well, he'll win Wimbledon."

Not if I had anything to do with it! I didn't take Tatum to Wimbledon: It would've been too much for her, for us, and for me. When I got there, I thought, "I've come here to play. I'm not here to mess around. I can stay in my room; I don't have to go out. I can just focus on the tennis."

It didn't help. The tabloids, American and British, kept on churning out the crud—whether it was lies about Tatum, or her mother's substance problems, or other cockamamie stories. They were in the papers, and I'd say, "I don't want to look at them"—and then someone would say, "Hey, John, did you see that story in the *Sun*?"

I felt I wasn't being beaten by any opponent that year; I was being beaten before I got on the court. In the quarters I played Kevin Curren, who was a very difficult opponent on grass. I'd defeated him at Wimbledon a couple of years earlier, when his serve had looked daunting, but he'd done a lot of improving since then. He also had a new graphite Kneissl racket, which was giving his serve even more pop—as if it needed any! With the new rackets, it was becoming more and more apparent that when a guy was already a big hitter, things were going to become problematic.

Curren overwhelmed me with his serve. I just couldn't get any rhythm going on the return. The score wasn't even close—6–2, 6–2, 6–4. I felt old out there. Old at twenty-six.

By the time Peter and I made it to the semifinals of the doubles, after Curren had crushed me, and with the pressure of all the tabloid stories, all of a sudden I got sick. I walked around hunched over from the stress, ill to the point where I was literally losing control of my bodily functions.

I remember sitting in the locker room before the doubles semifinal, bent over, feeling so bad that I thought, *I've got to get the hell out of here*—but I wasn't going to default on my partner.

It didn't matter: We lost anyway.

And Becker beat Curren in the singles final. He was seventeen years old.


I PLAYED HIM not long after he won Wimbledon, in an exhibition in Atlanta, at the Omni. There have been some great exhibitions over the years: Atlanta was like Milan—phenomenal crowds, incredible energy. Boris ended up beating me 7–5 in the third, and I thought, *This guy's got the biggest serve I've ever seen in my life. No one has ever hit a bigger serve.*

He hadn't played like that in Milan. Now he had won Wimbledon, and he had more confidence. It wasn't just that his serve was big—it was that he knew where to place it. Curren had had a huge serve at Wimbledon, but this kid's service was heavier, and had more spin, and was more unreadable, more unpredictable. He backed it up with that presence of his, and his nutty willingness to dive for shots. (It helps to be a teenager!) He had some pretty big groundstrokes, too.

Becker was simply a physical phenomenon. For someone that young, it was incredible how big his legs were. That's what amazed me. He still hadn't turned eighteen. I was getting old, and the future was moving in fast.


IN AUGUST, I beat Lendl in straight sets in both warmup events for the U.S. Open: Stratton Mountain, in Vermont, and the Canadian Open. He was fighting hard to take number one from me, and it was all coming down to Flushing Meadows, where, frankly, I thought my chances for a fifth title were extremely good.

I advanced routinely to the semifinals, where I played Mats Wilander. It was a match that would change my whole life.

We went out onto the court at eleven A.M. on Super Saturday. It was incredibly hot out, but I stayed calm, knowing I'd have to conserve every ounce of my energy. I was right: It was a long, tough, five-set match. Mats threw a lot at me, constantly mixing it up—I've always thought he's one of the most intelligent players I've ever played. Down two sets to one, I threw everything I had into it, and I managed to win the last two sets and pull out a victory.

It's hard to describe how tired I was after that match. Then came a long women's final, then Lendl didn't get out there against Connors until almost seven P.M., when the heat of the day had tempered, and then Connors was gimpy—something was wrong with his ankle. Lendl beat him in three easy sets, barely breaking a sweat.

I couldn't believe how bad I felt the next day. The truth is, my body hadn't felt right for the last four or five years, but this was the worst it had ever been. I'd pulled a hip muscle in early '85, and I'd started getting it strapped up by the trainer every time I played. That comforted me to the point where I could go all-out, but something was still just a little bit off. I thought it would go away, but it never did.

What had happened was that my body had started tightening up through all those years of pounding. Although people always said my style looked effortless compared to Lendl's (one sportswriter wrote that when he closed his eyes and listened to the two of us play, Lendl sounded as if he was moving furniture, and I was almost inaudible), effortlessness takes work.

I'd always prided myself on my movement. There was a catlike quality to it, I liked to think; I got the job done, even though people rarely said, "Hey, this guy's really fast." I didn't place a great deal of strain on my body, because I didn't think it could take a lot of strain. My legs were always powerful (even in my early teens, I could press an incredible amount of weight on a leg machine), but I didn't have a lot of upper-body strength. I'd always recovered pretty quickly. So if I just had enough time, I could win.

However, recovery time starts to decline as young men age, and the process accelerates in world-class athletes. Time was running out on me.

The next day, a little after one P.M., I was in my house in Oyster Bay with Tatum and her brother Griffin, watching the Giants game on TV. It was pouring rain, and for the first and only time in my life, I was praying that it would rain the entire day. Normally, you're so stressed out at the prospect of a big match that you just want to get it over with, but today I knew that my body wasn't right. I prayed for a postponement.

Then, all of a sudden, there was bright sunshine on the television.

"Oh, Jesus," I said, throwing my clothes and equipment into my tennis bag as fast as I could. We all went down and got into the car—and then, after we'd gone five blocks, Griffin said he'd forgotten his camera. Could we go back and get it? I turned around, he got his camera, and then we wound up sitting in U.S. Open traffic on the Grand Central Expressway and getting to the National Tennis Center at three-fifteen, forty-five minutes before my final. There was barely time to get taped up and stretch.

I'm not sure exactly how, but I actually got off to a good start against Lendl, going up 5–2 in the first set. Then suddenly, on the changeover, I stood up and . . . This is hard to explain. But when people describe out-of-body experiences, I understand completely. Because I stood up and walked over to my side of the court, but my body was still back in the chair.

I had gone totally dead. I had nothing left. Zero. I had set points against Lendl, but I lost 7–6, 6–3, 6–4.

It was a huge turning point. Lendl had lost in the final here three years in a row, twice to Connors and once to me. Now, once and for all, he had proved to New York that he wasn't a choker. His confidence soared after that match (he would go on to win two more U.S. Opens, and was in eight consecutive finals, from 1982 to 1989—an incredible record), and mine dropped away. I would never win another major tournament.

He had knocked me off the mountaintop. He was number one.

You can pick a handful of athletes, over time, who have changed the public's perspective on how a sport is played. Lawrence Taylor did it in football with the position of outside linebacker; Ivan Lendl and Martina Navratilova did it in tennis. Lendl had trained like a maniac to reach number one; he had lost fifteen pounds on Dr. Robert Haas's diet. My not-very-funny joke at the time—that I'd gone on the Häagen-Dazs diet—showed that I could no longer take number one completely seriously. I had lost the will to do what it took to stay on top: The territory up there was simply too punishing.

I needed a rest.

When tennis players saw what Lendl had done to edge by me in 1985—especially after the way I'd played in '84—they were ready to sign on. People said, "Wait a minute, I'm going to train harder; I'm going to do more off-court." And they did. Today's tennis stars, male and female, are bigger, stronger, faster, and more durable than ever before: They're the direct result of Lendl's example. The combination of fitness and racket power had left me out in the cold. The master of the wood racket was heading toward extinction.


IMMEDIATELY AFTER I lost to Lendl, Tatum and I went back to California. I needed a couple of days to rest before I played the tournaments in Los Angeles and San Francisco. And then the night before the semifinals in L.A., we found out that Tatum was pregnant.

It was very strange: That same night, Tatum's mother cooked us a very rich casserole for dinner, and then the next morning, I literally couldn't get out of bed. I was sick as a dog, and I had to default the semifinal. I was in bed through the weekend, and was able to play San Francisco only because the tournament had a Wednesday start, but I was still sick enough there to lose to Kriek in the quarterfinals.

I don't know if I was reacting to the casserole or to Tatum's news, but it was bizarre: In a certain way, I was totally happy. I was going to be a father! Whenever I was able to stop retching, I couldn't stop smiling.

Four days after we'd heard the news, my mother received a phone call from *People* magazine, and was asked to comment about a report that Tatum was pregnant. Was it true? My mother said she doubted it, because her son surely would have told her.

Why didn't I? Because I panicked. In fact, I hadn't told her because, although my parents were often affectionate with Tatum, I knew, deep-down, that they didn't approve of her. She was an actress, her parents were divorced, she was too young, she hadn't gone to college. I suspect they knew other things about her, too; things that Tatum and I could never discuss with them.

And then, beyond all that, to have a child out of wedlock! My parents were churchgoing Catholics: My brothers and I had all been baptized and confirmed, and I had gone to Mass every week until I was eighteen. Even though I had decided for myself that organized religion was a sham, and that God, if He exists, must be deaf, dumb, and blind—Catholic guilt doesn't go away easily.

Finally, several days later, I called her to wish her happy birthday. We talked for a little while—and I said nothing. I hung up, and felt awful.

More Catholic guilt! I couldn't stand it. I called her back, and I said, "By the way, I forgot to tell you you're going to be a grandmother." And that's how she finally found out. It's been the story of my life, in a lot of ways: Many great things have happened to me, but all the attention I've

been paid has often had a way of turning good to bad. Suddenly, after I'd
been feeling so ecstatic, the world felt sordid.


IN NOVEMBER OF 1985, I played six one-night exhibitions with Borg,
as part of the Tennis Over America tour I'd been doing for the past four
years. This was the first time that Bjorn had come along. It was six cities
in six nights, a tough grind, and, to put it mildly, my old friend and adversary no longer had the same severely regimented personality that he'd
had when he'd dominated world tennis. To be perfectly honest, I was a
little concerned about his ability to get through the week. Still, there
was an enormous demand out there to see us re-create the old rivalry, so
off we went to make a little money.

The first night, in Minneapolis, we must have had fourteen or fifteen
thousand people out to watch us play. It was an incredible crowd, and it
was absolutely packed with Swedes. Essentially, I threw Bjorn a bone that
night—there was no way he could lose in front of the Swedish crowd.

Soon, though, I found myself carrying him in every match. He was still
in amazing shape; he was still one of the fastest humans on earth.
However, he just could no longer hit a tennis ball the way he used to: His
heart wasn't in it.

One night we were having a drink, and I started waxing philosophical about losing the Open and being bumped from the number-one spot
by Lendl. Maybe it wasn't such a bad thing to be number two, I mused.
There was a hell of a lot less pressure, and number two wasn't exactly
chopped liver! Maybe I should hang it up as number two and call it a
good career, or—here was another idea—what about just regrouping for
a while, then going for the gold again?

He interrupted me, shaking his head. "Number one is the only thing
that matters, John," he said. "You know it as well as I do. If you're number two, you might as well be number three or four—you're nobody."

He motioned me closer, and lowered his voice, even though the music was blaring in the hotel bar. "You've got to go win the Australian!" Bjorn whispered, fervently. "If you win down there, then come back and win the Masters, it'll put you back on top again."

"Huh," I said. I blinked, thought about it a moment.

"You're going to be twenty-seven, John," Borg said. "Getting on. Grab it while you can grab it." He nodded slowly and solemnly, with absolute certainty. I was listening. I felt he was about the only person I could've discussed these things with who really knew what he was talking about. I decided then and there to go Down Under. He had convinced me I could still be number one.

THE AUSTRALIAN OPEN was horrendous: I never should have gone. I was way too burned-out to keep playing. I wasn't mentally stable.

But I flew there anyway. With my twenty-two-year-old pregnant girl-friend close by my side. I had briefly entertained the idea of going alone to Melbourne—if I was really serious about winning this title, I needed as few distractions as possible—but I could tell right away that Tatum wasn't having any of it. A pregnant woman, and especially a very young pregnant woman, wants to be with her mate. So I grew philosophical again. Maybe I should just relax, not worry so much about my results in the tournament. Number two in the world might be a disappointment, but no matter what Borg said, it still wasn't bad.

A car picked us up at the Melbourne airport and took us to the hotel—where we walked into a lobby full of paparazzi. I was furious, but contained. I demanded to see the manager, and said, "Get rid of these people, now. Please—give me a break. I've just flown here from the United States, and I can't deal with this." I was burning inside, and exhausted from the flight.

When we got up to our room, however, I could tell right away that I didn't like this hotel. It just didn't feel right. If they had let those people into the lobby, then there wasn't going to be any kind of control while we stayed there. I had to do something.

Tatum was upset. I said to her, "Listen, let me take care of this. I'll go back down and talk to the manager." She looked at me closely: She knew how I could get, and where it could go. I had cooled down, though. She trusted that I would go and handle the situation.

However, when I got back down to the lobby, one of the photographers was still there, and he immediately began taking my picture again.

I lost it. I grabbed the guy by the collar and pushed him over to a couch. "Listen, asshole," I growled. I don't know what I was going to do. I don't know what he was going to do. As I held the paparazzo by the collar, I suddenly heard one of the bellmen say, "There's another photographer coming."

Clearly, it was a setup. One of them was supposed to provoke me, so the other one could photograph it. I immediately let go of the guy, but the picture that immediately went worldwide was of the photographer lying on the couch, and me standing there, my hands open, holding on to nothing. That provoked an interesting phone call from my father a couple of days later! "Hey, how's it going down there? Uh-huh . . ."

It became a miserable ten days for me. I felt like such a jerk! When I went back up to the room, Tatum asked me how it had gone, and I had to tell her. "I thought you were going to take care of everything," she said. I stammered something lame—and then, of course, she wouldn't leave it alone: "That was really smart, wasn't it?"

That was another time I wished I had been with a team. With a team, you wouldn't be exposed to those things so early in a trip, when you're so fatigued. You'd have other people around you, to deflect, to protect. I was always out there all by myself—I never liked entourages. It was just Tatum and me.

That entire Australian Open was a succession of matches I was trying to lose—and I couldn't lose! In the third round, I played a Nigerian named Nduka Odizor. In the first game I served, he was hitting unbelievable returns—he broke me without any apparent effort. As far as I was concerned, I was out of there. I was as far away from it as I've ever been on a court. Then, the next game, he served two double-faults, missed a volley on top of the net, and handed it back to me. The next game, he was hitting screaming winners by me again. This went on for at least six games, then finally I thought, "I can't lose to this guy. I cannot do this, even if I want to."

It went on. In the round of 16, I played Henri Leconte, who was always a character and a crazy guy to play, and I got behind, one set to two and 1–4, two service breaks against me. I was totally down and out, but somehow I got back to 6–6. Then I got down 1–5 in the tiebreaker, and I won that! Poor Henri was so freaked out that I rolled over him in the fifth set.

In the quarterfinals, I faced Slobodan Zivojinovic, of Yugoslavia. Bobo was six-foot-six and 200 pounds, with a serve to match: In June, he had upset Wilander in the first round at Wimbledon. "Fine," I thought. "Here's my ticket out of here." Of course, I immediately went up two sets to one—and wound up losing love–6 in the fifth. By the end of that match, in my time-honored fashion, I had taken the crowd from cheering me to booing me, as I gave them finger-salutes.

So that was the end of my great Australian campaign of 1985. The beginning and the end were absolutely abysmal. The middle wasn't a whole lot better. It finally made me realize, "I need to pull myself together and get some time off, because I'm heading off the deep end." And that was the moment I chose to go to the Masters and lose to Brad Gilbert for the only time in my career.

# 10

I WAS STANDING ON THE SIDELINE of the playoff game between the New York Giants and the Chicago Bears, at Soldier Field in Chicago. My Chicago Bears buddies Kenny Margerum and Gary Fencik had set me up with a sideline pass. It was so cold, I felt as though I was about to get frostbite: seventeen degrees below zero. I vividly remember thinking, "Thank God I'm a tennis player."

Unfortunately, my momentary feeling of euphoria didn't last.

As you've probably figured out by now, I've had a number of nemeses in my tennis life (including, all too often, myself). However, nobody got to me the way Brad Gilbert did.

I played him fourteen times, and the one time I lost to him was the straw that broke the camel's back. I looked up to the heavens and thought, "Someone is telling me something here. Because if I can lose to

Brad Gilbert, something is seriously wrong. I've got to take a look at my-self. I've got to reevaluate not only my career but my life."

What was it about him? It mostly boiled down to this: I've never seen anybody as negative on a tennis court. Eeyore had nothing on Brad—he had a black cloud over his head from the moment he walked out there, and he never seemed satisfied until he got you feeling pretty gloomy, too. It almost seemed to be his game plan. He'd look like he was going to commit hara-kiri in the warmup. Then he did a running commentary while he played, berating himself on every single point (as if people cared), and justifying every mistake he made: "I can't believe I hit that backhand down the line instead of crosscourt." "Why didn't I hit a drop-volley there?" "Why didn't I hit my first serve wide instead of going up the middle?"

As an opponent, you'd hear everything he said, because he'd say it loud enough for the people in the stands to catch every word. It would get under your skin and infect you.

The other part of it, though, was: He could play. He was a better ath-lete than people realized. He was a pusher—his second serve was a melon, his volleying was fairly shaky, but he got everything back. He'd push the ball, you'd come to net, then he'd try to pass you. The style of play reflected his personality: He'd bring you down, and suck your en-ergy dry. You'd never lose to him if you were playing up to your level, but you had to guard against falling into that whirlpool.

It didn't always work. I saw top-ranked players just melt before my eyes. A perfect example is when Gilbert beat Becker at the 1987 U.S. Open. By the end of that match, Boris couldn't beat his way out of a paper bag, and it looked like he was ready to jump off the Empire State Building.

I'm sure Gilbert won a lot of matches by bending the emotional rules. Some people feed off negativity. For a long time, that was something I did myself. I couldn't appreciate when things were going well; I was always expecting the next bad thing to come, and I was constantly getting on myself in order not to let it happen. It's hard. When you're involved in a one-on-one game, it's very difficult to completely convince yourself that if you let down for an instant, the other guy isn't going to take advantage of it. I don't care who you are—you're going to get into situations that make you question yourself.

Perhaps there was something about Gilbert that made me look into myself and think, "Oh my God, can I possibly be that unbearable?"

I know I could be frustrating to play, but I'd always justify it by thinking that my style of play was attractive to watch; I also believe that people elevated their games when they played me. Counterpunching is a different mentality. Wilander and Borg were brilliant at it, always willing to wait for you to do something, then say, "I can do it better than you."

I preferred to take the initiative. Take the ball on the rise. Lay it out and just see if the person could handle it. I took it to people, which I think is more exciting—win or lose. Obviously, I always preferred to win.

However, 1985, after starting so well, had turned into a long year of defeats, culminating in the disastrous trip to Australia. Tatum was pregnant, and I felt exhausted and unsettled. Going into the Masters, I figured, "Well, maybe I can at least end the year on a good note."

My first-round match against Gilbert began well enough: I took the first set, 7–5. Then things began to deteriorate. Slowly and irreversibly, I let Gilbert's negativity get under my skin. It was almost as if he had become a kind of distorting mirror, reflecting my worst image of myself. By the time I'd lost the second set, 4–6, I simply didn't want to be there anymore.

The very lowest point came at the beginning of the third set, when I saw some people in the stands cheering for Gilbert. They weren't doing anything wrong, just encouraging him, but something in me snapped, and I actually heard myself mutter an ethnic slur. No one heard it but me. And I thought, "You have now officially gone over the edge."

That was diametrically the opposite of how I had been brought up, of everything I believed in. It wasn't me. But it had come out of my mouth. It was pathetic enough that I was losing to Gilbert, but this was a new low.

I completely fell apart, and lost the set, 1–6. I walked off the court, left the Garden, and drove uptown to my place on East 90th Street, which I was renting to my friend Ahmad Rashad at the time. I walked in and said, "Ahmad, that's it; I've had it. I'm not playing anymore. I can't handle it." And that was the last tournament I played for six months.

TATUM AND I SPENT the first few weeks after the Masters traveling around the country to a few exhibitions I'd promised to play. I didn't enjoy them very much, but the money was good, and once they were over, they were over. Then we went back to the beach house in Malibu.

For a while, I didn't do much more than decompress—watching the waves, marveling at Tatum's growing belly, going to parties. One of my favorite places to spend time was a private club called On the Rocks, owned by my friend Lou Adler. Located on the floor above the Roxy Theater on Sunset Boulevard in Hollywood, it had only fifty members or so, and it was a place where I could really let down my guard. It was also the site of the only surprise party ever thrown for me, given by Tatum in honor of my twenty-seventh birthday. More and more, I was spending time with the same A-list cast of characters. I had grown into my role, become comfortable with it: I was a star, they were stars. We were all stars together.

At the same time, it was beginning to occur to me that I wasn't doing very much training. My body certainly felt better for a while, but then I began to miss the movement. I played a bit of tennis, and could feel the usual aches and pains start to return. All the while, I couldn't help sneaking peeks at TV and the sports section, to see what was happening on the tennis tour. I was still plugged in to the tennis grapevine: Some people,

I was told, were starting to say, "McEnroe's finished; he's going to retire." It was very strange—not completely painful, but not quite pleasurable, either—to think about the caravan rattling on without me. I wondered: *Should I go back? And if I do go back, when would be the right time?*

If I did return to the tour, I knew I had to do something different. I was approaching thirty, that outer boundary for tennis players. I thought of last September's Open, and how Lendl had outlasted me in the final. Until that point, I had joked about training—but afterward I wasn't smiling. Did I need to train more myself?

One evening, I was sitting on my back porch with my old friend Tony Graham, a former UCLA player who'd also been on the tour for a while. My porch is right on the beach, and it was a perfect evening, with the kind of Pacific sunset that fills your whole soul. It was getting to be high tide: Some big waves were starting to roll in.

Tony and I had hit a few balls earlier, and now we were just sitting on the porch, in a quiet, philosophical mood, watching the waves and the gorgeous sky. I was talking about how the Gilbert match at the Masters had seemed like a sign from God that I needed to stop for a while; I wondered aloud about my future. And Tony said, jokingly, "There's got to be some other sign from God that'll let you know."

And just at that moment, a wave rolled all the way up to the porch and left a tennis ball sitting right at our feet.

Tony picked up the ball. We looked at each other, wide-eyed. "My God, man, there's your sign!" he said.

And I swear, for the whole rest of the night, not a single other wave came even close to the porch.


I WANTED NUMBER ONE BACK, so I started training. I wanted to get stronger, in order to be able to compete on a more equitable basis with players like Curren and Becker, so for the first time in my life, I began lifting weights. All the wise heads in sports training said you needed to be flexible, too, and so I also started doing yoga. In addition, for the first time, I briefly hired a coach, Paul Cohen, who had written a fantastic motivational letter to me while I was on hiatus. "I'm going to be better," I thought, as I jumped rope and pumped iron. "I'm going to be better." I was *convinced* of it. I thought about Lendl out there, doing what he was doing—I was going to train every bit as hard, if not harder. From here on in, Häagen-Dazs was out, along with every other dessert, and beer. From here on, it was fish and white meat skinless chicken, fruit and veggies. I began to lose weight again.

For five months, it was yoga in the morning, tennis in the afternoon, stationary bike and weight-training at night—day in, day out. And at the end of every one of my very full days . . . I was exhausted. I kept thinking, "It's going to come back, it's going to come back, it's *got* to come back." After all, I was training like a boxer: Whenever I watched a boxing match, I would look at those men and think, "My God, they have so much energy." I thought that sooner or later, that would happen to me— I'd be like Jim Carrey as Andy Kaufman, in *Man on the Moon:* "Here I am!" I thought I would have energy to burn. It never happened.

I overtrained, I think. A lot of it is mental—you've got to love it, or you can't break through the pain. I never enjoyed it enough. Lendl loved it—but in the end, that wasn't me.


ON ONE OF THE very first afternoons Tatum and I spent at my new house in Malibu, we were playing Frisbee on the beach when a neighbor came over and said, "Hey, there's someone dug in over there, taking pictures of you." I looked and, to my astonishment, about fifty yards away, a man in a bunker in the sand was pointing a huge telephoto lens at us.

I had thought this was private property, but I quickly learned otherwise when I walked over to the photographer, who informed me that any part of the beach below the tide line was public domain, and that he was perfectly within his rights.

I suppose I should have just blown it off and gone inside, but it seemed so outrageous! I started yelling at him, throwing sand at him. Ridiculous—but what were my alternatives? I was furious, but my rule with photographers was always *Don't hit the guy.* You can do practically anything else—spit, throw sand, hurl invective—but *don't punch the guy,* because you'll get sued.

The photographer was working for the English papers, and he eventually became an acquaintance—not a friend, mind you. I know his name to this day. When Tatum became pregnant, he said, "Look, you can do this the easy way or the hard way. Because either way, we're going to be around. So if you want to make it miserable for yourself, you can, but . . ." It turned out that he was getting a retainer of $1,500 a week just to follow me—whether he got a picture or not! I thought, "Who the hell am I? I'm just some tennis player. What in God's name is going on here?"

It turned out that he was being paid the retainer to get the first pictures of Tatum with the new baby. I asked him how much he was going to be paid if he got the pictures. Fifty thousand dollars, he told me. So I cut a deal with him. I said, "Listen, I'll let you get the first pictures—but you give me twenty-five thousand dollars, or I'm going to release the photos for nothing."

And that's exactly how it worked out. He took the first couple of pictures when Kevin was a couple of days old—and kept the other paparazzi away—and I donated half the fifty thousand to charity, so at least I could feel he wasn't getting all of it, and that I was making something positive out of an embarrassing situation.

Kevin Jack McEnroe was born at St. John's Hospital in Santa Monica on May 23, 1986. That day—that whole period—was the happiest I'd ever been. There's nothing comparable to the birth of your first child. First, there's the miracle of just watching him come out: You think, "My

God, how does that *happen?*" Then comes the relief that he's healthy. You feel grateful, weepy, blessed.

I also felt very good that he had been born during a period when I was taking time off. I was firmly convinced that that was the right thing to do, and I was positive it was going to better my career.

*I've got to smell the roses here,* I thought. *I've got to regroup.* I knew I needed some time off, and I knew that when I eventually came back, I'd be better off for it. Being a father for the first time would help me put things in perspective. I strongly believed that you could have a child and be number one. There was no doubt in my mind that I could do it. It felt exactly like all the other challenges I had set for myself in life. I had attained those goals; why not this?

At the same time, Kevin's birth made the picture much more complicated. Suddenly, tennis didn't feel as all-encompassing. There were even strange moments when it seemed trivial. I'd be in the Malibu house looking out the window and I'd say, "This is amazing—I'm on the beach in Malibu, and the sun's going down, and it's this incredible color."

Suddenly, my profession and my life had become two separate things. I kept trying to get my mind around it. *It's like singles and doubles,* I thought. *Like Davis Cup and Wimbledon. They're not the same.* My career thus far had been incredibly intense, but there was nothing to compare with the intensity of life itself.

And that was the moment—I didn't realize it at the time—when my passion for tennis began to shift in another direction.

In 1986, when I didn't go to Wimbledon for the first time in nine years, I remember thinking that somehow the sport was going to come to a complete standstill—I literally almost convinced myself that the tennis world was going to stop without me.

I thought I was making a point: "I'm not going to put up with this nonsense until something changes," meaning the paparazzi, the tabloids—the way they were all over me. Obviously, a fair amount of it was self-induced, but I felt, nevertheless, that it had gotten completely out of hand.

It gradually dawned on me, over the course of that year and the next, when I didn't play Wimbledon again, that not only was tennis going on without me, but—as Becker won once more in 1986 and Pat Cash won in 1987—that the game was changing radically: Power tennis was taking over. Suddenly, I thought, "Hey, they're still playing Wimbledon," and there I was, sitting on my behind, and I hadn't proven anything. In a certain way, I felt I had wasted two years—but then I realized what a mistake it was for me even to think that. . . .

One afternoon in late June of 1986, while Wimbledon was going on without me, I was at home in Malibu and there was a knock on the door. I opened it and a man said, "I'm from the *News of the World*," one of those English papers that were always tormenting me during the Wimbledon fortnight.

I thought, *No! This is my* house. *They're knocking on the door of my* house." I thought I was going to punch this guy's lights out, but I was sharp—I looked across the street for the photographer stationed there to catch a *picture* of me punching this guy's lights out. Sure enough, there he was. So I just said to the reporter, "Would you please step in here, because I have a little question to ask you. . . ."

He started to edge away.

"Come on in!" I said.

He ran across the Pacific Coast Highway.


WHEN I FINALLY ADMITTED to my mother that Tatum was pregnant, the first words out of her mouth were, "You're going to get married, right?" I said, "Yeah, of course"—even though, to tell the truth, marriage was never the first thing on my mind. I knew I wanted to have a family, but back then, I wasn't sure whether the formalities mattered to me or not.

Pretty soon, though, I realized that they did matter to Tatum, and before I knew it, I was promising my mother that we'd be married in the Catholic Church. Tatum actually sort of tried to become a Catholic for a while. She met with a priest, took instruction: It eventually petered out.

We were married on August 1, 1986, in St. Dominic's Roman Catholic Church, near my house in Oyster Bay. We had a tent put up so that people could enter the church privately. I wasn't about to try to make things easier for the paparazzi.

Some of the reporters and photographers started yelling, as we came out of the church, "Just smile; come on, just pose for a few pictures! You're happy, right? Come on!" And that was the last thing I wanted to do. Whether I was happy or not had nothing to do with it to me. Maybe it should have. I'm still not sure.

We ended up posing anyway: There are pictures of us, outside the church. I'm sorry we did it—I felt pressured to prove my happiness, which is completely ridiculous, when you think about it. I hated every minute of it.

Then some of the photographers wanted to pose a whole crowd, the wedding party and all the local onlookers, outside the church: Once again, it felt very uncomfortable. I don't know exactly why. Why couldn't I have been more relaxed on such a joyous day?

However, this day, especially, felt intensely private to me, and it was unbelievably hot in the church, and with all those press people outside, and the helicopters flying overhead, I just couldn't relax. I even wondered (I'd become so cynical) if there was someone inside, even some so-called friend, who might talk to the press or take a picture. All the hounding had taken on a life of its own that removed some of the pleasure from the occasion.

Maybe it doesn't matter, ultimately, if someone takes a photograph of you. I guess if you can get to the stage where it doesn't matter, then it doesn't matter. But I couldn't get to that point. That was the problem. It always mattered to me.

I NEVER FELT I was going to retire from tennis. Yes, I could afford to. But I just planned to take time off until I was ready, once more, to enjoy the feeling of being a professional tennis player. It's a magnificent job— but it had become a case of diminishing returns for me, even as the money kept rolling in.

My plan, at first, was to come back when I was ready, but then I started worrying about my contracts: Nike said I had to play eight tournaments per year, and Dunlop wanted me to play a minimum of six. Was I going to lose that, not get paid? And what about my ranking?

I should have waited out the year, but I didn't have the nerve.

I forced myself back, because of money and pride. It was a classic mistake that a lot of people make. Instead of thinking, *Have confidence; take a year off, then start from scratch—you could come back even better than you were* (and then people's expectations would have been lower anyway), I panicked—my ranking was slipping!—and I went back when I was absolutely unready, mentally and competitively, to go back.

I decided to play the Volvo Open Tournament at Stratton Mountain, Vermont, in early August.

When I told my parents about it, I could hear in their voices, right away, that they were relieved. I think they really believed I was going to quit. My mom said to me, "Now you can buy some diapers for Kevin."

I snapped at her. I said, "Mom, how much is enough? Tell me. How much money do I have to make before you don't have to say things like that? Give me a specific number. Is it five million? Ten? Fifteen?

Twenty? Tell me a number, so when I make it I won't have to hear about this anymore!"

This is where I have to remind myself that as difficult as Tatum could be, I didn't make things any easier. Instead of going on a honeymoon—which, God knows, you should do when you get married—we went to a tennis tournament. We were married on a Friday, and the following Monday, we went up to Stratton Mountain—it was like, "Quick-quick-quick, let's get married, because I love you and want you to know I'm committed, but now I've got to go play tennis."

I thought it would be a nice, relaxed place for us to stop, for me to phase back in. Vermont was so mellow—I had always enjoyed the tournament before. When we got there, though, there were paparazzi in the woods, looking to take the first picture of the newlyweds.

It was just so crazy, so uncomfortable, that I became more and more frazzled. I was in a very fragile state to start with—I was overtrained, over-tense, underweight. I gave a couple of interviews while I was there, which I now realize I shouldn't have done. I was trying hard to be honest—I've always tried to be honest—but I ended up feeling I had been far too candid about my confusion at that point. I felt the writers took advantage of my vulnerability to spin out their own take on what was going on with me, and even to insinuate things that weren't true. That was when the rumor started that since I was so thin, I must be on drugs.

After dispatching a very young (sixteen-year-old) André Agassi in the quarterfinals, I ended up, ironically enough, playing Becker in the semis, and I was just all over him verbally, trash-talking on every changeover. In retrospect, it had more to do with my brittleness at the time than anything else, and I probably picked the wrong person, although it made for an exciting match. I can't even remember exactly what I said to him—I've blocked it out. It was nothing terribly original, I'm sure. "You don't know who you're dealing with," or "I'm going to kick your ass"—which, by the way, I didn't do.

Trust me on this: I've been guilty of many verbal escapades, but trash-talking was something that didn't occur that often in my matches. I wish it had. Every once in a while, an opponent would say, "Hey, come on, stop yelling at the umpire," and I'd respond with a "Screw you—worry about yourself." But that was the extent of it.

This was on a whole new level. And then all the anxiety and negative karma got to me. The match went to a tiebreaker in the third set, and I was up 6–3 in the tiebreaker. Two serves to me. I double-faulted on the first. On the next, I came to net and hit a beautiful volley just inside the baseline, and Boris just barely got his racket on it, and as I was about to put away the ball to win the match, I heard the linesman say, "Out!"

Then I fell apart and lost the match.

The ball was clearly in, I knew it, and they screwed me on match point. I was positive of it: *They're out to get me. They're screwing me.* That's exactly what I thought. *Everyone's against me.* I was fighting a totally uphill battle. The paranoid part of me, the part that felt everyone—linesmen, umpires, other players, reporters, paparazzi—had it in for me, now saw it really happening.

When you tell people enough times to piss off, they're not exactly going to go out of their way to help you out. Even though I *may* have been wrong a few times about calls that I protested, I'm also sure that with all the marvelous goodwill I'd built up, there were umpires and linesmen who, given the chance, would look the other way or miss a call—and not in my favor. There's no question that that ball was in. However, it was close enough that, in his own mind, the linesman could justify calling it out.

Even paranoids have enemies.


IT WAS ALL DOWNHILL for the next month. I went to the Canadian Open and lost to Robert Seguso in the third round.

I hit bottom, physically, at the end of August, just before the Open began. I literally felt unprepared to play a best-of-five-set match. Something was way off in my body chemistry. I was too thin, I had no endurance.

It showed in the first round of the Open (I was seeded ninth), where I lost in four to Paul Annacone, who would become Pete Sampras's long-time coach. As icing on the cake, Peter Fleming and I got stuck in traffic and were defaulted in the doubles for showing up a few minutes late.

McEnroe and Fleming defaulted at the U.S. Open, for being two minutes late! That felt like the ultimate, sickening proof that everyone was against me. They'd all been trying to screw me, starting from my first tournament back, at Stratton Mountain. They just didn't want me back, I felt.

I said, "I'm out of the tournament—to hell with it. I'm going to have a cheeseburger and a beer!"

On my new cheeseburger-dessert-and-beer diet, I promptly won three tournaments in a row, in Los Angeles, San Francisco, and Scottsdale, Arizona.

I couldn't keep it going, though I was under tremendous pressure. I had been number two in the world in February of '86, and simply from the events I hadn't played over my six-month absence, I had dropped to number ten.

Then, as soon as I got back, I had a whole pile of ATP points to defend—after all, in 1985, I had won Stratton Mountain *and* the Canadian, *and* made it to the finals of the Open. Well, in 1986, I got to the semifinals at Stratton, the third round at the Canadian, and the first round at the Open. Coming out of the Open, I had dropped to number 20 in the world.

The three wins were a good start, but I needed to play a very heavy schedule if I was to have any hope of fulfilling my next goal, making the Masters. The trouble was, playing heavily meant traveling heavily. Tatum and the baby were traveling with me, and none of us was enjoying the grind. We went to Paris for the indoor tournament: I lost in the quarter-finals to a qualifier named Sergio Casal. Over to London, where I needed to do well—and lost in the first round to Pat Cash, who was on his way to winning Wimbledon in six months. ("God, you served like shit," he said, when we shook hands at net. I later found out that that was his puckish sense of humor.)

We flew back to New York. If I won the Houston Open in November, the Masters was a possibility. However, it was a tense time between Tatum and me. When I mentioned one more trip to her, she looked me in the eye and told me that if I went to Houston, I was going alone. I pulled out of the tournament, and we returned to Malibu.

I'd played only eight tournaments that year. If the ATP had divided my total points for 1986 by the number of events I'd played (which would have seemed logical), I would have been number six on their computer. But their formula at the time called for a minimum of twelve tournaments, so I came out number fourteen in the world.

Number fourteen, and not in the Masters—I felt furious at life.

WE FINALLY WENT on our honeymoon, to Hawaii, at Christmastime. At last I had given myself time to put aside all the nonsense that had taken place from August to November: It was as if I had taken a deep breath and said, "OK, let's start the new year fresh and just kick some ass."

We were staying on Oahu, at the home of a Japanese man I'd met playing golf. On New Year's Day, we woke up to a glorious Hawaiian morning, a velvety blue sky, and a fresh breeze blowing. And Tatum turned to me and said, "I'm pregnant."

"There goes nineteen eighty-seven," I said.

# 11

THERE WAS A WEDGE between us. It wasn't just my undiplomatic comment; it was the sentiment behind it, which we both understood: I felt I had blown 1986, and I couldn't afford to blow another year.

We hadn't intended to have another child right away, but we hadn't been trying especially hard *not* to have one. We were just kids, really—mature beyond our years in some ways, quite young in others. Tatum had just turned twenty-three in November, and I was still twenty-seven. We had had to try for six months before conceiving Kevin, so it had stuck in our minds that making a baby was never going to be easy for us.

Well, this time it was all too easy.

I seriously wondered whether we should go ahead with the pregnancy. Tatum asked me what I was thinking about, and I said, "Are we prepared to deal with this?" She couldn't stand the question, let alone the answer.

When we weren't locked in long silences, we began having screaming arguments.

All couples fight—couples need to fight—but our quarrels were nasty, and they escalated fast. We both had tempers, and Tatum was no shrinking violet. She was a tomboy from a tough household: Her father was a frustrated boxer, and her brother was quick with his fists. As our relationship grew more contentious, I noticed that whenever I raised my voice, she would flinch, as if I were about to hit her—except that I never had, or did.

I think she compared all men to her father, which put me in a tricky position. At first, she saw me as a better version of Ryan, but as things became tougher between us, the comparison got less favorable. She said then and later that I bullied her, but the truth was, she always gave as good as she got.

It got harder and harder to feel good about the pregnancy. In the last three or four months of her pregnancy with Kevin, I hadn't played tennis at all, which had made it much easier for us, but I didn't feel I could stop playing now, because I was trying so hard to come back. I was starting to develop back problems because of the tension; I was having trouble just focusing.

Then, in early February, something happened: Tatum started bleeding profusely. Our doctor told us that this kind of bleeding led to a miscarriage about 20 percent of the time, so I began to prepare myself for the possibility. Just before the bleeding had begun, I'd still been thinking, "Are we ready for another child?"—but when I took Tatum to the doctor, to my amazement, I suddenly burst into tears. I realized how much I wanted this child, and how frightened I was of losing it. I felt tremendous relief when it turned out that everything was okay.

That still didn't translate into a new attitude about my career, however—it simply wasn't fun to get out there and play. That was when

I again decided to hire a coach. I was under a huge amount of stress, and I needed a boost. My first thought was to ask Borg's coach, Lennart Bergelin, to work with me, and to this day, I wish I had, because I know that he would have nurtured me, and nurturing was what I badly needed at that point. I felt awkward about asking him, though, because I still wasn't 100 percent sure that Borg wasn't going to play again, and it felt strange, simply because Lennart had been with Bjorn all those years.

I wish I had just talked to Bjorn about it. People switch coaches all the time—it wouldn't have been that odd. Then again, I wasn't thinking straight about many things in those days. Maybe, too, I just didn't want to work that hard.

And maybe something in me knew that I was reaching for some kind of magic that was no longer there.

I called Tony Palafox. Tony, of course, was a touchstone in his own right: a mentor, a friend, a calming influence, the chief connection (along with Harry Hopman) to my formation as a tennis player. His quiet personality always dovetailed perfectly with mine: When I was a raging teenager, Tony just stood there patiently as I swore and smashed rackets, waiting for me to let it all out so we could go on with the practice. I badly needed that kind of calmness around me now.

Tony agreed to come work with me full-time—but almost as soon as he began, I could see that it wasn't working out. On the road, he was like a fish out of water: He simply preferred his routine, and he was so shy that it killed him to call and set up a practice court.

In May, Tony was with me at the Nations Cup in Düsseldorf. I was playing Miroslav Mecir, and I was at the end of my rope: tense and angry, the crowd booing me and rooting for Mecir. I kept thinking, "What's wrong with these people? Last time I was here, they were rooting for Lendl against me, and now it's goddamn Mecir!" It was driving me nuts.

Mecir was Mr. Smooth—he ran like a deer, and had incredible movement. We split the first two sets, I was down a break, and yelling, and finally the umpire said, "Point penalty, Mr. McEnroe; game, Mecir." I said, "That's it."

I went to the umpire, and said, "My shoulder hurts." Tony came over and asked what was wrong. I said, "I've had it," and I just walked off the court and defaulted. I said, "I'm not playing anymore. To hell with these people. That's it."

Tony went home.

But I went on. What else could I do? Usually, even when you're at the end of your rope, you find a little more rope.


I KEPT LOOKING for help: After Tony, Peter Fleming actually coached me for a while; later, I would work again with Paul Cohen, but his intensity was over the top even for me. None of it panned out, though, for me, or for the people who worked with me. In my desperation, I went against my gut feelings. By lifting weights and trying to change my game and hiring coaches, I was getting away from what I believed in. And I paid the price.

What happened to me is more or less the same thing that's happened to everyone who's been on top. Once you've lost it, everything spirals out of control, and it's difficult to find your way back. The process is gradual rather than sudden, and the whole way down you keep telling yourself that things are going to change. Little by little, however, the bad days at the office start to outnumber the good ones, and pain begins to replace the pleasure you once took in your profession.

Maybe if I'd taken the whole year off in 1986, my life would have been different. Maybe not.

The one thing that stayed the same for me, for a long time, was the money. The money made things very complicated.

Maybe Borg had the right idea—to cut the cord quickly and leave when people were still going to miss him. I chose a different route. I chose world-class mediocrity for the last five or six years of my career. I just couldn't walk away from that kind of money. What the hell else was I going to do? Being number eight or nine or ten in the world felt a lot better than sitting somewhere on my behind.

I LOST in the first round of the French Open to a twenty-year-old Argentinean named Horacio de la Pena. Just a couple of weeks earlier, I'd beaten him easily in Rome. It felt like yet another last straw. I said, "The hell with it; I'm not playing Wimbledon. Can't do it."

Part of me also felt content not to go. I had a baby at home and another on the way. Tatum needed me there. Of course, I had to come up with a reason to withdraw. My back was bothering me, my shoulder was hurting, my hip was tight—but I'm sure it was nothing worse than any other touring pro my age was going through. I was not too injured to play.

What I really wanted was for the world to read between the lines, to see my little son and my pregnant wife and know what I was thinking and feeling. I wanted to show everybody that certain things in life were more important than another Wimbledon title. I was groping my way toward that understanding: Couldn't the rest of the tennis world understand it along with me?

And of course, the word I heard back was, "McEnroe has gone over the edge."

I HAD ELECTED to sit out Davis Cup in 1985 and 1986, the Code of Conduct years. In the meantime, Arthur had left the captaincy and Tom Gorman had taken over. Tom had been a reasonably good player himself, though no shooting star, and I had the feeling he was really the USTA's man—a company guy. He certainly wasn't about to rock the boat and lift the Code, and since I was one of the main reasons the Code had been instituted in the first place, I didn't expect my phone to ring.

However, after the U.S.A. lost for the third year in a row in 1986, the USTA moved into fence-mending mode. Gorman called me early in 1987 and asked me if I could play our first-round match against Paraguay.

"Paraguay!" I said. "You don't need me for Paraguay—you can win it easily with the B-team. Besides, what about the Code?"

"What if it wasn't an issue?" Gorman asked. "Would you play?"

"Not this time, Tom. You don't need me."

Well, we got beaten by Paraguay. Aaron Krickstein and Jimmy Arias went down there; Arias was up 5–1 in the fifth set of the fifth and deciding match, and then he lost to somebody named Hugo Chapacu, who was ranked around 500 in the world! I remember it, because I was playing an exhibition in Lisbon, Portugal, and someone came up to me and said, "America lost three–two to Paraguay." I said, "You must be joking."

Suddenly, we were faced with elimination. The next tie we were to play was a relegation match against Germany. In Davis Cup, if your country loses a relegation match, you get bounced down from the main sixteen countries into zonal competition, which is the minors. You have to fight your way back. And Germany would be tough—Becker had won Wimbledon the last two years in a row.

I thought, "OK, enough's enough; I'm going to get back on the team." I missed Davis Cup—it was the last little vestige of team sports in my life. I called Gorman and said, "OK, I'll play."

He said, "Let me call you back."

Well, that didn't feel right. When Gorman called back, he told me, "Listen, I want you on the team, but you need to play a tournament in South Orange the week before." He was talking about Gene Scott's tournament in South Orange, New Jersey—the first tournament I'd ever played, eleven years before, the place where I'd collected my first ATP points. It was a nice tournament, but it wasn't exactly the big time. And what was this, anyway, an audition?

I said, "What are you talking about? What's that going to prove?"

Gorman said, "I'm sorry, I can't pick you unless you play there, because I want you to get a couple of matches under your belt."

I counted to ten. "Tom, I've won four Davis Cups and a few majors. Do you think I might know how best to prepare myself?"

"I'll get back to you," he said.

Gorman eventually called me to propose a compromise: Paul Annacone, Tim Mayotte, and I would play off, and the two winners would be on the team.

I swallowed my pride—a big swallow—and said yes. I wanted to go back to Davis Cup. Mayotte and I made the team.

And we lost to Germany, 2–3.

Tatum was due to give birth right around the quarterfinals of the U.S. Open, and—if it was possible—I was more on edge than I'd been the whole year.

I couldn't not play the tournament. Skipping Wimbledon had been a big enough gesture—I wasn't about to announce my retirement.

I was damned if I did and damned if I didn't. I went with "did," and made a colossal mess of it, in my third-round match against my nemesis from the 1985 Australian Open, Slobodan (Bobo) Zivojinovic. I had won the first set, and I was serving for the second at 5–3. Not once but twice, Zivojinovic hit shots that clearly landed over my baseline—I saw both of them with my own eyes—but the linesman said nothing, costing me the game.

My relationship with tournament officials had grown progressively more adversarial with each year since 1977, but since I'd returned from my layoff, things had worsened radically. I recognized that my problems with umpires had more to do with me than with them. Linesmen weren't the problem; I was.

They were fallible at the very best, but I had known that for a long time. Now, however, I had decided that because they were unable to make good calls, they were trying to screw me, and that, therefore, they were the enemy. I didn't think, *Look, these are human beings making mistakes.* I thought, *They are adversely affecting my career, therefore every one of them is an opponent, just like the person I'm playing against.*

Arthur Ashe would always say to me during Davis Cup, "Listen, calls end up evening out." That was his theory: Over the course of the year, you're going to get a hundred bad calls that work against you, but you'll get a hundred that work in your favor.

I didn't agree, to put it mildly. To me, the *timing* of bad calls always felt crucial. If a linesman or an umpire corrected a bad call when I had a comfortable lead, it didn't matter (and no lead ever felt comfortable to me). It was the times I was down break point in a tight set that mattered.

The second set against Zivojinovic was one of those times. After that second shot landed over the baseline without a call, I screamed something foul, and the umpire issued me a warning. Zivojinovic broke me, we changed sides, and I let the umpire know, in what had become my customary terms, what I thought of the officiating in this match.

Point penalty. Zivojinovic served three straight boomers (three was all he needed) to make it 5–5.

I was still boiling, and when I double-faulted to go down 5–6, I walked up to the umpire and let him have it again. What really got me going, however, was a CBS technician who pointed a boom mike at the umpire's chair while I ranted. I gave the microphone man—and all of America— one hell of a sound bite.

I made a complete ass of myself for the umpteenth time, but somehow I managed to hit a new low, using a penalizable obscenity approximately six times in the course of the minute-and-a-half changeover. I say "approximately" because, I promise you, I've never looked at the tape, and I lost count in the heat of the moment.

And now the umpire said, "Game penalty, Mr. McEnroe. Game and second set to Mr. Zivojinovic, seven games to five."

I stood and thought for a moment. I had now taken three steps: warning, point penalty, and game penalty. The next step was a default. I think back on that umpire—a young man named Richard Ings, just twenty-two years old with an Australian accent—with severely mixed feelings: On the one hand, he had been helpful by lumping together all my obscenities into a single offense, when he could have defaulted me after one or two expletives. I believe he was trying to dignify the occasion (as well as himself and me) as much as was possible under the circumstances.

On the other hand, he acted the way tennis usually did where I was concerned: weakly. Once again, it would have been better all around if I had been defaulted the first time I went so dramatically over the edge. It probably would have happened far less often after that, if at all. As it was, though, officials didn't want to lose their big ticket-seller at the moment, so they just made me someone else's problem by slapping my wrist. Then, when I accumulated enough fines, I had to miss the next tournament, which wound up hurting smaller events, not me.

I calmed down in the next set (one of my strengths was that I could always snap back into focus almost instantly), but lost in the tiebreaker. Then Zivojinovic started missing a few first serves, and I won the last two sets to take the match. The victory tasted like ashes, however.

I restrained myself after that (amazingly, since Tatum was due any minute), and wound up defeated by time instead of my own temper. In my quarterfinal against Lendl, Ivan the Terrible brutalized me with topspin lobs—it was the most phenomenal such exhibition I ever witnessed. He had to have hit it over my head fifteen times.

Expert gamesman that he was, Lendl picked up on my edginess about the imminent birth. Also, as the match wore on into dusk, I found that for the first time in my life I was having trouble seeing the ball. Was there something wrong with my eyesight? Was that an excuse? Was he just better?

After I'd lost that match, I was forced to realize that Lendl had been able to victimize me mainly because I wasn't moving well. My back was tensing up on me again—I had a sacroiliac problem. Sometimes I felt I could barely make it to the court. I know a lot of it was psychological, but whatever it was, it felt awful. Suddenly I was losing to guys like Wilander and Mecir on indoor carpet. On clay, it was a different matter—they had more of an advantage there—but on any other surface, even a slow one, I knew I should be winning.

I kept thinking, "This is impossible. There's no way I can be losing to these guys." But it was happening anyway.

The most difficult thing for me to accept, when my body started letting me down, was that I wasn't able to cover the net as well. Suddenly there was a whisper along the tennis grapevine: *He's fragile.*

That was hard to take, because at my peak, I was quicker than people realize. Borg had the speed of a great sprinter; Vitas moved differently, in quick little steps, but was also very fast; and Johan Kriek was one of the fastest human beings ever to step onto a tennis court. There were others, too. But I still always felt I was one of the quickest players out there, certainly in the top 10 or 20 percent.

Then I wasn't anymore.

As I lost a bit of my speed up to (and back from) the net, I had to rely more and more on my craftiness, which worked reasonably well for me until the big hitters started taking over the game. Becker was the first; then along came Agassi and Sampras. I wasn't used to having that pace generated at me from the baseline, or facing a serve that consistently hard.

When I played Sampras in the semifinals of the 1990 Open, I was convinced that I didn't need to be so aggressive; that I could actually afford to stay back. I thought I was solid enough from the baseline to bring it off. It may seem crazy now, but I believed I could just bide my time:

Instead of coming in and feeling unsure because I'd lost a bit of my quickness, I felt I could wait it out an extra shot or two if necessary.

I thought I had a great chance to win it, that I could wrap up my career with a fifth Open. I couldn't have been more wrong. Who would have thought it? Pete was nineteen; that was the first year he ever won a Major. He had beaten Lendl in the quarterfinals, and he beat Agassi in the final. I don't think I have anything to hang my head about; he's turned out to be a great champion. But at the time, I was really disappointed at how poorly I played, how badly prepared I was.

What I didn't realize was this: It's never possible to be prepared when the future takes over from the past.

AFTER THE 1987 OPEN, I was fined $7,500 for my tirade during the Zivojinovic match (plus another $350 for ball abuse earlier in the tournament), which, because I'd already been fined $18,000 that year, resulted in an automatic two-month suspension. To date in my career, I had amassed $80,500 in fines, almost half of it—$38,500—in the horrible year of 1987.

In another way, though, the year turned out to be wonderful: Sean Timothy McEnroe was born on September 23, at NYU Medical Center in downtown New York City. One part of me thought of the two-month suspension as paternity leave.

IT WAS A BRIEF PERIOD of calm in an ever more turbulent time. We now had two babies in the house, a toddler and an infant, and even though we could certainly afford nannies and other people to help around the house, we both felt more and more overwhelmed. I was trying to get my tennis career back on track; Tatum, barely out of adolescence at twenty-four, was trying to figure out who she was, and what it meant to be a mother.

She didn't have the strongest of foundations on which to build a sense of motherhood. Her own mother had had such problems with alcohol and pills that she'd barely been present when Tatum was little; for a time, Ryan had carried most of the burden, to the best of his limited ability, while pursuing a full-time acting career.

As Tatum told it, though, once she'd entered her teens, her father seemed to lose interest in fatherhood, especially after he'd gotten together with Farrah Fawcett, who appeared lukewarm at best about being a stepmother, surrogate or otherwise, to Tatum and Griffin. Once Ryan moved to Farrah's place, Tatum said, she and her brother were frequently left alone in their father's beach house in Malibu.

And now here she was, alone much of the time with two small children of her own, and back in Malibu.

She was still very conflicted about her work—or her lack of work. Her acting career had tailed off pretty sharply after she came out of her teens. The transition to adulthood is perilous for every child actor: Very few make the jump successfully. As a young woman, Tatum just couldn't seem to bring the same charm to the screen that she'd projected as a little girl, and even as a teenager. She'd finished her last movie, *Certain Fury*, just before we met—it had vanished quickly, to the relief of everyone involved in it, including Tatum, who refused to do any press or publicity for the picture.

Sometimes she thought it would just be a good idea to leave it at that. She would often say, "Will you love me if I never work again?" Trick question! I wanted to say that I would feel fine about it, but if she then decided she did want to work, I didn't want to be the one who had told her, "You can't do it."

The one thing I felt strongly about was that I never wanted both of us to be working at the same time. Even that was tricky, though, because I made up my schedule every September for the coming year, and acting jobs tended to come up on the spur of the moment. I wanted to plan out well in advance when Tatum might be working—but I didn't think agents, producers, and casting people were likely to be very concerned about my tennis schedule.

At the same time, Sean's arrival made all of that academic. With two babies in the house, Tatum couldn't suddenly turn around and tell Hollywood, "OK, I'm ready to work now."

Still, she continued to be conflicted. With Sean's birth, she had naturally gained weight, and in the months afterward she seemed obsessed with taking it off. She had grown up in an environment where being thin and beautiful meant everything—employability being one of those things—and she'd suffered terribly when she'd gone through a chubby phase as an adolescent. In the first months of 1988, I kept feeling worried that her obsession about losing weight was taking her back to bad habits she'd cultivated as a teenager.

I suggested that she try working with a trainer again, and because we were friendly with Madonna and Sean Penn, Tatum hired Rob Parr, a trainer who had worked with Madonna. Madonna was thin and successful—maybe some of that would wear off on her.

Moderation was never one of Tatum's strong points, though. Soon she was training like a maniac, lifting weights and running six miles a day. She was in amazing shape, but I felt concerned when she started complaining about knee problems. I said, "I think you're running on pavement too much." She kept going anyway.

And she kept feeling frustrated that work wasn't dropping into her lap. Part of her knew that if she wanted to get acting jobs, she would have to go out and try hard for them—but with two small children at home, she wasn't in a position to do so. She blamed me for this, and I just saw it as our life. Later on, when things got much worse, she would say, "Oh, John doesn't want me to work," which wasn't true. I didn't want her to be filming while I was playing Wimbledon, but I did try to be supportive. In fact, in a way, our situation was ideal, because it allowed her to feel her way back into acting without the pressure of having to make a lot of money. Couldn't she be happy about developing her craft and gradually establishing herself as a mature actress?

I said, "Look, financially we're in pretty good shape. I'm not winning, but I'm still making the same money I was in eighty-four. You haven't worked for a while. Why don't you start small? Work with good actors in small projects, so you can be around them?"

She would snap at me then: "Who the hell are you? I'll do what I want." And then she'd go up against the hottest actresses of the moment, Demi Moore and the like, and she'd get rejected every time.

One night we had dinner with Madonna and Sean, during a period when I'd been pestering Tatum about taking acting lessons. "I can't not practice and then think I have any sort of chance of winning Wimbledon," I told her. "You've got to work at your craft." I'd say that over and over—I'd try to be the sensible guy. She'd brush me off: "What do you know about movies? You're an athlete."

Then, at dinner, Madonna said, "You know, Tatum, there's this great acting class I've gone to—you should give it a try."

"What a great idea!" Tatum said.

I sat there thinking, *That's what I've been saying the last three years, but thanks for taking credit.*

Then Madonna told her, "You can have a career and be a mother, too—you can do it all." I couldn't help thinking, *What the hell do you know about it? You're the most career-obsessed person I've ever met in my life.* Not to mention that she hadn't even had a child at that point!

Tatum kept auditioning and auditioning, and never getting any parts. A little while later, after the movie *Working Girl* was a big success, someone decided to do a TV series based on the film, and Tatum tried out for the lead role. She decided to do her reading in a heavy Brooklyn accent, and the producers said to her, "We want to give you the part, but come back tomorrow and just speak in a normal voice." She went back—and did the same accent again. I thought, "Why would she do that?" The only answer I could come up with was that somehow, she really didn't want the job—or to work at all.

We were together eight years, and over that time, she acted in three projects. One was a play with William Hickey that ran for a week. One was a strange independent movie, *Little Noises,* with Crispin Glover, which went straight to video. The one project that had any sort of an audience was a 1989 after-school special with Drew Barrymore and Corey Feldman. It was called *Fifteen and Getting Straight,* and it was an anti-drug movie.

It was Tatum's twenty-sixth birthday, November 5, 1989, and I was playing Boris Becker in the semifinals of the Paris Indoor. Tatum was seated at courtside. And both Boris and I had come down with a hacking cough.

Let me explain. Ever since he had burst onto the scene in 1985, Boris had had a locker-room reputation for suddenly going into a loud coughing fit at key psychological moments in a match—say, when you were serving at break point, or when he needed a rest before his own serve. He was a big guy, with a big chest, and his hacking was deep and resonant—it wasn't something you could ignore easily.

He was at it again this year in Paris, and before we met in the semis, I decided to give him a taste of his own medicine. As soon as we began to play, every time Boris began to cough, I would answer with an even louder and longer bark of my own. It was a little childish, maybe, and it might have had something to do with the fact that, at number two, Boris was now two spots above me in the rankings. Still, in my mind, the coughing was just a new form of trash-talking. I wanted to teach him a lesson.

Naturally, it backfired. I must have echoed him ten times in the first set alone, and in my time-tested fashion, I once again managed to alienate the crowd: Every time I coughed, they began to rustle and boo. On a changeover near the end of the set, Boris said, "Come on, John—give me a break. I have a cold."

"You've had a cold for four years," I said.

With the crowd against me and Boris annoyed—and now trying harder than ever—I had put myself in a perfect position to blow the match, which is exactly what I wound up doing, losing in three sets.

In our hotel room afterwards, Tatum was furious with me. "How could you embarrass Boris that way?" she said.

"Whose side are you on?" I asked her.

I guess I know the answer now—she wasn't on my side.

At the moment, though, I elected (even though I felt I was right) to smooth over a fight with my wife rather than stand on principle. I went to Boris's room—he was in the same hotel—and apologized. "Listen, Boris," I said. "I'm sorry. I did it in the heat of competition."

He was extremely gracious. "I understand," he said. "To me, it's over already—don't even think about it."

For me, though, that fight with Tatum on her birthday, and on the day of a big match, was a down note on which to end the year. I had started 1989 at number eleven, and I'd fought my way up to number four; with this loss, and my subsequent loss to Becker in the Masters a few weeks later, my ranking would once more begin to slide.

And, after that year, the men's Masters would never again be played at Madison Square Garden. In a remarkably shortsighted move, the ATP traded prestige and media attention for dollars, and moved the tournament to Germany when the German Tennis Federation came up with a bigger contract than the Garden was willing to offer. As far as I was concerned, moving the event had destroyed it. It was the end of an era.

It was also the end, for all intents and purposes, of my top-ten ranking. In early 1990, Hamilton Jordan, the executive director of the ATP,
instituted a change in the ranking rules that ran counter to the wishes of
the top players. The new rules rewarded pros who played more events.
Only their top fourteen results were counted, even if they had played
thirty-five or more tournaments. These rules obviously weren't designed
for a player with a wife and kids.

I didn't agree with the change, I didn't feel it was in my best interests
as a husband, and I knew that it would hurt my ranking. Ultimately, I felt
that the rule change hurt the game, and my personal feeling was that, in
the ostensible interests of generating more tennis action, Jordan had sold
us out. Had the players been more organized, we might have started boy-
cotting tournaments in protest, but once the change was in effect, apathy
set in.

IN JANUARY 1990, I was playing Mikael Pernfors in the fourth round
of the Australian Open. At one set all, I disagreed with a call a lines-
woman had made, and I walked over to her. I didn't say anything; I just
stood in front of her and stared at her, bouncing a ball up and down on
my strings. "Code of conduct warning, Mr. McEnroe," the umpire announced. That seemed debatable to me, and so I debated it for a few moments. The umpire prevailed, and I calmed down and won the third set.

Then, serving at 2–3 in the fourth, I hit a forehand approach wide.
Suddenly, on that very hot Australian afternoon—it was 135 degrees on
the court—I saw red. I slammed my racket to the ground. The frame
cracked. "Racket abuse, Mr. McEnroe," announced the umpire. "Point
penalty." My anger did not subside. I went up to the umpire, let him know
how I was feeling for a minute or two, then demanded to see the tournament supervisor. The supervisor materialized, and calmly said that a

cracked racket frame was an automatic penalty. That was when I broke some new ground. As the supervisor turned away, I made an extremely rude suggestion, in a very loud voice. There was a gasp in the stands— McEnroe had topped himself.

"Verbal abuse, audible obscenity, Mr. McEnroe," the umpire said. "Default. Game, set, and match, Mr. Pernfors." It was the only other time in my career, besides the doubles at the 1986 U.S. Open, that I had been defaulted. I had also made history by becoming the first player defaulted out of a Grand Slam event in the Open era.

I plead idiocy—but I also plead ignorance. If you look at my career, you'll see that in dozens of matches (and I'd say that it really was only dozens; people might be surprised to hear it), I took matters to that edge where if I incurred one more penalty, I was gone. However, the one and only time that I went over the edge, I literally didn't realize that the default rule had been changed, from four steps to three.

At the moment the words flew out of my mouth, I thought, "Okay, I've lost the game." I thought that it was going to be four games to two in the fourth, but that I was still up two sets to one. I still felt certain I'd win the match. But when the umpire said, "Game, set, match," the first thing I thought was that my agent, Sergio Palmieri, had forgotten to tell me about the rule change.

Obviously, I can't just say, "It happened because my agent forgot to tell me about the change." Of course I have to take the responsibility for the whole incident. I truly believe, though, that if I had known the new rule, I would have contained myself. I sometimes went off the rails, but I always knew where I stood.

I LEFT AUSTRALIA, wife and two small boys in tow, swamped by photographers wanting to get one last shot of a humiliated McEnroe fleeing the country. I had seldom been so happy to get back to Malibu. I stewed about the default for a couple of days—until one morning, when I was watching CNN for results from Down Under, I saw something that put my problem in perspective.

Tragically, an Avianca Airlines passenger jet had crashed near Kennedy Airport in New York. Incredibly, the anchorwoman soon said she had an uncomfirmed report that the plane had crashed on John McEnroe's home in Oyster Bay. I was stunned. My first thought was to worry about my parents, who also lived on the property. But they were on vacation in Egypt, and my two brothers, I realized, were also elsewhere.

The newscast then went to a reporter on the scene, who was talking to an Oyster Bay neighbor of mine, whose first words were, "The plane did not crash on John McEnroe's house—but they're using his yard as a morgue."

Talk about mixed emotions! I felt, all at once, relieved, spooked, sorry for the victims, and guilty at worrying about my property. It was then and there that I decided to sell my Oyster Bay house. Life is too weird.

ONE NIGHT in the summer of 1990, Tatum said, "What about a third? Want to go for the girl?"

I was back from another tournament. Kevin was four, Sean almost three. I felt as if we were just beginning to get a grip on our lives. "I don't know," I said, hesitantly.

"Come on," she said. "What are you, chicken?"

I said, "Chicken? You're the one who's got to go through it, not me. And you're the one who's always talking about how difficult it is to have a career. Do you think having another child is going to solve that problem?"

As it turned out, the conversation was academic. Emily Katherine

McEnroe was born on May 10, 1991. At first, we felt, "This is perfect; we've finally got two boys and a girl. This is the answer." But then we found it wasn't the answer.

Maybe we were too spoiled. We had more than enough money, and fame, and we enjoyed the good things that money and fame brought us. At the same time, we aspired to live like normal people, and that just wasn't possible. It seemed that there was never enough calm in the house. Too often, Tatum was upset and embarrassed by my latest outburst on a tennis court—and the outbursts got worse as the tension at home increased. My answer to all this was to over-indulge in marijuana. I thought it would relax me and help me appreciate my life more. Unfortunately, it often had the opposite effect.

It was very confusing—in our way, we were both trying to be good parents and good partners to each other, but her career was in eclipse and mine was in decline, and you need to feel reasonably good about yourself before you can be kind. We loved our children, but it felt harder and harder all the time to come up with any kindness for each other. . . .

THE HIGHEST MY RANKING ever got again was number four, at the end of 1989. I saw I was being overwhelmed by some players, whether it was Becker on a good day, or Edberg or Lendl, but that my game was finally coming back. It had taken three years. I ended 1986 at fourteen in the world; in 1987 I was number ten, and in 1988 I was number eleven. By 1989, I wasn't playing a lot of tournaments, but at least I had gotten to the point where I was contending. Contending, but not winning the big ones. I was knocking on the door; I just wasn't able to get in.

My drive stopped. My commitment waned. There could be no better example of this than my idiotic decision, the week before Wimbledon in 1988, to play an exhibition with Mats Wilander for GOAL, a Dublin-based charity. What was the idiotic part? For starters, I hadn't played

Wimbledon in the previous two years, and while the GOAL event did feature tennis during the day, it culminated with a boxing match between Mats and me at night! In my mind (after a few shots of tequila), I won a unanimous decision: I threw a lot of punches, but I couldn't lift my arms for the next three days.

Needless to say, tuning up on the grass at Queen's would have been a slightly better preparation for Wimbledon that year, where I lost in the second round to Wally Masur.

My motivation suffered from a combination of having kids and, for lack of a better term, going Hollywood. Appreciating the good life. I couldn't seem to focus as intently on the job at hand. It became less important to be number one—so I settled for number four. I was still making a ton of money; I was still the biggest guy in tennis. I just wasn't the *best* guy. Yes, I might have lost a step, but before, I had always found a way to do what it took with what I had. My ferocity had gotten me there. Now my ferocity seemed like something I had to unlearn if I was going to be a good husband and father.

I tried, hard. In my darker moments, however, I sometimes wonder why I went to the effort, because it ended so badly. Sometimes—I can't help it—I feel as if I wasted my time. Ultimately, I have no one to blame but myself. I'm the one who chose that life, that wife. Nobody made me do it. I naïvely believed that this person actually thought along the same lines as I did—and maybe she did, for a while. In her own way, Tatum tried hard, too, but ultimately she just didn't have the wherewithal to bring it off. She was so young! *We* were so young. As angry as I get, I do feel for her—when I can get through the anger.

## 12

"WHAT DID YOU EXPECT?" a guy named McEnroe said. It was the press conference before the semifinals of the January 1991 Australian Open. "Edberg versus Lendl, McEnroe against Becker." The only difference was: I wasn't the one saying it. Patrick McEnroe had then proceeded to give Boris Becker a good scare, winning the first set in a tiebreaker before succumbing in four.

One of the nicer surprises of the beginning of the '90s was my baby brother Patrick's reinvention of himself as a tennis player. He had followed a strong junior career—at one point rising to as high as number three in the nation—with a not-especially-distinguished varsity career at Stanford. I think that when he did so well in the juniors, it was the first time people started paying him a lot of attention in his own right, and so he wilted a bit when he got to college. When he got to his senior year, our mom told him to forget about his dreams of playing professional tennis: It was time to look for a real job.

I had a talk with Mom. I said, "Listen, you lay off him. He's got to try to play professional tennis. It's gone too far now; he'll regret it the rest of his life if he doesn't do it. Everyone's comparing him with me, and he's really his own man. And I think he can make it if he just puts his mind to it."

Our tennis games are as different as our personalities. Patrick is a right-hander, with that same two-handed backhand he used as a little boy. He tends to stay back more than I do, and his best stroke is his backhand return of serve. He's easygoing and soft-spoken; I'm—well, you know how I am. As I've mentioned, he started playing much earlier than I did, and at first it looked as though he might go even further. One year, our parents took us all to Miami, for the Orange Bowl, where I played the 14-and-unders and Patrick played the 12-and-unders—at age six! He lost in the first round (to a twelve-year-old), and walked off the court dejectedly. Another spectator turned to my father and said, "He doesn't have to worry—he's got six more years in the twelves."

When he actually did turn twelve, Patrick was even better than I'd been at that age, but then he didn't do as well in the fourteens and sixteens. By the time he was seventeen, he was significantly stronger. In 1983, he lost two extremely close three-set matches to Stefan Edberg in the semifinals of the juniors at both Wimbledon and the U.S. Open. He was wild-carded into a couple of ATP tournaments early in his career, but part of him wondered if he deserved it. The first time we ever played each other on the tour was at Stratton Mountain in 1985, in the first round. He was nineteen; I was twenty-six, and number one in the world. I behaved myself, like a nice older brother, and won, 6–1, 6–2.

He struggled for his first couple of years on the tour, but then when he hit his mid-twenties, he recommitted himself to the game and really improved his ranking, ultimately rising as high as number thirty-one in the world. He wound up more successful at doubles than at singles, but he had some excellent singles results. Along with his semifinal in Australia, he won one career singles title, at Sydney in 1995, and later that year, he had a great run at the U.S. Open, getting as far as the quarterfinals, where he gave Becker a very close match (a match for which I did the television commentary—with some bias, of course).

After I'd left the tour, it was definitely easier for me to root for Patrick. I'd once thought that if I had to lose to someone, it would be best if it were someone I was close to, my brother or a friend. When push came to shove, however, things felt different. I always wanted my family and friends to do well—just not as well as I did. I learned that when Peter Fleming beat me a couple of times. When Patrick and I played that first time at Stratton Mountain, it was a mismatch. Six years later, in Basel, Switzerland, it was a different story.

That was the year he'd gotten to the semifinals in Australia, so he was more of a contender. This was also the third round, not the first, and so I was in one of my more intense modes. He'd never seen that from me before, and I think it took poor Patrick aback. I just couldn't help myself. I really laid it on—dirty looks, the whole routine—and he basically folded, the way most people did. I was outplaying him, too, so I'm sorry I had to do the other stuff. It was a compliment, Patrick!

The one other time we played was in a final, in Chicago, in February of 1991. A final was a different matter altogether. I thought, "God, if I lose to Patrick, that's it. I'm jumping off the Sears Tower." I couldn't lose to my little brother!

Yet I felt bad about it, too. At that point I had won seventy-six tournaments, and Patrick hadn't won any. He had established his own identity, but he was not going to be a Grand Slam winner. I wanted the best for him—but not at my expense.

I really didn't know how to feel.

This time, I behaved myself. I thought, "You've got to just play. Don't make any trouble." I remember feeling like I was going to explode, though—it was almost impossible for me to keep everything in. I was ready to have a meltdown.

It was a well-played match, and he took the first set, 6–3. I won the second, 6–2, but the third was neck-and-neck until 3–3. Then I broke his serve. I was serving at match point when suddenly a phone rang at court-side. That was when, for one of the few times in my life, I actually said something funny. I looked at my father, who was courtside. "Dad, Mom's on the phone." Everybody laughed. Patrick laughed. "Tell her I'll be home soon," he said. He was right—I served out the match.

Why was I able to joke that once? I think I was so tense about the oc-casion that I just needed to do *something*. I didn't feel good about win-ning, but I couldn't imagine losing. I would have much preferred not to have dealt with it at all.

It was the last tournament I ever won, and I had to beat my brother to do it.

THERE WAS NO paternity leave after Emily's birth. Two weeks later, I was out on the road again, mostly going through the motions. At the end of May, I headed off to Paris, where I lost in the first round to Andrei Cherkasov, a Russian journeyman. I'd taken 1990 off from playing Davis Cup to make room for some new guys named Agassi, Chang, and Jim Courier, but I went back in June and lit a bit of the old fire by winning two matches in our successful tie over Spain.

That fire was sputtering, however. I could no longer pull off the big ones—I'd occasionally play a big match and beat the defending cham-pion, or get to the semis at an important tournament, but then I'd lose to some young buck. Not only was I not winning the big ones; I sometimes wasn't even playing the small ones: After I'd made a rude remark to a woman who had overstayed her time at a practice court at Queen's Club in 1985, I found out that the woman was the club president's wife— Queen's ended up rescinding my membership, and even though I was reinstated a few years later, the self-inflicted wound never completely healed. I no longer played this key Wimbledon warmup.

At Wimbledon that year, I was soundly outplayed in the round of 16 by Stefan Edberg, who made my net play look inadequate. I remember thinking, "Weird forehand, kick serve that's under a hundred miles per hour—and he's kicking my ass." At the Canadian Open, I lost to Derrick Rostagno in the third. At New Haven, I lost to a huge-serving young Goran Ivanisevic in the quarterfinals.

And at the U.S. Open that year, nineteen-year-old Michael Chang beat me for the only time, in five sets in the third round, using the top-spin lob against me as effectively as Lendl had four years earlier. It killed me to watch those spins go over my head and land right inside the baseline. It was as if Chang had read right through me: *He's lost a step. He can't get back fast enough.* The helplessness was terrible.

However, I still took pride in the fact that opponents—even the young bucks—were always very up when they played me. Maybe I was a notch in their belts; maybe they felt, *This guy's a prick; I'll show him.* I like to think it was because I was a great champion. Such enthusiasm, however, certainly made it more difficult toward the end of my career, when those young guys were as keen for my blood as sharks in the water!

That blood was evident at an indoor tournament in Birmingham, England, in November. I had been wild-carded into the event, and been paid a substantial guarantee to show up. I certainly failed to give Birmingham its money's worth, however, playing a pitiful excuse for a tennis match in my first-round loss to the German Alexander Mronz (who would later achieve his greatest fame, briefly, as a boyfriend of Steffi Graf).

I thought I had hit a new low. When I returned to New York, however, as I walked off the plane, the customs agent said to me, "You hear the news?"

"No," I replied.

"Magic Johnson announced he has AIDS."

Suddenly, the loss to Mronz didn't seem so significant anymore.

By the time I played an exhibition against Agassi at the Los Angeles Forum, a few weeks later, I realized that I needed some help. Hiring coaches might have gone against my instincts before, but when the dynamic former touring pro Larry Stefanki approached me after my lackluster match, I was ready to listen. Clearly, whatever I was doing wasn't working.

"You really shouldn't bother playing at this point, Mac, unless you're ready to make a real effort," Larry said. I was listening. Larry had been a solid enough player, but it was his energy and enthusiasm that were electric: He was like a walking cup of espresso.

To begin what was to become my last stand on the circuit, I put together Team McEnroe: Larry as my coach; Rob Parr, the trainer who had worked so effectively with Madonna and Tatum; and a young Canadian masseur named Derek Nobles. I rented a house across the road in Malibu for my support group and hunkered down to prepare for the 1992 Australian Open.

It worked. Larry and I flew down to Melbourne in January, where, in the third round, I had one of my best wins ever against Boris Becker, 6–4, 6–3, 7–5, a month before my thirty-third birthday. I eventually made it through to the quarterfinals before being beaten by Wayne Ferreira—a disappointing end to a potentially great run. Still, the tournament felt like a good strong step back toward winning.

Another disappointing aspect of the trip was when I read in the newspaper that I had not been selected for the Olympic team. In 1988, the first year since 1924 that tennis was included in the Olympics as a medal sport, I had felt lukewarm about the position of professional tennis in the games. Instead of participating, I'd chosen to play my regular touring schedule. Now I felt my Olympic days were numbered, so I had been hopeful that Tom Gorman would pick me for the singles squad. I had discussed it with him, and requested a return call only if he planned to offer me the doubles slot. He hadn't called.

I was away from home for two and a half weeks on that Australian trip, the longest I'd ever been away from my kids, and I missed them badly. I flew to Hawaii to meet my family and prepare for the first-round Davis Cup tie against Argentina, my debut as a doubles specialist. As soon as I saw Tatum, however, I noticed she was acting odd around me. I chalked it up to my long absence, but the feeling hung around over the following weeks and months.

The strangeness only deepened when five-and-a-half-year-old Kevin came down with what at first seemed to be severe food poisoning, but then turned out to be a rare childhood disease, Heinlein purpura, which caused him to miss six weeks of school. It was a scary time, and it should have drawn Tatum and me closer together; instead, we seemed to be pulling farther and farther apart. I felt perplexed and concerned.

My state of distraction didn't help my tennis. As 1992 moved along, Team McEnroe began to feel less helpful than unwieldy—it was nice to be able to get a massage every day, but there were days when I felt I was doing it only because I was paying the masseur's salary. My uneasiness about my home life also made training more difficult. Larry was a superb coach—he would go on to work with Marcelo Rios, Yevgeny Kafelnikov, and Tim Henman—but ultimately, I was in no emotional shape to lead a team. By June, it was just Larry and me.

On Saturday, the fourth of July, 1992, I played my last singles match on Centre Court at Wimbledon, having defied all the naysayers and advanced to the semifinals against twenty-two-year-old Andre Agassi, who had yet to win a Grand Slam tournament. It was fifteen years, almost to the day, since my 1977 semifinal against Connors: the amazing run that had launched me into the tennis heavens.

This, too, was the end of an amazing run. For fifteen years, I had been a presence—terrible or wonderful, but never boring—at Wimbledon, stirring conversation and controversy even when I didn't show up. In my own inimitable way, and without even willing it, I had become part of Wimbledon's tradition.

There would be no controversy this year. As in certain key matches in the past, I would need all my energy for playing. In the end, I was simply unable to find the answer to Agassi's blistering returns of serve, and to his big groundstrokes: He seemed to take the ball on as short a rise as I ever had in my prime, and to hit it twice as hard.

The final score was 6–4, 6–2, 6–3. I gave young Andre a hug at the net, and said, "Why did you listen so well?" A couple of weeks earlier, I had given him some grass-court tips, and I now saw that he had been all too astute a pupil. He was still so wet behind the ears that I had to remind him to bow to the Royal Box on his way off the court. Here was a kind of sweet poetic justice: In my final Wimbledon singles match, I was teaching manners to the next generation!

Andre would win his first Grand Slam title the next day, beating Goran Ivanisevic in the final.

The sweetness wasn't over for me yet, though. Two days later, Michael Stich and I won the darkness-delayed doubles final against Jim Grabb and Richey Reneberg, 5–7, 7–6, 3–6, 7–6, and 19–17. It was the longest Wimbledon final ever in terms of games—eighty-three!—and the energy of the crowd, which had been let in for free on the extra day, made me forget how tired and stiff I actually was.

Not too shabby for an old man.

. . .

IT WAS MY LAST HURRAH. My Wimbledon result had lifted my ranking from 30 in the world to 17, but I had to face the fact that I wasn't winning tournaments anymore. That summer, I told Tatum, "If I don't win a big
one this year, I'll stop playing. I'll step back and allow you to step forward."

She couldn't let go of the idea of rekindling her acting career. In
September of 1992, an interviewer had asked her about her dream for the
future, and she said, "I guess it's that when John's tennis career is finished, he takes care of the kids while I make two pictures a year and get
to pick my scripts and work with whomever I want, and that our kids go
to great schools and live happily ever after."

I wanted to help Tatum feel fulfilled, but we should have talked about
that dream for the future and tried to get on the same page. It was close
to my own dream, I guess—I certainly wanted a lot more to do with taking care of our kids than I had had to date—but she had overlooked the
restlessness of my soul. My years as a touring tennis professional might
have been coming to a close, but I never wanted to stop *doing* things, and
if that meant travel, then so be it. Once that bug is in your blood—once
you're used to moving around the world and feeling important—I don't
know if it's ever possible to come to a full stop.

I would learn to appreciate staying at home—once I had a happy
home. But my home wasn't happy now. From this distance, the anger and
desperation between the lines of Tatum's dream are painfully clear.

Between my frustrating quest to rekindle my own career and the huge
pressures that having a third child had put on our marriage, we had
grown impossibly far apart. Too often, when we were together, there was
anger and distance instead of intimacy. If she was angry enough, she'd
tell me to just go and do whatever I wanted. Well, that *wasn't* what I
wanted.

Then, with things between us completely unresolved, I'd have to go off to events for weeks on end. It had been fun when I was young and single, but now I felt a wrench in my heart. I was agonizingly lonely—it's not an excuse this time, but a fumbling toward an explanation—and I did things I wasn't proud of.

And I never knew just what Tatum was doing back at home, or who she was spending time with. I mostly tried not to think about it.

In October, I was in Australia, playing the Sydney Indoor tournament. At this point, my tennis focus was wavering more and more: I'd have flashes of my old flair, then I'd lose to people for whom I had little respect. By now I barely had respect for myself. I lost to Edberg in Sydney, in the quarterfinals. A decent enough result—but just decent.

One night, Tatum called from New York (once Kevin and Sean had started preschool, we'd decided to move back east, keeping Malibu as a West Coast base) and, in the course of the conversation, mentioned that she was planning a fund-raising event for Bill Clinton. It would be held at some artist's studio, and Stephen Stills was going to play. . . . "Uh-huh," I said. "That sounds nice." I was half-listening to the usual music of a domestic conversation, when suddenly Tatum spoke three words that changed my life forever. "You're not invited," she said.

Now I was paying full attention. "I'm not invited?" I asked. "Why not?"

She hastily tried to put a better face on the situation. "You can come, but I'm sure you wouldn't even want to," Tatum said. "It's just a bunch of people you wouldn't be particularly interested in—I've only invited a couple of friends of mine, from acting class."

*Friends from acting class*—the phrase stuck in my head. Now I was thinking about things I didn't want to be thinking about.

Then, almost absurdly, she mentioned that her mother had been in a car accident, and had lost a couple of fingers.

I started laughing. I couldn't help myself. It all sounded so crazy. Her poor mother, Joanna Moore, had had such a sad and disordered life that almost no possibility seemed too strange. "What's the *next* thing you're going to tell me?" I asked.

Tatum got furious—I can't say I totally blame her. "How dare you be so insensitive?" she shouted.

I tried to smooth things over, but I sensed it was far too late for that.

When I flew back from Australia, I rented a car and drove to Palm Springs, where Tatum's mother lived. Joanna had indeed lost two fingers—to this day, I'm not sure it had anything to do with a car crash. The story was that she had gotten off at an exit, gone through a guardrail and over an embankment, and plunged twenty feet to the bottom of a gully—and that she'd been completely uninjured except for the loss of the fingers.

As I sat with Joanna, the talk turned to Tatum and our difficulties. "Tatum is going through something, but you've got to stand by her," Joanna said. "You've just got to stand by her—it's going to be OK." She seemed to know a lot more than she was saying—certainly a lot more than I knew. I left feeling profoundly unsettled.

We spent the rest of October in chilly silence: Tatum had clearly made up her mind. At the end of the month, we decided to separate officially—I couldn't stand the thought of a divorce, even though I knew, in the pit of my stomach, that there was no other next step.

I was devastated.

The real killer was that, for the short term at least, I had to go on with my tennis life. I was committed to three more tournaments, the Paris Indoor, Antwerp, and the Grand Slam Cup in Germany, as well as the Davis Cup final against Switzerland, in Fort Worth.

It was the end of my marriage and the end of my tennis career, both at the same time, and almost nobody knew about it except Tatum and me. I felt as though the bottom had dropped out of the world. I couldn't go on, but I had to go on.

In Paris, I was literally crying on the changeovers. I would put my head in a towel and fake being angry. It was an easy enough deception—

I was always worked up about something, anyway. I couldn't have told the truth and asked for sympathy: I think I would have fallen over if I'd done that. What saved my life in Paris was the presence of Patrick, the one person there whom I could begin to talk to about what I was going through. We played doubles together at that tournament, for only the third or fourth time in an ATP event. And significantly, though I lost in the second round of the singles—and though Patrick and I hadn't done especially well together before—teaming with my brother at that moment gave me the strength to play on. We won the tournament!

Then I went on alone to Antwerp, and lost once again in the second round. I would barely be able to function for the next six months.

My final Davis Cup tie, in Fort Worth, was a brief, strange respite. I had brought along a support group: my parents, my brothers, all three of my children, a nanny, and my agent, Sergio Palmieri. I needed every one of them. A few days before, I had been staying at Andre Agassi's house in Las Vegas, telling Andre, "I don't know if I can do Davis Cup— I just can't function."

The news of my separation had leaked to the press—a couple of photographs of Tatum out kicking up her heels with new friends had fanned the flames—and it was all the reporters wanted to talk about. I spent the days before my first match (I was there to play doubles with Pete Sampras) trying to practice and spend time with my kids as I dodged inappropriate questions.

The strain showed when I finally got on court to play. The atmosphere inside the Tarrant County Convention Center was the kind of chaos I'd once loved in Davis Cup—American fans waving flags and sounding boat horns at lederhosen-wearing Swiss fans chanting and rattling cowbells—but now it felt all too much like the chaos inside me. I doublefaulted at set point in the first-set tiebreaker, then dropped my serve again at 5–4 in the second set, which Pete and I went on to lose in another tiebreaker.

I felt furious and humiliated. This was my final Davis Cup; I couldn't go out on a loss—to the Swiss! (It was the first time they'd ever made it to a final.) I began yelling at Pete, trying to psych him up; trash-talking at Jakob Hlasek and Marc Rosset, the Swiss team. Somehow we managed to hang on and take the third set, 7–5, but by the time we went into the locker room for the ten-minute break, I was in some kind of altered state. All my fear and anger and frustration and sorrow had built up to the point where smoke was practically coming out of my ears.

*"We're going to go out and kick some ass!"* I screamed, at Pete and Jim Courier and Andre Agassi. *"We're going to go out and kick some ass!"* I repeated. I screamed it over and over, like a war chant, until my voice was hoarse.

And when Pete and I went back out, that was exactly what we did. Every time we won a point, Agassi and Courier would shout, "Answer the question!"—a little phrase I occasionally used to shout at umpires. Pete—imagine it; Pete Sampras!—was shouting, pumping his fist. The fans in the stands were going crazy, the boat horns drowning out the cowbells. We won the last two sets, 6–1 and 6–2. When it was over, Pete hugged me. "I love you, Mac," he said.

I rested up my voice that night, then screamed it hoarse again the next day as Jim beat Hlasek in four sets. When it was all over, I took a big American flag from courtside and ran around and around the court, waving it high from both hands, as the crowd went nuts. It was as happy as I'd ever been.

Then I went right back to being the saddest I'd ever been, all over again. I returned to New York with my parents, my brothers, and my kids—and then, the very next day, flew to Germany for the Grand Slam Cup. I could hardly imagine playing tennis: I was barely putting one foot in front of the other.

Before I got on the plane at Kennedy, I went to a newsstand to get something to read for the flight and divert my mind from the only thing

I could think about. And there, staring me in the face, was *People* magazine, with Tatum and me on the cover, and the caption, "End of the Love Match." I picked up a copy in spite of myself—I couldn't help it—and read the article. I can't even remember the piece, it made me so angry: The thrust appeared to be that the end of the marriage had mostly been my fault, for holding Tatum back from her career.

ABOUT A MONTH into our separation, Tatum and I went to the premiere of the movie *Malcolm X*, in Manhattan. We were still living in the apartment together, with the kids, even though we weren't staying in the same room. It was a very strange time, I didn't know which end was up, and so when she suggested we go together, I said, "Why not?" I suppose that, just as I'd once harbored a secret hope, a decade earlier, that Borg would return to the tour, some hidden part of me held a tiny hope that Tatum and I would get back together.

I regretted going as soon as we got to the theater. What had I been thinking? There were cameras everywhere, titillated reporters shouting questions. For reasons only she could understand, Tatum was absolutely glowing that night, while my smiles were as fake as could be. As soon as the lights went down in the theater, the floods started again—I sat there weeping, thinking, *Why aren't we together?* And, *Why doesn't she feel bad, even if she does believe this is the right thing to do?*

After the movie was over, Tatum looked at me with something almost like sympathy. "Someday you'll thank me for this," she said.

I wondered about that for a little while. Then I understood what she'd meant. I think she'd realized she was such trouble, and so incapable of being the wife that I wanted, that eventually I'd be happier with someone else.

At that point, though, I couldn't imagine being with anyone, ever again.

I also resented the way she'd said it. While I was falling apart, she seemed to be feeling better about herself than she had in a long time, and so her words conveyed a certain superiority. It was almost as if she was drawing power from my weakness.

The last thing I felt like doing was sticking around while Tatum went through her latest phase of self-discovery. I wanted to try to work things out, or split for good.

After returning from the Grand Slam Cup, I told her I was staying in my apartment, and that if she, in fact, wanted to separate, she would have to move out. She did. It was over.

It's almost hard to understand from this distance, but at the time, I was shocked and devastated by how suddenly it had all happened. I did feel responsible, but at the same time, I felt furious at Tatum—how could she have made this decision when I had already told her I was going to stop playing so she could work more?

However, the question I kept asking myself over and over was, What had I been thinking in the first place? If it had all been meant to come to this, why did I ever think we could really function as a couple? I felt dumb, and it hurt. Love is blind, they say; now I really knew what they were talking about. I'd thought Tatum was a diamond in the rough, that I was going to be the guy to polish her up and help her shine. Now it all just seemed idiotic.

I had never cried so much in my life—I would start thinking about everything, the tears would come, and I wouldn't be able to stop until I had cried myself out. In early February, Arthur Ashe died, and the news only seemed to add more weight to a burden I could no longer bear. Arthur and I had had our differences, even our clashes, but I'd had a huge amount of respect for him as a man, a black man, and a positive force for world tennis. I realized too late that he was the greatest ambassador our sport had ever had, and I was determined to try to do better myself.

Almost as soon as I'd returned from Germany in December, Tatum had gone to make a TV movie—reinforcing the appearance that I'd been the one holding her back from her career. She'd insisted on taking one-and-a-half-year-old Emily with her for virtually the entire two-month shoot. I thought it was a huge mistake, but there wasn't much I could do about it. Kevin and Sean and I all slept in the same room together the whole time: Sometimes one of them would wake up and see the tears on my face. Then, one morning, Kevin said, "I don't want to see you cry any-more, Dad."

I WALKED OUT into the fresh air of 1993 and began my new life. Now that I was no longer touring, I had a lot of time to devote to ventures I'd begun earlier. One of them was broadcasting.

At the 1991 U.S. Open, a couple of rounds after the match where Michael Chang had topspin-lobbed me to death, I had stopped by the USA Network's broadcast booth to visit my buddy Vitas Gerulaitis, who'd begun a promising new career as a tennis commentator. At the time, I'd thought Vitas was head and shoulders above almost any of the tennis broadcasters out there—which wasn't saying a lot, since I felt (and still largely feel) that most of them stank: Virtually without exception, they were arrogant, dry, pompous, or just plain boring—take your pick.

Vitas, on the other hand, was anything but boring. It wasn't just that he knew pro tennis inside and out—he had the wonderful gift of being himself on the air, Queens accent and all. He had a conversational style and a funny, irreverent personality that simply drew you into the match.

Jimmy Connors was playing a lanky young Dutchman named Paul Haarhuis in a quarterfinal that night, and though Jimmy had been wild-carded into the tournament at the astounding age of thirty-nine, he was giving Haarhuis one hell of a match. Vitas was doing the commentary, along with Ted Robinson, and, not knowing enough about broadcasting to be afraid, I fell into a natural give-and-take with the two of them. At one point in the match, Jimmy started throwing up lobs at Haarhuis, Haarhuis kept hitting smashes—and Jimmy kept running each one down and throwing up another lob. This happened several times in a row, until Jimmy ended the point with an incredible running winner, which drove the Flushing Meadows crowd into a frenzy. That was the greatest point I ever saw at the U.S. Open.

It wasn't just a hell of a match (Connors wound up winning in four), it was a hell of a match to begin my commentating career with. USA liked what I'd done so much that they offered me a contract. We signed a deal in 1992, based on my availability, since I was still playing at the time. I also signed with NBC to broadcast the French Open and Wimbledon. With each network, the agreement was that I could start broadcasting as soon as I had been eliminated from the singles in the tournament. Unfortunately, my availability was increasing all the time!

Now, in 1993, my schedule was wide open. I re-upped with USA. I had once told myself that after my playing career was over, the two things I would never do were commentary and Seniors tennis. Never say never.

Early that year, I also briefly considered coaching Andre Agassi, but I worried that it wouldn't give me time enough with my kids—who I was actually getting to see for weeks at a time, now that I was no longer touring. It became a moot point when Andre hired Pancho Segura (I would later learn, after brief fiascos with Sergei Bruguera and Boris Becker, that being a traveling coach was not my cup of tea. I'm good at putting on diapers, but not with people over eighteen.)

Another new venture was music. All through high school, I had been an impressive (to me) air guitarist, and from time to time I inflicted my singing voice on friends who had put together rock bands. When I started on the tennis circuit, however, and suddenly found myself with hours and hours to kill in hotel rooms all over the world, it occurred to me that I should actually try taking up the guitar.

Way back in 1981, I had bought a black Les Paul, which I broke into pieces in frustration the first week I owned it, after seeing Buddy Guy play at the Checkerboard Lounge in Chicago, where I'd been taken by my friend Gary Fencik. Next I bought a 1962 white Fender Stratocaster formerly owned by Elliot Easton of the Cars. I managed to figure out a chord here, a song there, and pretty soon I could play a little. Very little.

I would eventually get private guitar lessons from my friends Carlos Santana, Eddie Van Halen, Stephen Stills, Alex Lifeson, and Billy Squier, among others; bass lessons from Bill Wyman of the Rolling Stones; and piano lessons from the legendary songwriter Jimmy Webb. I would also get to jam with the likes of Stevie Ray Vaughn, Buddy Guy, Joe Cocker, and Lars Ulrich of Metallica (whose father, Torben, had played on the tennis circuit and for the Danish Davis Cup team). I would love to say that some of the brilliance of these amazing musicians rubbed off on me, but I can't go that far. I will say that I advanced from miserable to . . . mediocre.

Now that Tatum had moved to my other apartment on East 90th Street, I sometimes had my whole place to myself when the kids were with her, or at school—all four floors, including an incredible two-story tower penthouse with a 360-degree view of Manhattan. I turned the penthouse into a music studio. My musician buddies, both great and unknown, would frequently stop by to jam, and I began to try my hand at writing songs. I even sat in on a few of my friends' gigs at downtown clubs that spring and summer.

Restless character that I am, I also branched out in an entirely new direction. Mary Carillo hadn't known what she was starting when she took me to those Paris art museums back in the spring of 1977. One Saturday afternoon in 1980, I'd gone gallery-hopping in SoHo with Vitas, who was collecting photo-realist paintings at the time. We wound up at the Meisel Gallery, where he bought a number of pieces, and what I saw there excited me. Part of me was tempted to emulate Vitas and buy a canvas, but I didn't want to spend a lot of money on something I didn't completely understand. As a result, for the next year or so, in every city I played, I stopped into galleries and museums, slowly educating my eye.

I found myself most attracted to modern American painters—people as diverse as Alice Neel, Marsden Hartley, Arthur Dove, Richard Diebenkorn, Philip Guston, and Agnes Martin, as well as much younger artists such as Eric Fischl and the graffiti-influenced Jean-Michel Basquiat and Keith Haring. I bought a photo-realist canvas by Tom Blackwell, and gradually began to make some other purchases.

As I approached the end of my tennis-playing career, it had scarcely occurred to me that someday I might want to open a gallery of my own. I liked the idea of going into business, but I didn't know if I wanted to be in the business of buying and selling something that could appreciate significantly in value—but could also drop like a ton of bricks. In 1992, I'd bought a residential loft in an old cast-iron building on Greene Street in SoHo. After my separation, I began to consider converting the big loft into a viewing space.

As with buying paintings, however, I knew I couldn't go into the art-gallery business half-cocked. I now knew a little bit about art, but I didn't know much about buying and selling it. And so, at the end of 1992, Larry Salander offered me a nonpaying job at the Salander-O'Reilly Galleries on the Upper East Side. You can't learn the guitar without learning the basic chords, and you can't learn the art business without knowing the nuts and bolts.

But I was often lonely. I dated a bit after Tatum and I separated, but it gave me a terribly hollow feeling, and, at the same time, I really wasn't ready for anything more serious. Even dating was tricky, since the last thing I wanted was publicity while I was getting divorced. That would be a long and very messy process: twenty-two months–plus, to be exact.

OVER CHRISTMAS VACATION that year, I took my kids to stay at the Malibu house for a couple of weeks. It's hard to beat Manhattan at Christmastime, but it was a moody holiday for me that year, and I felt we all needed some sun and fun.

Not long after we arrived, I got a phone call from Lily Gross, a beach friend from Malibu. Lily told me that Corky Grazer—the former wife of Brian Grazer, the movie producer—who lived in North Malibu, was having a party on Christmas Day for her friends and their kids. Did I feel like bringing my brood along?

Sure I did, I said. It sounded like fun.

"Patty Smyth's going to be there, with her daughter," Lily said, in a significant, slightly teasing way.

Well, that was interesting. I had loved Patty Smyth's band, Scandal, in the eighties—her big hit "Goodbye to You" was one of my favorites—and I knew she had recently released a solo album that had sold a million copies. I thought her voice was tough and sexy, and I had seen her videos. . . .

This was interesting.

The party was a mob scene, full of noisy kids running around a Christmas tree placed, slightly surreally, near a big picture window overlooking the sun-sparkling Pacific. As usual, there were lots of Hollywood people, a number of well-known faces, but I was intrigued by Patty, who didn't seem like anyone else there.

I'm a New Yorker, and I can always tell a fellow New Yorker, and I could see and hear in an instant that that was Patty. She had grown up in Queens, she told me. So had I, I said. She had moved to the Coast the year before, she said, as her daughter, Ruby, was starting first grade. Patty had been divorced from Ruby's father, the musician Richard Hell, "forever." She had come west not just because she was making the album with a Los Angeles producer, but because life as a single mother of a six-year-old in downtown Manhattan was becoming just a little too colorful. She had witnessed a shooting and a stabbing in her neighborhood, and she'd had to punch a guy in the face after he touched her on the street—while she was holding Ruby's hand.

She had all of a native New Yorker's reservations about L.A., she said—the endless flirtation and lack of sincerity drove her crazy—but she had a little house up in Topanga Canyon, and her own washer and dryer, and a car, and her daughter was happy in school. . . . Things could be a lot worse.

I liked her right away. Over years of being famous and infamous, I had developed very sensitive antennae for when people were overimpressed by me, or were trying to get something, or thought I was a jerk—and Patty was up to none of that. She was real and cute and sexy, but she was a woman, not a girl; someone who had lived life and knew the score. And as an aspiring musician, I was impressed by *her*.

So I told her about myself, simply and directly. I knew she knew who I was, so instead of talking about my history, I told her about a couple of my new ventures. I said that the interior of my SoHo loft was almost re-furbished, and that I was going to open my gallery there in a few weeks. I told her about the end of my career and the end of my marriage, about sleeping in the same bed with my kids, about Kevin telling me it was time to stop crying. I wasn't trying to impress her (or depress her); I was just speaking from the heart.

One of my kids ran up and interrupted us. We both smiled. I knew, and knew she knew, that we had made a connection. But at the same time, we both knew that the last thing (and on some deeper level, the first thing) either of us was looking for at that point was a serious relationship.

It was all too complicated. Even our smiles were complicated. The party, and the children, pulled us off to different corners of the room. Awhile later, I saw her smiling and talking with a man I didn't know—and already didn't like. I pressed my lips together and shook my head.

As the party began to break up, I couldn't just let her go. I made my way through the parents and kids and put myself in front of Patty. "Can we get together sometime?" I asked. "I'm out here for another ten days." I gave her my best boyish grin. "I'm not doing anything New Year's Eve."

She sighed. "I'm going to Florida tomorrow," she said. "Key West. I really don't want to go, but I have to—I promised a friend."

"So don't go," I tried.

She shook her head. "I wish it were that simple," she said. We looked at each other for a second, trying to figure out what to do. I wasn't sure how to read her signals—or if there were any signals. "Listen," Patty finally said. "I go to New York a lot. I'd really like to see your gallery—maybe I'll stop by sometime."

That was my cue, I realized afterward. That was the moment I should have looked for a pencil and paper, scribbled down my phone number, and handed it to her. But I was scared; I was frozen; I was not a fully operating human being at that point in my life. So I smiled and nodded. "That'd be great," I said.

She smiled back, then took Ruby's hand and walked out the door.

# 13

IF THERE WAS ANY DOUBT that my ATP career was over, I dispelled it in February of 1994 with what turned out to be my final tournament, in Rotterdam: I lost in the first round to the then-tenth-ranked Magnus Gustafsson of Sweden. The real disappointment, however, came when Boris Becker went through the motions in our semifinal doubles loss. Had I won that match and the next, I would have broken the all-time doubles record held by the Dutchman Tom Okker (and, interestingly, would have had to beat two other Dutchmen, Paul Haarhuis and Jacco Eltingh, in the final to do it).

I was now thirty-five, officially old enough to play Seniors events, and I kicked off my Seniors career soon afterward with my first trip to Russia, for a four-man event with Borg, Connors, and Vilas in St. Petersburg. It was a depressing, slightly eerie trip: The tone was set right away when the lights inside our Aeroflot plane flicked off as we landed.

I was sobered to find St. Petersburg's great art museum, the Hermitage, heatless and dilapidated, and to see that the lobby of my hotel was crawling with prostitutes, who seemed to be even more interested in finding a way out of Russia than in making a few rubles. The tournament itself was no less strange: The organizers didn't seem to want to admit anyone but family and friends, and refused entry, to the people waiting outside who could afford to buy tickets. Sadly, not many could afford them. We played in front of nearly empty stands.

Much more successful was my first ever—though admittedly non-paying—music gig, in Paris, during the French Open. Yannick Noah had started his own career as a singer-songwriter (and has since become a bestselling recording artist in France), and was holding the first in what turned out to be an annual series of music-and-tennis events for his children's charity. The John McEnroe Band—yours truly on lead vocals and rhythm guitar; the youngsters Chris Scianni on lead guitar and Rich Novatka on drums; and, just for that trip, Matt Kramer on bass—played in front of four thousand people!

It was a rousing start for my rock-and-roll career, and things got even more exciting a few nights later when we became only the second live act ever (after, if you can believe it, Prince) to perform in La Bandouche, a big Paris nightclub. To my amazement, as we played, Joe Cocker actually jumped up on stage and sang a few songs with us.

I wasn't sure if we were headed for the top, but I felt encouraged when Sergio Palmieri booked us for a two-week tour of Italy, in July. The money wasn't much—sixteen thousand dollars, split four ways. Still, it was money: We were playing for pay, just like a real band, and it was a serious schedule, twelve gigs in fourteen nights in Sardinia and seaside resorts on the peninsula's west coast. It was quite a tour.

In my original concept for the band, I wasn't the front man. My first impulse, again, had been to be a team player: I just wanted to play rhythm guitar, maybe take a few solos, sing a little backup, and leave it at that. The idea had been to lend my name and presence to a solid group effort.

One of my mistakes was to assume that, somewhere out there, a good, unknown lead singer would see an opportunity in working with me— would think my energy and enthusiasm and notoriety could lift both of us to legitimacy.

Never did I picture myself as lead guitarist/vocalist: When it came to actually doing it, it was like that joke line about not being able to walk and chew gum at the same time—I was literally unable to focus on singing and playing my guitar at once. I would forget to breathe, then come in at the wrong place on the vocal, or sing off-key, or hit the wrong chord.

I had figured that if we went places where they didn't understand English, my roughness around the edges wouldn't matter—people would just be happy that I was there. They would come out to see the spectacle of John McEnroe playing guitar and singing. I knew I had to be bad before I was good, so I was willing to try to get my feet wet by being *really* bad and taking some abuse.

Little did I realize what kind of abuse I was letting myself in for.

When we rehearsed in New York in June, I brought in a new band member, who had toured with some serious rock musicians. I thought his professionalism would be the glue we needed to hold the band together. He had been on the wagon for years, and this was the moment when he suddenly fell off. It didn't seem especially significant until we got to our first gig, in a seaside town called Rapallo, at a pretty club where, it was said, Frank Sinatra had once performed. As we prepared to play our first number, I looked around and noticed that our guy was missing.

I found him at the bar, well-oiled. When I told him we were about to play "I Got the Blues," a standard twelve-bar blues number we'd played dozens of times before, he asked me what key it was in. I blinked. "E," I said.

"What are the changes?" he asked.

My heart sank. When your very experienced bandmate is asking you for the chord changes to a twelve-bar blues tune, you're in big trouble. I had no idea, though, what kind of real trouble we were in.

He was our foundation: If we couldn't depend on him, we couldn't put together a credible performance. And if you don't believe in yourself in some way, no one is going to believe in you. Soon the audiences lost interest in us. They booed; they threw things. It was about as bad as you could imagine—and then it got worse.

Halfway into the tour, he went missing. We were scheduled to leave for our next gig, in Forte di Marmi, at noon; by one-thirty, he was nowhere to be found. First we felt worried, then we turned cynical: We told Katia Lesmo, Sergio's assistant, to call the hospitals and the police station. Sure enough, he turned up in the emergency room of the local hospital. We were later told that the police had found him unconscious, face-down on the pavement outside a nightclub. He claimed that someone had put LSD in his drink. Amazingly, he played the gig that night. Rock and roll will never die.

The rest of the tour became a survival test. Finally, after two long weeks, we flew home with our tails between our legs. I did not read the Italian reviews. For the first time in my life, I was happy I had never learned a foreign language.

IN EARLY AUGUST, not long after I returned to New York, my divorce became final. I felt as though a huge weight had come off my shoulders (and out of my checkbook!), but my heart still had a gaping hole in it. Soon afterward, I got a call from my friend Lily, in California. She was just phoning to check when I was coming out west, but as soon as I heard her voice, I naturally thought of Patty Smyth. It had now been seven months since I'd seen Patty at the Christmas party, and we hadn't talked once. I'd kept hoping she might actually stop by my gallery, but she never had. I even went to Los Angeles in April to play an exhibition, but since I was semi-involved with someone at that point, and Patty and I hadn't seen each other or talked, I figured it just wasn't going to happen, so I didn't call her.

I was a fool. I was scared. I had often hidden my fear behind bravado or feigned nonchalance, and here was another instance. No woman I'd seen since my separation had been nearly as impressive as Patty, had caught my soul the way she had, and I was simply frightened she would turn me down if I sought her out.

And so, midway into the conversation with Lily, I said, as casually as I could, "How's Patty Smyth?"

There was a slight pause. "Oh, she's fine," Lily said, with something in her voice I couldn't quite decipher. The female mafia has its own secret codes.

"She has a boyfriend or something, right?" I said.

More of that odd tone from Lily: "Not that I know of," she said, in a singsong voice.

"That's interesting," I said.

"Oh, yeah?" Lily said.

Something had gotten under my skin—but I was still scared, and I hated to be scared. My solution was to try not to think about Patty. That didn't work very well.

I went to the U.S. Open that year as a veteran broadcaster of four years' standing. It was an exciting tournament: Number-one seed Pete Sampras was upset in the quarterfinals by Jaime Yzaga, and unseeded Andre Agassi beat Michael Stich to win the championship.

One week later, I beat Agassi.

It was in an exhibition, in Phoenix, five days after he had won the Open, and I know Andre was probably still a little tired and deflated—

but so what? I was thirty-five years old, and I had beaten the twenty-four-year-old United States Open champion in a tennis match. The old dog had some tricks in him yet!

Exhibitions are funny: They always contain that uncertain line between entertainment and serious tennis. In this instance, I think that Andre figured he could have his cake and eat it, too—have fun, make me look reasonably good, and win. I know he was probably toying with me to some extent, but then I put pressure on him after he let down his guard, and I was pumped up, and then it was over. I think he was a little annoyed after that match.

I, on the other hand, was feeling pretty good about myself! Even though I had been around the block quite a few times by now, and I'd learned I wasn't the king of the world if I won Wimbledon, or the pits of the world if I lost, it was always hard to avoid falling into the trap of basing my self-esteem on my results.

Especially when I won big.

And this seemed reasonably large to me. Suddenly, I wanted to celebrate. When I got back to the hotel that night, I phoned Lily in Los Angeles and asked her for Patty's number. That took all the courage I had at the moment. The next morning, when I got to the airport in Phoenix— I was on my way to L.A. for five days, before going to Mexico City to play an exhibition with Borg and Gerulaitis—I took a deep breath and phoned Patty. I don't know why I expected to get her machine on a Saturday morning: Part of me, probably, hoped that I would.

She answered, sounding a little sleepy and annoyed.

"Patty?" I said. "This is John McEnroe. Listen—I'm coming to town for a few days, and I just wanted to know if maybe you'd like to get together."

There was the tiniest of pauses. "Sure," she said. "I'm going to a lesbian party tonight. Wanna come?"

Now it was my turn to pause. Was she trying to tell me something here? "Um—sure," I said. "Are you, uh, sure it's OK if I come?"

She laughed. "Don't get any ideas," she said. "It's just a birthday party for a friend of mine who happens to be gay, and a lot of her gay friends are going to be there, but I'm sure there'll be plenty of straight people, too. If that makes you feel better."

Just hearing the welcome in her voice was making me feel better already.

I picked her up in Topanga Canyon at dusk—a golden Pacific dusk— and we drove up the coast to the party. It was strange: We hadn't seen each other in eight months, so theoretically we should have had quite a bit to talk about. But I was still tired from the match with Agassi, and the flight, and the drive, and I didn't have a lot of conversation in me. I explained to Patty, and apologized for my quietness.

"That's okay," she said. "I'm pretty wiped, too, actually."

We rode mostly in silence—but oddly enough, it was comfortable silence, the kind of quiet that two people who've known each other a long time can enjoy.

It was a big Hollywood party, with a slightly different crowd than I was used to, but it was Hollywood. Buck Henry was there. So was Tom Scott, the saxophone player from L.A. Express, and his wife Lynn, and it turned out that they were close friends with Patty. When the two of us walked in, a big cheer went up: later, Patty told me that she'd sworn off dating quite a while ago and had started going everywhere with Tom and Lynn—to the point that people had begun calling her "the other Mrs. Scott." That afternoon, she'd phoned them to say she was actually bringing a date to this party, and guess who it was?

The party had a warm feeling, and I felt completely comfortable being there with Patty. At one point, we were sitting in the living room talking with some people, and I put my arm around her shoulder—and was suddenly surprised at how totally natural the gesture felt. Fortunately, Patty seemed to feel good about it, too.

I started to yawn, and she hit me playfully on the shoulder. "That's rude!" she said.

"I'm sorry. I've really had it," I said.

"We'd better get you back home," Patty said.

I asked her if she would drive my car, because I was so tired. She agreed, a little grumpily. "What do you live out here for?" I asked her as we rode. "You're a New York girl. It's not right that you live out here."

I was giving her a hard time, half joking and half serious. The serious part was that I wanted to spend more time with her, a lot more time, and my kids were in school in New York, and Ruby was in school here. It was adding up on so many levels, but the logistics stank.

I dropped Patty off at her place, and we kissed for a long time at her front door. "This was really, really nice," I said. "I really want to see you again."

"OK," she said.

"How about tomorrow night?" I said.

"God, you move fast, Mr. McEnroe."

"Hey, that's why they pay me the big bucks," I said.

I had to fly to San Francisco the next day, to play an exhibition with Michael Chang for Michael's Bay Area charity. The whole way up there, I couldn't stop thinking about Patty. I had looked at the airline schedule and figured out that if the match ended by eight o'clock, I'd be able to fly back to L.A. and drive over to her place. I could barely wait—I would let Chang bulldoze me, if that was what it took.

When I got to the auditorium, Michael told me the event was sold out. It seemed like a good sign—*all* the signs were good. *My luck is finally changing,* I thought. I felt euphoric as I stood in the locker room putting on my tennis clothes.

Then someone walked in and told me that Vitas had died.

No one knew any details, but I later learned that his body had been found on Sunday morning in Marty Raines's guest house, in Southampton. Marty was a real-estate developer whom both Vitas and I had known for a long time: I'd bought my 90th Street co-op from his organization. Apparently Vitas had been in the Hamptons to play in a charity tennis clinic, had taken a nap at Marty's, and had never woken up.

I was staggered. Vitas had just turned forty in July: he was still a young man. I had worried about him for a long time, but lately he seemed to have turned his life around. He was taking better care of himself, and so my first natural suspicions just didn't add up. (It later turned out that Vitas had died in his sleep of carbon-monoxide asphyxiation from an improperly vented space heater in the pool house.)

I went numb. I kept thinking, *Oh my God, this is so bad. This isn't possible.* I walked onto the court, numb. Was I going to play tennis? Apparently, I was. I started to hit with Michael, just going through the motions I'd gone through a million times before—forehands, backhands, volleys, overheads. "Mr. McEnroe has won the toss. He has elected to serve."

I served, still numb. Ace. Fifteen-love. I served again. Numb. Thirty-love. Two more points. "Game, Mr. McEnroe. He leads, one game to love."

I simply couldn't miss. I can't explain it. *I couldn't miss anything.* The tension of what I had come to do had totally evaporated. Nothing mattered anymore. I could see the odd look on Michael's face: He was trying as hard as he could, but there was nothing he could do against me.

I won the first set, 6–4, gathering speed, and before I knew it, I was ahead, 5–1, in the second. It was five minutes after seven. I let Michael win a couple of games, to make it look better, and then the match was over, 6–4, 6–3. I had destroyed Michael Chang, number five in the world. I'd cleaned his clock.

I showered, dressed, went to the airport, barely made my plane, and flew back to Los Angeles. I got to Malibu by ten. I called Patty.

"Can I come over and see you?" I said. "I really need to see you."

"Well, it's kind of late," she said. "I'm in my pajamas already—why don't you come over tomorrow."

"I want to see you now," I said.

"What's the hurry?" Patty asked. "Why do you have to come over now?"

"Because I just have a feeling about you and me, and my friend died tonight, and I really need to see you," I said.

"OK," she said. I went over, and we've been together ever since.

I pulled out of the Mexico City exhibition, and stayed close by Patty's side until I flew back east to Vitas's funeral on Long Island. It was a long day that went by in a blur of tears. Jimmy Connors, Mary Carillo, and Vitas's sister, Ruta, all gave touching tributes to Vitas, but at the moment when I might have gone up and said a few words myself, I found myself too undone to move. I've regretted it ever since.

THAT WAS THE WEEK that brought Patty and me together for good, but consistent physical proximity (which, I've learned at long last, is absolutely essential to a relationship) took a little while to work out. After all, she lived in Topanga Canyon; I lived on Central Park West. Ruby was just starting the fourth grade at Topanga Elementary; Kevin and Sean were in the third and second grades respectively at Trinity, and three-year-old Emily had just started preschool at Rodeph Sholom, on the Upper West Side.

It may sound like *The Brady Bunch,* but it wasn't funny. It was a bumpy start.

We did the bicoastal-relationship thing for a while: Occasionally, Patty would fly east to visit, and when I had my kids for a week or two at a time, over vacations, I'd take them out to Malibu. It was wonderful when we did manage to get together, but it could be very rough when we were apart, which was most of the time. Even when we did meet, there were adjustments and difficulties—any couple knows you don't just shift into happy gear the second you see each other, and it's all the more problematic when you're both regretting the many obstacles of living three thousand miles apart.

And there was more. The custody battle between Tatum and me had been protracted and ugly, and much of it got aired in the always-helpful tabloid press, which only worsened things, especially for the two boys, who were old enough to begin to understand what was going on. Tatum had tried to get full custody of the children, claiming that my emotional abusiveness—my anger problems, as differentiated from her anger problems—and my protracted absences for tennis business made me an unfit father.

I countered with the simple statement that though I did still do some business traveling, I was no longer a touring tennis pro. I had stopped touring not just because my career was ending, but because I'd realized there was no way I could be a real father to my kids if I was on the road thirty weeks a year.

Soon after the separation, I asked my assistant at the time to go to the New York Public Library and check every study on children and divorce they had. The studies suggested overwhelmingly that the best-case scenario for the kids was that the father spend as much time as possible with them—and that in most cases the father didn't. Joint custody, the studies said, was better for children by far, both in terms of the way they viewed the divorce, and the parents' involvement with them. Over and over during the proceedings, I said to Tatum, "Show me a single case where it says the mother should have full custody of the kids when the father is financially independent and not working a nine-to-five job." And there weren't any.

I had the research done because I needed to back up, for her and for me, what I felt in my heart: I didn't want to be a father who wasn't with his kids.

Even after the court decided on joint custody, however, there were constant border wars between us about arrangements, and every time I said an unkind word to her, threats by Tatum to sue for custody because of my anger issues.

This is what Patty was walking into the middle of.

She was also walking into a relationship with someone whose life's ambition was to become a rock-and-roll musician. Patty didn't want to burst my bubble, at first. She wrote a song for me right around then, called "Wish I Were You," contrasting, with some amusement, my enthusiasm for music and her distaste for the business.

Almost from the start it had seemed beautifully obvious to me that Patty Smyth was the lead vocalist I'd been looking for ever since I first picked up that black Les Paul guitar. But the harder I pushed, the more she resisted. When I first said, "Hey, can I play in your band?" she said, "Why don't we play mixed doubles at Wimbledon?" I thought, *Oh my God, am I that bad?* Patty didn't even play tennis!

She had hit a wall in her own music career: Despite the success of her self-titled second solo album in 1992 (a single from the album, "Sometimes Love Just Ain't Enough," which she sang with Don Henley of the Eagles, became a number-one hit), Patty had found herself struggling for motivation and fed up with the record business. She had decided to take a break to think things over.

Just as our relationship began, Patty was asked to sing a movie theme song. In October 1994, she recorded, "Look What Love Has Done," which she had co-written with Carole Bayer Sager, James Ingram, and James Newton Howard. The song was used as the theme for an Arnold Schwarzenegger movie, *Junior*, which came out a couple of months later, and not long afterward, to Patty's amazement, "Look What Love Has Done" was nominated for an Academy Award.

We then proceeded to go through a fiasco which, somehow, seems all too emblematic of my music career. After I had pestered her many times about our playing together, she decided to throw me a bone. To my vast excitement, she told me that she would allow me to play acoustic guitar in the band backing her up when she sang "Look What Love Has Done" on the Academy Awards telecast—in front of a television audience of a billion people!

I learned every note of that song, rehearsing it over and over with my bass player John Martarelli, who was also an excellent guitarist. Patty and Ruby had come east for a school vacation; now they and I and my kids all flew west for the big broadcast.

We were scheduled to rehearse for the telecast on the day we arrived. Since our flight had come in a little early, we decided to drop the kids off at the beach before we went back to the studio in Hollywood. Early quickly turned into late, though; we were delayed getting to the rehearsal, and when we walked in, Gil Cates, the director, told us that the band had already rehearsed the song.

"You rehearsed the song without the singer?" I asked, incredulously.

Cates looked at me uneasily, but didn't respond.

I asked the question again, with a little more agitation. Once more, Cates said nothing.

"Let's just get out of here," I said to Patty.

As we walked outside, I was congratulating myself on keeping my cool—but Patty felt that in fact I had made a scene, over something that wasn't a big deal. That evening, we got a call from one of Cates's assistants, who told us that if I planned to play with Patty, she would be replaced on the telecast by James Ingram. I was, the assistant said, "a distraction."

Patty decided I wasn't going to distract anybody. She was going to sing that night, and I was going to watch. The night of the telecast, as I sat proudly in the fifth row, I felt more nervous than I would have been if I'd been up there playing. Patty sang beautifully, but Elton John won for "Can You Feel the Love Tonight," his song for *The Lion King*.

A month later—look what love had done—we were expecting.

We were both marriage-shy, for a number of reasons. Happy marriage simply wasn't something in Patty's history. Her mother had left her father when Patty was a little girl; she had never lived in a conventional nuclear family. To top it off, her father had died when she was eight. Patty and Ruby's father had split up when Ruby was still a baby, and, like her own mother, Patty had learned to live as a single parent. That was what she knew; that was what she was used to.

I've already listed my reasons. Once you've gone through the pain and the difficulties and the maneuvering and the lawyering and the high emotions of a long, bitter divorce, you literally feel as if you've been through hell. You can't help being jealous when you hear the stories of amicable divorces, when you run into men who say, "My ex-wife and I get along well." Something down deep in you says, "Never again." And the best way to ensure that is never to marry again.

Having children outside of wedlock is complicated. But Patty and I were committed to each other. What wasn't complicated was my absolute determination to stay faithful. It seemed to me that there was no other way. If that made me an anomaly in the world of macho married tennis players, so be it.

In September, Patty and Ruby moved to New York to live with me. We were a family of four—and on a regular basis, a family of seven. The big apartment wasn't empty anymore.

The end of 1995 brought a minor distinction and a major miracle. The minor distinction was that, after having toured Hawaii, Japan, South America, and the U.S., my band had become the most-traveled unsigned band in the history of music!

The miracle was the birth of Anna Smyth McEnroe, on December 27th. Nine weeks before the due date, Patty experienced a pain in her stomach. It felt to her like a muscle pull, but for the next day or two, she didn't feel the baby moving. We went to the doctor to ease our fears, but instead, Patty was ordered to the emergency room at Lenox Hill Hospital. For the next two weeks, she hung on like a champ as the fetus continued to develop. Finally, the doctors felt they could wait no longer.

After Anna was born, seven weeks early and in the midst of one of New York's snowiest winters ever, she spent the first month of her life at Lenox Hill. Finally, after a huge thank-you to all the doctors and staff, and a not-so-kind word to the paparazzi outside, Patty and I brought Anna home.

IN OCTOBER OF 1996, I stood in the living room of an unpretentious middle-class house in a quiet suburb of Johannesburg, South Africa, and shook Nelson Mandela's hand.

I remember handshakes, especially when they're important ones. Both Muhammad Ali and Larry Holmes disappointed me with mushy, almost fishy grips. Maybe boxers think they need to protect their hands! Both Pete Rose and Joe Theismann almost broke my hand. But Nelson Mandela was different: He had a big hand, and it felt soft, yet strong. It's hard to explain, but an almost magical warmth seemed to emanate from it.

It was the first time (at long last) that I'd gone to South Africa: I was there for a Champions Tour Seniors tennis event, and Patty was there with me. Bjorn Borg was also in the event, and so was Yannick Noah, who—somehow appropriately, I thought—won the final. Patty, Bjorn and his girlfriend, Yannick and his then-wife, and a few other people were standing in Mandela's living room. But he was shaking my hand, and saying that it was an honor to meet me.

I had to restrain the urge to look to either side when he said that, to say, "Who are you talking to?"—I knew (even if I couldn't quite believe) that he was talking to me. We sat down on his couch and chatted for a few minutes. He said that while he was in prison on Robben Island, he had heard about my 1980 refusal to play in Sun City. And then he said the most amazing thing: that he and the other inmates on Robben Island had listened to my 1980 Wimbledon final against Borg. That gave me chills. But I knew that the main reason I was sitting on Mr. Mandela's couch was my visceral decision fifteen years earlier to follow my conscience instead of the money. Sometimes what goes around really does come around.

WE FELT SOME STRAINS at the end of 1996: My ex-wife was continuing to have drug problems, and Kevin, Sean, and Emily, who were spending a lot of time with us then, were feeling quite anxious about her. There were days when I was off traveling for the Seniors tour—I was starting to play a bit more often now—and Patty was the one in charge of five kids, ages twelve down to two. She would find herself going to school conferences for the boys in the slightly staid halls of Trinity, and feeling a little strange about it.

"I feel too weird," she would tell me. "Here I am, the rock-chick girlfriend, at Trinity. I can't do this and be just your girlfriend."

Meanwhile, my kids kept asking Patty if we were going to get married.

I'd been grappling with my fears about marriage for a while; my usual solution was to change the channel and think about something else. But now the channel-changer was stuck: There was no getting around the issue.

*Forward, always forward*—just like that, I made up my mind. I loved her. Who else was I going to spend the rest of my life with? My proposal wasn't one for the ages. Yes, I did get on my knees, but it was in front of our Traulson refrigerator in the kitchen. I took off the friendship ring I had given her early in our relationship, held it in my hands, and asked her to marry me.

Patty said yes.

I followed that with, "I don't have to get you another ring, do I?" Always the diplomat.

However, all's well that ends well: I did give her a proper engagement ring during our Christmas in Sun Valley.

We decided to have a very small wedding, just immediate family and about as many friends as could come on short notice. And we wanted to get married in Maui, so we could stay right there and honeymoon afterward.

A week or so later, Bjorn called and asked me to play an exhibition with him in Houston. I told him I would do it if he and his eleven-year-old son, Robin, would come to my wedding. I thought it would be a good way for our kids to get to know one another, and for Bjorn and me to spend some time together. He said we had a deal.

My innate discretion and good breeding prevent me from disclosing more than a few details about my bachelor party. Let's just say I remember two things: The strippers were ugly, and the shots were flowing freely. If the express purpose of the party was to get me as sick as a dog for the next day's ceremony, then the occasion was a roaring success. I think the cigars are what finally did me in.

Nevertheless, I was well enough to smile and say, "I do" the following afternoon, May 23, 1997, under a tent on the back lawn of the Maui home of our old friend Libby Titus and her husband Donald Fagen, of Steely Dan. The tent was surrounded by plantings to screen the ceremony from the inevitable tabloid photographers, with their giant telephoto lenses, in boats just offshore. It was pouring rain that day, which made me smile inside, because I knew it made the photographers' lives miserable; but more important, rain was said to be a sign of good luck for newlyweds.

This time around, I was happy.

. . .

EVEN THOUGH we were wearing rings now, there were still bumps in the road—what happy couple doesn't encounter them? I was the cause of one of the biggest problems, though, in continuing to pursue my ever-elusive rock-and-roll career.

I thought I had built up a real head of steam with my music. I was happy, I was excited about being married, and about being married to Patty Smyth. I took voice lessons, and I wrote more songs. In Patty's honor, I changed the name of my band to The Johnny Smyth Band. I hired some real musicians and a real producer, Eddie Kramer, whose claim to fame—which I thought was a pretty good one—was having worked with one of my all-time favorites, left-hander Jimi Hendrix. I recorded a few tracks. We continued doing gigs.

The reaction was a little better than the reaction to my ill-fated Italian tour. A little better. (At one engagement, people threw tennis balls at us. At another, a guy in the audience yelled, after our first song, "You suck!"—and then our equipment exploded. A sign from God?)

Now that we were married, all the kids were living with us most of the time, and Anna was growing up, Patty became less amused at my musical ambitions. She felt (rightfully) annoyed that I was off playing on the Seniors tour and running my art gallery and playing gigs with my band while she was at home taking care of her child, our child, and my children. She felt the music was taking me away more, and she needed me to be away less.

One day, she said to me, "You know, you're doing what I'm supposed to be doing. This isn't your job. This is my job. And I don't have five minutes to think about doing my job, because you're off doing fifteen things." Patty looked me in the eye and said, "It's not going to happen. You're not going to sell a lot of records. People aren't going to suddenly decide that you're a great musician. It's time to stop."

I'm hardheaded, and I kept playing for a while. That was the lecture, not the fight. The fights happened when I kept nagging at her to sing with me at our gigs. One night, at a party in a club in Paris during the French Open, she relented. She got up on stage. And as she was in the middle of a song, I walked out into the audience with my guitar—oblivious to the fact that you're not supposed to take attention away from the singer.

That didn't go down well. What Patty finally said to me was, "Number one, I've never worked with anyone I was involved with, and I never will. And number two, the Lord doesn't let you be one of the greatest tennis players that ever lived and then be Keith Richards. It just doesn't work that way."

I looked in the mirror and knew she was right. I still have my guitars, I still jam with my friends, but my gigging days are over. Yes, the world is a safer place.

# 14

BACK IN 1993, Jimmy Connors had started the Champions Tour, a/k/a the Seniors tour, for players over thirty-five who'd compiled notable records in their days on the circuit. Jimmy, who co-owned the tour with an entrepreneur named Ray Benton, had actually kept earning ATP points into that year, and so even though he was forty-one, he was still match-tough, had only lost a step or so, and was as insanely competitive as ever. Accordingly, for the first few years of the Seniors, he beat almost everybody in sight.

Then I came along. I played my first Seniors tournament in April of 1995, in Moscow, and I won the event. Because of my complicated life, though, I played only a few events each season for the first couple of years, whereas Jimmy, who was the co-proprietor, was out regularly, racking up the wins. Once Patty and I were married, however, and my life had settled down a bit, I started playing more and more, and winning more. Patty got me started in the right direction. Noticing how badly I'd been taking the losses, she had urged me on: "If you're going to do it, do it right," she'd said. Nineteen ninety-eight was my first big year, the year I surpassed Connors and won more events than anyone else. And Jimmy didn't like it.

Things have always been competitive and complicated between us, from that first encounter in the Wimbledon locker room to the present day. Jimmy's a strange character: One minute he's your best friend; the next minute he's not speaking to you. He's lived his own life in his own way, resisting the pitfalls of celebrity, largely staying out of the limelight, and making a lot of money in the process. (He eventually wound up selling his interest in the Seniors tour to International Management Group, in 1997, for a hefty sum, though he held on to control over who played in the events he participated in.)

Jimmy has that real gambler's spirit—the legend is that a few years ago he played Martina Navratilova in a match in which he only got to use one serve and she got half the doubles court; he apparently bet his entire guarantee on himself to win in straight sets, and won. I always thought he and Pete Rose were separated at birth, only Jimmy did a lot better.

Things came to a head between us in September of 1998, at the finals of the event in Dallas, in what turned out to be the most interesting match I've ever played on the Seniors tour. It was broiling hot, he was ahead 3–2 in the first set, and I hit an in ball that the linesman called out. Sound vaguely familiar? I went up to the umpire and did my usual shtick—it's almost part of the deal now, really; the crowd is disappointed if I don't explode at least once a match. (My joke is, they used to fine me if I lost my temper; now they do if I don't.) In this case, however, I was also genuinely ticked off, since Connors was my main tour competition at that juncture, and he didn't need free points. I argued, but the umpire didn't give me the point. Just as Connors was about to go back and serve, someone yelled out, "Be fair, Jimmy!"

"Who said that?" he yelled. But the guy wouldn't admit to it, so Jimmy was sort of huffing and puffing, and then finally, after about a minute of walking around and staring into the crowd, he called, "Whoever said that, raise your hand!" No one raised a hand—so I did.

I was just trying to be funny (for a change)—to make light of the situation, but Jimmy wasn't amused. "That's it!" he yelled. "I've had it!" He walked over to his chair, picked up his bags, and stalked off the court. Dead silence. Nobody knew what to do.

A couple of minutes went by. Finally, the umpire said, "Connors is defaulted; game, set, match, McEnroe." People were booing, but no one was leaving. Everyone looked anxious. I was, too. I just stood there, unsure of what to do. I didn't want it to end like this. A few minutes later, again I heard, "Game, set, match, McEnroe." I was starting to get annoyed at the whole situation. Then some guy called to me from the crowd, "That's why your ex-wife left you!" I swore at him. Things were spiraling out of control—how was *I* being blamed for this?

I took the umpire's mike. I said, "Listen, I don't want to win this way. I'm ready to keep playing. I want to say this for the record. I do not want to win this match by default. And I'm willing to wait to see if he comes back." Still no Jimmy. Meanwhile, the guy from the stands was hurling insults at me. I thought, "I'm not going to take this."

I went into the locker room, and Connors was sitting in a chair. I said, "Jimmy, what's going on? We've had worse disagreements in practice! What's the problem?"

He said, "Ah, I've had it. I'm too old for this shit; I don't need it anymore."

I said, "Come on, man; this is the Seniors tour! It's not exactly Wimbledon!" I reminded him that there were 3,000 people out there, they were pumped up, it was the final, and we couldn't just toss them after twenty minutes.

"Forget it, I'm not going to play," he said. But I could tell he was softening a little.

I wheedled a little bit. "Come on, Jimbo! Let's just go out and play!"

He gave me a funny look. "All right," he said. "I'll play if you'll win, 6–3, 6–2."

What? This was *Jimmy Connors* talking—was he trying to mess with my head? I said, "Forget it, man; let's go out and play." There had been times in the past, at exhibitions, when if one of us was clearly under par, we'd play the first set full-out, and then whoever won the first set would lose the second, and then we'd play out the third. Just to ensure that the people were getting their money's worth. You don't want to go out there and win an exhibition, 6–1, 6–2. This was different. It was extremely competitive out there—we were *playing*.

But Jimmy's incorrigible. He gave me that gambler's smile. "Fine," he said. "We'll split sets and you win in the third set."

I still didn't know what to think. "Let's just play, man," I said. But he didn't reply—he just took his bag and walked back out to the court. To huge applause.

We played out the first set, it went to a tiebreaker, and I won it. It had turned into pretty good tennis; Jimmy was back into it.

Then, in the second set, he started losing it again. He was obviously not there mentally. He wasn't even sitting down on the changeovers; he was talking to me—loudly—saying, "I'm just gonna tank it; I've had it. Just stand over there; I'm going to double-fault." Everyone could hear him. It was really awkward.

Then—the story of my life!—Jimmy started hitting winners, all over the place. It wasn't even that he was trying—on some level, he had checked out—but once the winners started coming, it felt good. And he wound up winning the match in a third-set tiebreaker.

When it was over, I said to myself, "There's no way on earth I'm going to shake this guy's hand." Then I looked up, and he was walking off the court, without offering to shake *my* hand! He even one-upped me there! And the crowd was eating it up.

I was so upset at what had happened, I skipped the press conference (I was afraid I'd say something I'd regret—like the real story, for starters) and went up to my room. It had been a two o'clock match, and I had a five o'clock flight; normally there would have been plenty of time to catch my plane, but because of the delay and all the other nonsense, I'd missed it—and after I'd told my kids, "Daddy will be home tonight, he'll take you to school in the morning." I was good and steamed.

I had to wait till the next morning to fly home—and when I picked up a Dallas paper in the airport, the headline read, "Jimmy Saves the Day!"

Connors and I were the Senior tour's big drawing cards; Borg had played on and off for years, but he had mostly been unable to recapture his past form and win matches. Now that Jimmy was starting to lose interest (he was also about to turn forty-six), the onus fell, more and more, on me. I never minded being the main attraction, and I liked the competition (and the money), but at the same time I felt restless. I had felt that this tour had a future, that the sport would be better off for giving its masters a legitimate forum.

However, when you put together a tour, everyone is obviously not going to be on the same level, and I found myself playing a lot of matches against guys I should beat—and who didn't really seem to care. More and more, I'd find myself losing my temper and not knowing if I was doing it because it was expected of me, or because I was really mad. There were times I felt like an old circus act, in a show that was attracting less and less interest.

I wanted something more.


AND, WONDER OF WONDERS, it began to come to me. Patty had become pregnant again in June of 1998, but by December, it had turned into a struggle: This time, the doctors ordered her to spend the last four months on her back. Between Tatum's drug rehabilitation and Kevin,

Sean, and Emily's concerns over the welfare of both their moms, in early 1999, tensions were high in the McEnroe household. I had to give up traveling for tournaments and exhibitions, and I found myself, for the first time, in complete charge of five children.

To our vast relief, on March 28, 1999, a healthy, seven-pound-eleven-ounce Ava Charlie McEnroe was born at Lenox Hill Hospital. We were a family of eight. Eight! I thought back to those days when, as a young, single touring pro, I'd dreamed longingly of having children. Be careful what you wish for. . . .

I loved being a father. It was also the hardest work, by far, that I'd ever done. When your children range in age from the teens down to the teeny, it feels as though you're in charge of a laboratory conducting multiple experiments, all of them dangerous and combustible, but just possibly lifesaving. Every day seemed to bring situations that would try the patience of a saint—let alone John McEnroe. Of course there were times I lost it (there still are), but when you're responsible to other people, and especially very young people, you quickly learn that you have to find ways to control yourself. However much you may feel the need to let off steam, the needs of people who depend on you for everything come first.

I was still very much a work in progress. But—at forty!—I was coming along.

I went to Wimbledon with a new purpose that year. Along with my TV responsibilities, I was actually going to play at the All England Club again, in the mixed doubles, for the first time since 1979. I was excited: My partner was to be one of the all-time legends, Steffi Graf. For years, Steffi's agent had been telling my agent about her desire to play mixed with me. My response had always been, "If she wants to do it so badly, let her call me herself."

Coincidentally, we had run into each other in the players' lounge at the French Open just two weeks before, during a rain delay in her incredible final against Martina Hingis, a match for which I was doing the commentary. During our chitchat, Steffi's mother, Heidi, said, "You know, it's always been Steffi's dream to play mixed doubles with you at Wimbledon."

I said, "Is that true, Steffi?" Steffi said yes.

I said, "OK, let's play, but let's do it under two conditions—let's try our hardest, and let's finish what we start."

It seemed people were excited about watching us play. Our early-round matches were packed with enthusiastic crowds, and we did well. In the quarterfinals, we played Venus Williams and Justin Gimelstob, who had won two Grand Slam mixed-doubles titles in the previous year. In the first game, I served, and I noticed that Venus was standing inside the baseline to receive. I was amused. I hit three unreturnable serves in that first game—one at her body, one out wide, and one up the middle. I could tell she wanted to swing hard on the returns, and I encouraged her on the changeover. "I like where you're standing," I told her. "Why don't you move in a little closer next time?"

Now Steffi was amused. Our relaxed state, along with the enthusiastic support of the packed Centre Court crowd, helped us advance to an easy straight-set win.

In the semifinals, we were scheduled to meet Jonas Bjorkman and Anna Kournikova. Everyone was coming up to me, people I knew and people I didn't, excited about the match. At five-fifteen that afternoon, I walked out of the NBC booth extremely frustrated at what I had thought was one of our more lackluster broadcast efforts that day, but I told myself, "Hey, forget about it. Just think about winning two more matches in the mixed doubles at Wimbledon." Just then, Bob Basche, a production assistant, handed me a note. "Call Steffi," it said.

I phoned her from the locker room. She sounded subdued. "John, I'm sorry," she said. "It's too much, and it's too late in the day—I'm defaulting." She had to save herself for the final tomorrow, she told me. For one of the few times in my life, I was speechless. I sat there for five minutes, silent. Then I started to get angry.

It was the end of the day, and only two people were left in the locker room besides me. I turned to them and said, "Can you believe what this [blanking] bitch did to me?"

The two people were Andre Agassi and his coach, Brad Gilbert.

It turned out there was a lot I didn't know at that moment. I later discovered that others may have known about Steffi's decision to pull out of the mixed before she informed me. What was more, Andre and Steffi had already begun seeing each other secretly, and had planned to have dinner together that night. I'm not sure if her desire to see Andre outweighed her desire to play our match, but—now that they're married and parents themselves—I forgive them.

ON JULY 10, 1999, a glorious early summer day in Newport, Rhode Island, I stood before a crowd of some 4,000 people on the big back lawn of the International Tennis Hall of Fame, and felt elevated and grateful beyond belief. It was the day of my induction into the Hall, and, because I'd always had such a sharp sense of the game's history, it was a day that meant as much to me as any in my career.

They asked me to speak for about four or five minutes that afternoon. As I had so often done in the past, I ignored the advice of the officials. Once Dr. Eric Heiden, the great Olympic speed skater (and a friend through my old college buddy Kenny Margerum), introduced me with the immortal words, "He's probably the most controversial player in modern tennis. He took whining to the next level—I think we ought to hold off on that induction until John apologizes," I was off and running. For the next forty-five minutes.

"Is it true that I have to apologize?" I asked the crowd.

"Nooo!" yelled four thousand people.

"That's what I thought," I said. "To hell with them!"

My parents were out there on the green lawn, and Mark and his wife, Diane, and their three kids, and my brother Patrick. Patty was there, looking beautiful in a white dress, and holding baby Ava, and Ruby, looking beautiful, too, and Kevin and Sean, handsome in their blue blazers, and lovely Emily and Anna. A lot of other people who meant something to me were on hand, too: Peter Fleming; former New York mayor David Dinkins; Doug Saputo, Tony Palafox, my old Stanford friend Bill Maze.

I thanked my parents, for getting me started in this great game and encouraging me every step of the way. I thanked Rod Laver, for inspiring me. And I mentioned everyone, alive or dead, who had meant something to my tennis career, from Tony to the late Harry Hopman to Gene Scott to Tony Trabert to the late Arthur Ashe. I mentioned the late Frank Hammond, and stated my belief that *he* should be in the Hall of Fame. I called Peter Fleming "the perfect partner for me, and the perfect friend to have." I acknowledged my great rivals Borg and Connors.

I even mentioned God. "If you believe in someone up above," I said, "that person, for whatever reason, wanted me to play tennis. . . . Believe it or not, I think God had an enjoyable time watching my tantrums. . . . I think my emotions were on my sleeve. I think that my drive and intensity were on display. But ultimately, I don't think people would have given a hill of beans if I hadn't been able to play.

"I'll never get away from the label of the next Nastase or Connors," I said. "I don't happen to think I was as bad as they were, but I was pretty darn close. But hopefully, in the end, I will be remembered because of the way I played."

My painter friend Eric Fischl was also there that day. Over the years, Eric had shown me the ropes in the art world, and I had given him tennis lessons in exchange for drawing lessons (his lessons, with a nude model, were a lot more fun!). I had asked Eric to paint a small tennis portrait of me to donate to the Hall of Fame, and we unveiled the (six-foot-by-seven-foot!) painting as part of the weekend ceremonies.

Unfortunately, the painting was too big to fit in the Hall; fortunately it now hangs in the living room of my summer home on Long Island. The following year, Eric's design for a sculpture commemorating Arthur Ashe was chosen from hundreds of applications, and the statue now stands outside the National Tennis Center in Flushing Meadows.

THE NEW PRESIDENT of the USTA, Judy Levering, was also there that day in Newport. And two months later, in a press conference at the United States Tennis Center in Flushing Meadows, Judy was introducing me as the thirty-seventh captain of the United States Davis Cup team:

"I believe that John is the best person at this time for the job as Davis Cup captain. It's as simple as that. There is nobody in the world more passionate about Davis Cup or tennis in general than John. He is perhaps the greatest Davis Cup player in the history of the sport. John's record as a player was fifty-nine wins and ten losses. That's remarkable. I think he will be just as successful as captain and bring that same passion and energy as he did as a player. John is certainly the most recognizable figure in the sport of tennis, the most outspoken advocate of Davis Cup, and for tennis. I think it all adds up. He has the respect of the players and everyone involved in tennis. I think this is great for Davis Cup and great for the sport. John joins an illustrious group of Davis Cup captains that include, among others, Bill Tilden, Bill Talbert, Tony Trabert, and Arthur Ashe. . . . That's quite a group, folks."

It sure was quite a group, one to which I was enormously proud to belong. I had received two huge honors in the space of two months, and I felt as if I had stepped up to a new level in my career, and my life.

The first of those honors would live with me forever. The second one also happened to be a job, however, and as I knew all too well from having played under three different Davis Cup captains, it was a very hard one. It was both a figurehead and a political position, and it called for someone with persuasive diplomatic skills. Players had to be wooed away from tournaments, exhibitions, and other lucrative commercial ventures to compete for their country, for less money than they might have been able to make elsewhere. They had to be coaxed to commit to a physically taxing and emotionally draining week at a time when they might be recharging their batteries. And the four separate weeks of Cup play invariably fell at times that didn't jibe with the players' schedules. Time and again, I had seen Connors and Vitas blow off Davis Cup, and I knew I was potentially facing the same kind of reaction from Andre Agassi and especially Pete Sampras.

For a few years in the early and mid-nineties, Pete had had some great moments as a Davis Cup player, including two spirited five-set wins in doubles with yours truly in 1992. In what was probably his best moment in Cup play, in Russia in 1995, he won the final just about singlehandedly, taking both his singles matches (including one on the first day, where he was cramping in the fifth set against Andrei Chesnokov), and dominating the doubles, all on an indoor clay-court surface that the Russians had specifically designed to try to defeat his game—just as the French had done against me at Grenoble in 1982, also to no avail.

He won that cup for us, and I knew he had wondered, Where was the recognition? Where was the cover of *Sports Illustrated*? I think Pete had come to feel about Davis Cup, "No one cares, so why should I?"

Well, of course, the reverse of that is, If the top guy doesn't care, then no one will. You've got to keep caring even when others have stopped. It's like the old story about the comedian: You prefer a thousand people in the room, but if there's just one person out there, should you not do the show? The answer is, The show must go on. If you believe in the concept of Davis Cup, of representing your country, it's got to come at a pretty difficult cost sometimes.

I remembered my own conflict, when I wouldn't or couldn't play during the Code of Conduct years, 1985 and 1986. I felt I was standing up for a principle, but I still wondered if I was doing the right thing.

I thought that if Andre and Pete and Michael Chang would listen to anyone, it was me. But I knew I still had an uphill battle in front of me.

I lost.

In part, I lost to some of the very powers that had helped enrich me: tennis's agents. The agents, who work every side of a big tournament, from the players to the TV coverage to the endorsements—damn the conflict of interest, full speed ahead!—see little advantage in their clients' playing for their country. So whenever a Sampras or an Agassi said, "Why should I care about Davis Cup?" there would be his agent, sitting on his shoulder like a little devil, saying, "You don't have to care! Nobody else cares! Go play Hong Kong for double the bucks!"

I think Judy Levering, the first woman to be USTA president, was and is a fine person, and really wanted to change things: Picking me as captain over a number of less controversial tennis figures who had lobbied hard for the job was a gutsy move.

In the end, I took us partway up the mountain, but I couldn't drag us to the top.

For me, Davis Cup was an exercise in mixed feelings: I loved representing my country again, I loved the camaraderie with the team members, I liked being a leader. That's a natural role for the oldest of three brothers.

What I hated was having to go through a song-and-dance to try to persuade stars to participate—and then, once they'd agreed, to see them drop out at the last minute. I may be many things, but I'm not a salesman. I hated having Michael Chang turn me down, not once but twice—first, at the desperate moment when both Todd Martin and Sampras had pulled out just before our first-round match against Zimbabwe, and then in July, against our semifinal opponent, Spain. (It should be said for Michael

that his conflict for the semifinal had to do with some clinics he'd scheduled for his religious group. Still, I couldn't help wondering: If anyone
was going to forgive you for playing for your country, wouldn't it be a religious group?)

I also hated the captain's lack of control over any but the most trivial
matters, such as tennis balls or practice courts. I wanted to coach my
team, but I quickly found that the players' own coaches were highly pro-
tective of their turf and weren't keen on my stepping in. As I sat at courtside, watching the matches unfold, I thought longingly of the days when,
with the ball on my racket, I could change the outcome of an entire tie.
Just sitting there, I couldn't change much. (Nor had I anticipated how
much I would hate *just sitting,* in what felt like the very worst spot on the
court, my head swinging back and forth, back and forth, like some guy
in a bad tennis commercial.)

More and more, I thought of poor Arthur Ashe, in his chair by the net,
his face a blank mask as I underwent my volcanic struggles on-court. He
always kept his emotions bound up so tightly that I never fully appreci-
ated the frustrations he must have been feeling. Until now.

After losing to Agassi in a five-set semifinal marathon at the January
2000 Australian Open, Sampras went to the tournament doctor complaining of a sore shoulder; the doctor advised him to take a few weeks
off. He reached me by phone while I was at a restaurant with Eric Fischl
and his wife, April Gornick, discussing the latest events in the tennis and
art worlds. The restaurant was crowded and noisy, and I could barely hear
Pete making his excuses. I was less than convinced, and Pete promptly
accused me of questioning his integrity. Things didn't feel good between
us when I hung up.

Fortunately, against Zimbabwe in February, Andre Agassi came
straight from his title at the Australian and played like a true champion—despite exhaustion and the personal turmoil of family illness, despite the incessant drumming that began on the first point of the first

match and didn't stop until the end. After Rick Leach and Alex O'Brien played their hearts out in a tension-filled doubles match, only to lose 6–8 in the fifth set, the tie came down, on the final day, to Chris "Country" Woodruff's match against Wayne Black.

On the first day, in his first Davis Cup appearance ever, Chris had frozen like a deer in the headlights and lost badly to Wayne's brother, Byron. I had been subdued—depressed—during that match, but now the whole tie was on the line. At one set all and down a break in the third, Chris was looking tired and panicky, so I decided to give him a taste of the real me. "Country, you can't let this [blanking] match slip away!" I yelled at him. "You've got to suck it up. You can *win* this thing!"

And that's precisely what he did, taking inspiration from my tirade and running off the next two sets, 6–2, 6–4, to win the biggest match of his career and seal our victory. I felt as if I had aged a month in a week—I wondered how long I could take all this prestige. Still, I felt I had made the little bit of difference that had put us over the top. During my TV interview after the match (with Patrick McEnroe), I dedicated the victory to Arthur Ashe, who had died on that very date seven years before.

Because our quarterfinal tie against the Czech Republic in April was at the Forum in Los Angeles, and because I strongly felt that our best players were needed in Davis Cup, I was able to convince (translation: butter up) Pete Sampras into playing. He made things a little more dramatic than I would have liked. He lost the first of his singles matches, and then—after Andre had once again won both of his singles—needed to beat Slava Dosedel if we were going to advance into the semifinals. Pete's first service game was all I needed to see: his serve was really booming, and Dosedel looked intimidated.

Then, as Pete changed sides at 2–1 in the first set, already up a break, he appeared to have pulled a leg muscle. He actually looked as if he were going to throw in towel.

Before he could say anything, I took him aside. "Listen, Pete, you can't quit," I said. "You've got to keep playing—if you keep serving this big, you'll be a hero, and you'll be off the court in an hour and a half." Somehow, Pete managed to play through the pain and do just that. He came off the court smiling.

The semifinal against Spain would've been very tough even if we'd had a full squad. In July, however, the day after Sampras won his seventh Wimbledon, he called me to say he was unfit to play the tie. That came on the heels of Andre Agassi's call saying he had been in a car accident on the way home from the airport after his loss to Patrick Rafter at Wimbledon. *And* Michael Chang had turned me down two weeks earlier. That left me with my Zimbabwe hero Chris Woodruff; Todd Martin, who had been fighting injuries the whole year; Jan-Michael Gambill, who was not a clay-court player; and Vince Spadea, who had been in the top twenty, but had just lost twenty-one of his previous twenty-two matches.

The crowds in Santander were rough, the heat was unbearable, and we never had a chance. Things were so desperate that I even considered putting myself in the doubles—not that it would have helped. In the end, we gave it our best shot, but we were outclassed and outplayed, 5–0. Spain won the Davis Cup that year for the first time ever.

DESPITE THE FACT that Vince Spadea was on his way to the hospital with severe dehydration and everyone else on the team was feeling pretty low, I couldn't get out of there fast enough. I felt burned out and beaten up: Everything that could have gone wrong that week had gone wrong. And I wanted badly to see my kids.

I left Spain feeling severely conflicted. As a captain, I should have stayed with my team; as a father, I needed to be with my family. I flew to Paris and took the Concorde to New York the next morning. As soon I arrived, I drove to Massachusetts to see my boys at camp, then turned around and drove back to Manhattan the same night.

The next morning, I was on the road again, heading to Connecticut to see Ruby at her camp, when a report came over the radio: A Concorde had crashed on takeoff in Paris, killing all aboard. Once again, a terrible tragedy had thrown my tennis misadventures into sharp perspective. I became more determined than ever to appreciate how really fortunate I was.

MY PLAY on the Seniors tour and my commentary work at the U.S. Open that year felt like a walk in the park after the intensity of Davis Cup. On the first Friday of the Open, I was broadcasting a night match for USA when somebody passed an envelope to me. Inside was a letter from Mr. Promoter himself, Donald Trump—his box was right next to the broadcast booth—offering me a million dollars to play either one of the Williams sisters at one of his hotels. I laughed. Earlier that week, a *New Yorker* profile of me, by Calvin Tomkins, had appeared, with a quote that was widely picked up and quickly fanned into a big brouhaha. Because the Williamses had been going around for a couple of years claiming they could beat ranked male players, Tomkins had asked me if I thought it was true. I'd responded that I felt *any* respectable male player, be it a top college competitor, a seniors player, or a professional, could beat them.

Here was the next step in the controversy—a million dollars! I thought, "That's a good start." Patty and I had a good chuckle about the whole thing when I got home. Still, the idea gathered further momentum after Trump phoned the *New York Times* and an article about the potential match appeared that Sunday. A few days later, the Williamses came to their senses and put out a statement that they didn't want to play against "an old man."

Once again, I felt severely conflicting emotions: In one way, I had no interest whatever in playing against women. I'd always thought that men's and women's tennis were simply apples and oranges. I didn't consider myself a hustler like Jimmy Connors or Bobby Riggs. On the other hand, I still had my masculine pride, and my tennis pride. I didn't appreciate the Williamses' lack of respect for the men's game, and toward me in particular. And I knew that, if push should ever come to shove, I would have no problem whatsoever in beating Venus or Serena.

But I still think it's apples and oranges.

A few years before, I had gotten into a not-dissimilar flap with my old friend Mary Carillo, who had become a tennis commentator back in the '80s. In the early '90s, I told a reporter that I thought men were more qualified than women to call men's matches. The comment was picked up by *USA Today,* and soon the whole thing snowballed, making Mary and me appear to be adversaries when in fact we were old friends, and making me look like a sexist Neanderthal into the bargain.

The essence of what I'd said then was that I felt women were less able than men to understand what went on inside a male competitor's head— and vice versa, when it came to male commentators and female players! I also felt that anybody who did tennis analysis should have competed at the same level as the players being analyzed—and since Mary, in particular, had never advanced very far in her singles career, I didn't think it made sense for her to be telling the public about the inside of a top-ten male player's singles game.

You'll be glad to know that I've evolved since then—and my daughters are the reason why. Watching my girls grow up gave me a new appreciation for female athletics, and for the opportunities that trailblazers like Billie Jean King opened up for all girls and women. I've also come to understand that televised tennis is really entertainment, and that tennis broadcasting must be entertaining. Mary is a good example of someone who never starred, but whose effervescent personality and incisive wit add energy to a broadcast. Tennis needs all the energy it can get.

I must admit, though, that—personalities aside—I haven't always been so happy about working three to a booth. In case you haven't noticed, I like to talk! It would take an incident on Super Saturday of the 2000 Open to prove me wrong once again.

Mary, Dick Enberg, and I were in the CBS booth, broadcasting the Pete Sampras–Lleyton Hewitt semifinal, when someone passed me a note. It said—to my amazement—that President Clinton was in a nearby box and wanted to talk with me.

If I had been working alone with Dick or Mary, I simply wouldn't have been able to go. Now, however, I was. I left—gathering Patty, Kevin, and Anna along the way—and went to sit with the President for an educational half-hour. After a little while, one of the CBS cameras picked me up, and somebody noticed that, quite uncharacteristically, I was doing a lot of listening and no talking. A clock was started, and I was timed—on the air—saying absolutely nothing for eight solid minutes: a new record!

I was very impressed with President Clinton (which is more than I can say for Anna, who was bored to tears). He was much more knowledgeable about tennis than I would ever have imagined, and he just generally knew so much about so many things that it was fun to talk with (or even listen to) him.

After a little while, to my disbelief, somebody handed me a note. I was pretty sure my producer, Bob Mansbach, wanted me back in the booth. Somehow I just couldn't imagine saying, "Excuse me, Mr. President . . . ." I didn't open it. Five minutes later, though, someone handed the President a note—perhaps a little more pressing than mine—and while he read his, I felt obliged to read mine. It was just what I'd suspected. "Mr. President, could you please fire my producer?" I said. "He says he wants me back in the booth now." We both had a good laugh over that.

When I got back, Mary and Dick were delightfully jealous—and I was delighted to tease them. "What did he *say*?" they kept asking. "Sorry—I can't reveal that," I told them.

. . .

SOON AFTER THE U.S. OPEN, Andre Agassi called me and said I shouldn't count on him for 2001. I knew Pete Sampras was a question mark at best. And so, when I met in September with Arlen Kantarian, the Chief Executive for Professional Tennis of the USTA, I suggested we go with youth in the coming year, mentioning the rising stars Mardie Fish, Andy Roddick, Taylor Dent, and James Blake. I told Kantarian I thought that for Davis Cup to become relevant to Americans and American players, it badly needed to be both more fan-friendly and more player-friendly. I said I believed strongly that unless significant changes were made in the format and scheduling, we should pull out of Cup play the following year. I also threw into the mix that I was very serious about wanting to start a national tennis academy to develop American youth. Kantarian nodded mechanically and told me my ideas were good, and I never heard from him again. For the next couple of months, I didn't even want to think about Davis Cup.

In November, I met with incoming USTA president Merv Heller and Judy Levering, presumably to discuss the next year's Davis Cup. It was there that I announced to them that after months of soul-searching, I had decided to resign my post. They offered no resistance.

It was a down note to leave on. Finally, though, the frustrations had been too great, and I really hadn't enjoyed myself. Life is too short to do things—especially big, important things—that you don't enjoy. I wanted to spend more time with my wife and six children, rather than banging my head against the wall. My dad the lawyer had helped me write my three-year contract with a provision for assessing my performance and my feelings about Davis Cup each year, and a potential out if I felt either was not up to par. I believed I had done my best that first year; I had been happy to donate my entire salary to my foundation. Now, however, the negatives were outweighing the positives. As much as I cherished Davis Cup, I had discovered the one role in it that I wasn't cut out for. It was time to go.

A lot of people, in the press and tennis, took potshots at me for quitting. Ultimately, though, I felt our Cup chances would be better served with someone other than me in the captain's chair.

And what a replacement they found.

On December 13, 2000, the United States Tennis Association named Patrick McEnroe as the thirty-eighth Davis Cup captain. Captain Patrick! Of all the ironies . . . my mind was a welter of emotions. But mostly, I was proud.

IF SOMEBODY HAD told me back when the All England Club was refusing me a membership that I would one day find myself playing Bjorn Borg in Buckingham Palace, I would have said, "Yeah, and I'll probably wind up playing Seniors tennis and doing commentary on women's tournaments, too."

Nevertheless—despite Pat Cash's statement that the only way I would ever get into Buckingham Palace would be by climbing the fence—on the middle Sunday of Wimbledon in 2000, I rode through the palace gates and up to a hard court in the middle of the magnificent grounds, where Bjorn and I proceeded to play a pleasantly relaxed charity exhibition in front of a small group of invited guests that included Prince Andrew and Sarah Ferguson. The person I really missed that day was Princess Diana, who had been so kind to me on the few occasions when we had met, expressing sympathy for my difficulties with the press at the end of my marriage—at a time when I knew it was a hundred times worse for her.

Stuffy old England—after all this time, I was getting to like it quite a lot.

WIMBLEDON, 2001. I was still sweating from my cardiovascular workout when I stepped into the BBC late-night-show studio to discuss the quarterfinal match between Goran Ivanisevic and Marat Safin. I had often arrived at the last moment before, but tonight, as I sat in front of the cameras, I suddenly found myself distracted by the fact that I was perspiring so heavily. Uncustomarily, I cut short my interview with John Inverdale, dismissing the match. Goran had been hitting his usual colossal serves, I said, and Marat was trying to push the ball back from the baseline, like a clay-court player on grass. I felt the match had seemed tailor-made for Goran to win, and that Safin appeared less than confident about his chances, perhaps satisfied with a quarterfinal result. It had been boring to watch, and I said so.

For years, BBC had been asking me to work for them during the Wimbledon fortnight, and in 2000, NBC had finally agreed that I could broadcast for both networks, as long as I made NBC my priority. So far, my work for BBC had gone even better than expected. My producer, Dave Gordon, had encouraged me to be myself, sensing that the British public was ready for a change in attitude. His guess had been right: The reaction in England had been overwhelmingly positive.

This was my first slip-up.

I felt slightly uneasy after I left the studio, but then I forgot about it. After Goran's third-round win over Andy Roddick, I went into the locker room and told him how happy I was for him. "You can do it!" I told him, in an unconscious echo of the very words my dad used to say to me.

Deep down, however, I didn't think he had a chance in the world.

Goran and I had a long history. We'd first played in the early nineties, as his career was beginning and mine was ending. That giant lefty serve of his, which started in a strange crouch and finished with an explosion, was the centerpiece of his game, and there wasn't much I or anyone else could do with it when he was on. His groundstrokes and volley were strong but inconsistent. The big Croatian was one of the few players with a winning record against me.

But I liked him. He was my kind of guy—funny, outspoken, hotheaded, and a little flaky around the edges. A typical left-hander, per-haps. His personality was like his groundstrokes: here one day, there the next. We played doubles together at Wimbledon in 1991, and for reasons I never understood, we were up a set and a break, and then he seemed to check out mentally, and we ended up losing.

I felt that we were friends, but there was something elusive about him. The two times I played Seniors events in Croatia, where he was an idol, I was disappointed that we couldn't get together. Goran had said he would show me around Zagreb—but he never called.

Still, I kept rooting for him. In the midst of all the blandness that overtook the sport in the '90s, Goran was a breath of fresh air: a player with the potential for greatness, who brought drama to the court every time he played. Too often, though, the drama turned to farce or tragedy, as he frittered away chance after chance. I felt horrible for him at Wimbledon in 1998, when, as the fourteenth seed, he blew his biggest—and, I thought, his last—opportunity for a title there in his five-set loss to Sampras in the final.

And now in 2001, he was back again, in a scenario almost too strange to be true. Either from a certain sentimentality about his past here, or a hardheaded appreciation of his entertainment value (or both), the All-England Club had wild-carded Goran into the tournament at number 125 in the world. They would live to regret it.

He had proceeded to plow his way through the draw, beating red-hot Andy Roddick in the third round, Greg Rusedski in the fourth, and Safin in the quarters. Then—with the Wimbledon Tournament Committee kicking itself around the block, I'm sure—he dispatched the last English hope, Tim Henman, in a three-day, rain-delayed semifinal marathon. Ivanisevic's 2001 Wimbledon had a look of crazy destiny about it.

In the press conference after his victory over Henman, however, still stinging from my remarks during the Safin match (which by this point, I had forgotten), Goran let me have it.

"John McEnroe was my idol," he said. "He was the player I really liked to watch but, as a person, I don't think too much about him. He says I only have one shot. That makes me a genius or that makes the other guys very bad. . . . [He] gives everybody shit. Who cares about John McEnroe now? . . . He's an idiot."

I felt rattled. This had been an especially intense Wimbledon fortnight for me. My old friend Richard Weisman had taken Patty, Ruby, and Emily on a camera safari in Botswana, and I felt excited for them, but also vaguely nervous about their being so far away. The two little girls were with me in London, and between my broadcast responsibilities and my responsibilities as a father, I was feeling ragged.

It didn't help that I had been trying for days to reach Patty by cell phone but hadn't been able to get through. You can reach practically anyplace by cell phone these days, but apparently the Botswana bush was pushing it. Worse still, I had left the safari brochure back in New York, and I didn't even know which outfit they were traveling with. I felt embarrassed and worried. Part of me felt sure they were all okay, but my imagination was starting to work overtime.

And in the middle of it all, I had to work, hard. This was a good thing. It was interesting to try to do the same job two slightly different ways. Of course, there are no commercials on BBC, which means you can talk during the changeovers: This alters the rhythm of the broadcast, and allows for a more natural, conversational style, with silences when appropriate.

American television, as we know, is a little more skittish about dead air, although you don't want to talk too much during a tennis match, either. The trick on American TV is finding just the right balance. I like to have fun, say what's on my mind, work the edges. When a streaker ran across the court at Wimbledon in 1996, Dick Enberg frantically signaled me not to acknowledge it. Me? "We've got to see that replay from all the angles," I told the audience.

Goran's tirade was the last thing I needed at that point. By the day before the Ivanisevic–Patrick Rafter final—which, because of rain delays, had been pushed back to Monday for only the second time since my 1980 final against Borg—I was in a very bad way. I had been unable to reach Patty for a week, and I spent that night doing a lot of tossing and turning (and crying) instead of sleeping.

I had to wake up at five-thirty the next morning to get Anna and Ava and their nanny ready to catch their plane. By the time the car came to take me to the matches, I was staggering—and my mental state wasn't helped by seeing the newspapers, which were still full of the McEnroe–Ivanisevic battle. The car dropped me off at the customary spot, a parking lot near Court 14 at Wimbledon. When I got out, I heard something unlike anything I had ever heard before at the tournament—it turned out to be the happy sound of ten thousand predominantly Australian and Croatian young people chanting their respective national anthems, all at once. These were kids who a week before would never have dreamed of attending a final at the All England Club, but here they were on a Monday morning, amped and ready to go.

The second I walked into the NBC area, my producer, John McGuinness, said, "Are you OK? You look horrible." Then he told me that, by the way, the BBC wanted to do an interview on-court with me immediately.

When I walked out to talk with BBC anchorwoman Sue Barker, the Centre Court crowd let out a roar at the sight of me. Suddenly, I felt good for the first time in days.

However, my worry and fatigue caught right back up with me as soon as I got to the booth, and I was struggling. My commentary comes from my gut, and that day I didn't have anything. During a break just after the first set, I reflexively picked up my cell phone and, for the umpteenth time, tried to call Patty.

And I reached her. In Johannesburg Airport.

A tremendous weight lifted from my shoulders. I was struggling not to weep, telling her how worried I'd been.

"Aren't you silly, John," she said. "It's a *safari*. We were in *Botswana*. You can't just chat on the cell phone whenever you feel like it."

The burden had been lifted. I happily went back to work, but I didn't have to do much talking after that: The energy of the crowd was so spectacular that I was able to let the match speak for itself.

Goran threw himself to the grass and looked up to heaven when he won the fifth set and his first Wimbledon. I knew exactly how he felt.

I flew back to New York that night with a smile on my face the whole way. Patty flew back from Johannesburg the next afternoon. The moment she walked in the door, my eyes filled with tears: I had never loved her so much.

This, I thought, was what it was all about.


A FEW MONTHS AGO, I was in my den, watching TV with my daughter Anna, when the phone rang. Anna jumped at the sound of the phone. I picked it up. The voice on the other end was instantly familiar: "John. Jimmy Connors."

I hadn't spoken to Jimmy for months, since he'd walked out of another Seniors tournament, in Stanford. We were supposed to have played in the final the next day, but Jimmy'd said he had hurt his back. It was the latest of several tournaments he'd pulled out of that year. I think his real reason for withdrawing was that he was annoyed that, since he'd sold it to IMG, the tour had gone from a twelve-man single-elimination format to an eight-man round-robin; it was essentially so that the sponsors and the promoters could squeeze at least three matches out of us.

Maybe, too, he didn't want to play me—I'd beaten him pretty badly the last few times. But now, on the phone, that was all forgotten: He sounded excited. He had a promoter, he said, who was ready to back a doubles match: Sampras and Agassi against the two of us.

I said, "Are you serious?"

Jimmy said, "You can cover three-quarters of the court, and I figure I can return and hold my own and do as well as Agassi, and I know you're a better doubles player than Sampras. Would you be interested in talking to this guy sometime?"

Now here's the amazing part. I said, "OK. I'll talk to him." What I should have said was, "Forget about it, Jimmy! Hang it up, man!" But there's still an allure, even to me. I thought, "This guy still believes he's better than anybody!" Part of it is, we *are* better—in a way. We're old codgers who could barely beat the local pro sometimes, but we still have these egos. Jimmy's amazing. I thought he was going to say, "Let's play the Williams sisters!"

It's very strange. You reach these highs at a young age, then part of you keeps searching forever to re-create them. Say you're Borg, and you're on the Swedish Tourism Board, and you're hanging around with the president of Sweden, trying to figure out how to encourage people to visit the country. Is that going to give you the rush of winning Wimbledon? Is playing the Seniors tour? So how do you get that rush again?

That's why bad things happen with athletes more often than with other people. They can't reach that high anymore, so they have to get it artificially, or, if they don't succeed, feel empty. My life feels good—and better all the time—but as good as it gets, sometimes it's hard to forget those tremendous victories. . . .

That's when I have to remind myself that I really had no one to share those victories with. That's when I remember how cold the top of the mountain was.

.   .   .

LATE FEBRUARY 2002, the middle of a weekday night: I was startled out of an unusually deep sleep by the sound of my youngest child crying. Patty was away, and so there was no choice: I had to get up and go to Ava, who had wet her bed and was half-asleep and hysterical. I changed her sheets, put on a fresh blanket, and got her a bottle to calm her down. She fell back to sleep in a couple of minutes—at which point, of course, I was wide awake.

I spent a bad couple of hours tossing and turning, worrying about everything. I had recently come back from California, where I'd completed shooting the thirteenth episode of my ABC TV show, *The Chair.* The show was a kind of curveball in my life: The idea had only come up just after Christmas, and less than two months later, I found myself the star of a prime-time broadcast, kind of a cross between a game show and a reality program.

But I ran into the real reality at home. I returned from the Coast just in time to celebrate my forty-third birthday, yet I felt burned out from making four trips to Los Angeles in six weeks, and my household and I had to do some readjusting to each other. I wanted to drive out to our weekend house on Long Island for my birthday, but my plan met with a less-than-enthusiastic response from my teenagers. "It's boring there, Dad," Ruby and the boys said. They wanted to go to their friends' houses on sleepover dates.

Meanwhile, Patty was once again exhausted from bearing the brunt of the childcare, and feeling farther away than ever from the million-selling artist she'd been before we met. Somehow, she also felt guilty about not having arranged a party for me—but mad that I had made her feel guilty (and never given her a birthday party)! It was all well and good for me to run around being a star, she told me, but now she needed some time to herself. She decided to go to a spa for a few days, for some decompression and pampering.

As I rolled restlessly in the bed that felt too big without her, I wondered: Was I selfish? A narcissist? *Still?* As a young and single tennis player, the center of my own world, I used to go to sleep at two A.M. and wake up at eleven, with nothing to think about but my practice, my meals, my match, and how I'd entertain myself afterward. As a young husband home from the road, I'd informed Tatum that I was available from seven in the morning until midnight, but that if anything arose between midnight and seven A.M., it was her problem. I needed my sleep. With Patty, I had hired nannies so I wouldn't have to get up in the night if she couldn't.

Now I was finding out what it really meant to be a parent: waking in the middle of the night to comfort children, grappling with my own demons—and then trying to find energy during the day to handle the rest of my life. Had I been too tough on Tatum? Was I too self-involved for Patty? Was my perfectionism driving my family crazy? Were my kids doing OK? Would I ever learn to relax? Why was I running off to do a game show instead of sticking around to attend to the real (and thankless and overwhelming) job of taking care of our children—a job that Patty had given up her own career for?

Finally, I forgot about sleep and went to my den, where I looked out the windows at the city, my city, as the sky grew light over Central Park. This was another mountaintop, I realized, one I'd had to struggle to reach—unlike the one I'd ascended so long ago, by the grace of my gifts, with such apparent ease.

I'd had an unsuccessful marriage; I'd been humbled in ways other than the gradual, inevitable deterioration of my career. I'd worked, harder than I'd ever worked before, at making a new marriage, at being a father. At long last, I'd actually begun to find myself. With any luck, I had a lot of future left in me.

It's funny: I took on the television show because I worried I was in danger of taking myself too seriously. Now I was worrying that it was pulling me away from the more important things in life. It seemed so hard to find a middle ground.

Still, I felt optimistic as I looked out at the city. The possibilities seemed limitless. Art, tennis, television . . . I thought again that someday I might even wind up in politics. Stranger things have happened. Hey, if Jesse Ventura could become governor of Minnesota, who knows how far I might go?

I'm totally serious.

# John McEnroe's Top Ten Recommendations for Improving Tennis in the 21st Century

1. Tennis should have a commissioner. Baseball, football, and basketball all do; why not our sport? (I'm available. . . .)

2. This country should have a National Tennis Academy. Flushing Meadows would be a natural site, but if the logistics there are too daunting, there are many other possibilities. Kids with potential should be brought in from all over the country, on scholarship if necessary, and they could be developed in much the same way I was by Tony Palafox and Harry Hopman at the Port Washington Academy. (I'm available here, too. . . .)

3. Players need to be more accessible to fans and the media (did I really say that?), the way NASCAR drivers are.

4. A return to wooden rackets would be a huge improvement for professional tennis. The biggest change in the game in the last twenty-five years—the replacement of wood by graphite—has been a bad

one. I happen to think that wooden rackets are beautiful aesthetically and purer for the game. Look at baseball: Kids start with aluminum bats in Little League, then move on to graphite or Kevlar or whatever in college, and then—and only then—if they make it to the majors, do they get to use these beautiful wooden bats that require greater expertise for success. Why not do the same thing in tennis? I think it looks great to have a little wand in your hand, instead of some ultra-thick club big enough to kill somebody with! Wood, to me, has glamour. You need strategy and technique. Tennis, these days, is sadly lacking in all those things: It's all (as David Bowie said) Wham, bam, thank you, ma'am.

5. Like other sports, tennis should have a season. I'd recommend February to October. For three months every year, there wouldn't be any tennis. Players could rest and recharge; fans could work up a little hunger to see the game again.

6. The Davis Cup's schedule also has to be brought into the real world. Should it be held for a week every other year, like golf's Ryder Cup? Or maybe once a year? Whatever the answer, the powers-that-be need to sit down and decide how to re-interest tennis's top players in participating in this great event.

7. Only tennis's top-notch amateurs should be allowed to compete in the Olympics. The lure of a gold medal would encourage young players to stay in college and wait longer to turn pro. The results would be more-mature professionals and a purer Olympics.

8. The service line should be moved three to six inches closer to the net. The serve has become far too important to tennis—especially at Wimbledon, where the best fans in the world sit patiently through long rain delays, only to have to sit through boring serve-a-thons.

9. Let cords should be eliminated. Having to play all let serves would speed up the game and make it more exciting.

10. Tennis players should be far more involved in charity work. The sport

should champion a couple of causes as a group and try to make a real difference—the kind of difference that Andre Agassi and Andrea Jaeger have made, Andre with his school for disadvantaged kids in Las Vegas, and Andrea with her Silver Lining Ranch for terminally ill children in Aspen, Colorado.

# My Top 25 Rock & Roll Moments: A Personal Outtake Reel

*(Some moments are just too great to leave on the cutting-room floor . . .)*

1. 1980 Rolling Stones tour, the Meadowlands: Vitas and I went together, and we soon found ourselves partying heartily with Ronnie Wood and Keith Richards, just the four of us. We then proceeded to hold up the show while we lit up with Mick Jagger just before the band went on-stage. The boys performed incredibly well—that's rock and roll!

2. 1980 TV special with Luciano Pavarotti: After he heard me sing, he decided we should do our comedy bit on the tennis court instead. He tried to jump the net and fell on his face.

3. Forest Hills tennis/rock charity event, 1982: During the tennis portion, in the afternoon, I played Meat Loaf—who also tried to jump over the net and fell on his face. (Moral: Fat singers shouldn't try to jump the net.) At night, as I stood onstage in front of 15,000 fans with Carlos Santana, Joe Cocker, and others, Santana started going

around the horn—pointing at people to play a lead. "Please don't point to me," I thought. (I only knew three chords at that point.) He pointed to me. I just kept playing rhythm.

4. In between rounds at Wimbledon in 1982, I struggled to learn David Bowie's "Suffragette City" and "Rebel, Rebel" in my hotel flat. I heard a knock on my door. It was David Bowie. "Come up and have a drink," he told me. "Just don't bring your guitar."

5. A 1982 Allman Brothers concert at the old Palladium in New York: After the show, I went backstage, and Dickie Betts said, "Hey, we saw you on TV!" Then Greg Allman said, "You must be the golfer." Paul Lynde had said the same thing to me on *Hollywood Squares* in 1979.

6. 1983: Another tennis/rock charity event, on a pier on the Hudson River, hosted by Vitas Gerulaitis and me. In front of 5,000 people, I jammed with the likes of Clarence Clemmons of the E Street Band, Steven Tyler of Aerosmith, and Alex Lifeson and Geddy Lee of Rush. Later that night, I jammed—or attempted to—at a studio with Stevie Ray Vaughan and Buddy Guy.

7. August 1, 1986: I and a bunch of fellow musical neophytes played with my buddy Mick Jones of Foreigner, who was holding down the fort at my wedding party.

8. February 16, 1991: On my thirty-second birthday, I was playing Pete Sampras in the semifinals at Philadelphia. Meanwhile, Tatum had planned a party at my home in Malibu, where a stage had been set up on the beach, and I was to jam with Bruce Springsteen, Bruce Willis, and Stephen Stills, among others. Tatum phoned me and said, "You're not going to miss this party, are you?" I didn't miss it.

9. July 1991: Pat Cash and I recorded, if you could call it that, a rendition of Led Zeppelin's "Rock and Roll," for the American Earthquake Fund, on which we were actually able to convince Roger Daltrey to sing. We were billed as Full Metal Racket. We subse-

quently played the song with Roger at the Limelight, a club in London. Needless to say, the single didn't make number one on the charts, but we did raise a little money and have some fun.

10. As I sat in the broadcast booth at Wimbledon in 1993 going through a pile of otherwise forgettable letters from old people asking for my autograph, I found a note saying, "Call George Harrison." Could this be real? I wondered. I called the number on the note, and it was George. He invited me to his castle in Henley the next day. I played tennis with his son and toured the premises, and then George took me over to a nearby studio, where I jammed with him and Gary Moore, the blues musician.

11. Bob Dylan concert in London, 1994: After the concert, I was invited backstage, where I walked into a room that had five people in it: Dylan, Chrissie Hynde, George Harrison and his son Dhani, and one guy I didn't recognize. I went up to the guy and said, "I'm John McEnroe, who are you?" He said, "I'm Bozo the fucking clown." It turned out to be Van Morrison. I'll never forget the first thing Dylan said to me: "I heard you can dunk a basketball, and you play great guitar, and I know Carlos Santana wouldn't lie." It pained me to have to disillusion him on both counts.

12. April 1994: I was in Buenos Aires, Argentina, playing a tennis exhibition on the night that Kurt Cobain killed himself. A friend got me on a live radio show, where, at two in the morning, I played the worst rendition ever heard of Cobain's "Come As You Are." His death had hit me hard, but at least my heart was in the right place.

13. May 1995: At the Chesterfield Bar in Paris, during the French Open, Patty Smyth came up and sang with me and my band for the first time. The song was her single about me, "Wish I Were You," which later appeared on the platinum-selling *Armageddon* soundtrack.

14. Halloween Night, 1995. The Johnny Smyth Band played at the an-

nual Maui Halloween Parade on Front Street in Lahaina, the biggest Halloween party in the U.S. As many as four bands were playing at once as 20,000 people went up and down the street: The energy was crazy.

15. December 1995, the Power Station, New York City, the studio where the Stones recorded "Tattoo You." The Johnny Smyth Band had a recording contract, and our in-house producers Steve Boyer and Tony Bongiovi told me and my bandmates Chris Scianni, John Martarelli, and Rich Novatka that we had a hit single on our hands with "Pressure." Three days later, the studio was rented to someone else.

16. Philadelphia, 1996: Patty inducted Joan Jett into the Philadelphia Hall of Fame. I played, and Patty sang, on two songs—"I Love Rock and Roll" and "I Hate Myself for Loving You."

17. A 1996 charity concert at my gallery in SoHo: After the set by Mississippi blues musician Johnny Billington, in walked my friend Lars Ulrich and two of his bandmates from Metallica, Jason Newsted and Kirk Hammett, and we jammed the night away. Needless to say, we took the decibel level up considerably.

18. 1997: I realized that my band's manager, Peter Gold, was clueless after the two of us heard Dave Grohl of the Foo Fighters singing on the Howard Stern show, in one of the most poignant live moments I had ever heard on radio—and Peter told me that I had a better voice than Grohl's.

19. April 1997: Nike asked me to do an appearance at the Orange Bowl in Miami. I sat on the sideline at the Brazil–Mexico soccer game, and then, afterward, I surprised Carlos Santana by jumping onstage mid-song. At last, I really did play lead with him. To my amazement, Carlos actually asked me to turn my amp up, and to my even greater amazement, I heard myself playing lead in front of 50,000 people.

20. 1997: Paul Allen's amazing party in Venice, Italy. First came the

masquerade ball, an event in itself, and then the concert, where Jimi Hendrix's bass player, Noel Redding, asked if I would play some Hendrix songs with him. What do you think my answer was? We jammed together on "Purple Haze," "Foxy Lady," and "Hey Joe."

21. 1998, the Hard Rock Café in New York: I played five songs with Billy Squier's band. Billy's career was clearly going down the tubes if he was putting me onstage.

22. 1998, Radio City Music Hall: My friend Chrissie Hynde, lead singer of the Pretenders, asked me to sit in on my favorite song of hers, "Precious." To make sure I knew the song, she had requested that I come to rehearsal—but I couldn't go. I assumed I wasn't going to play, and I didn't bring my guitar to the show. She saw me at the side of the stage during the show and announced to the crowd, "I have a special surprise for you." So I ended up picking up a right-handed guitar and playing it backwards! I did my best.

23. January 2000: Stephen Stills's fiftieth-birthday-party gig at the House of Blues in Los Angeles. Stephen asked me to come up and sing the encore with him, and when I got up on stage, the guitar that the tech handed me was totally out of tune. I stalled for time by getting the entire crowd to sing "Happy Birthday" to Stephen, at which point Stephen pulled me aside and said, "You're good—you've got a future in entertainment."

24. The World Sports Awards Show at the Royal Albert Hall in London, January 2001. I was paid a substantial fee to play guitar with other sports celebrities and Bryan Adams on a performance of his new single "We're Gonna Win." As it turned out, they really had hired me for my presence and not my musical expertise: My guitar was plugged in, but they didn't turn on the amp. Right after the song, I asked the emcee, Roger "007" Moore, if he wanted to hear another song. Apparently he misread the cue card, and said, "Sure." The produc-

ers put on the tape of "We're Gonna Win" all over again—much to Bryan Adams's chagrin. Despite this, about fifty people came up to me afterward and said, "Great playing! Incredible!" I guess that says it all.

25. July 2001: Played "No Changes" with Spinal Tap at the Beacon Theater in New York. I seemed to fit right in.

# Acknowledgments

There are so many thank-yous to go around that I don't even know where to begin. They range from the obscure to the obvious. Here's my best shot:

My kids, who keep me young and make me feel old at the same time: Ruby, Kevin, Sean, Emily, Anna, and Ava. You're the best thing that's ever happened to me.

Mom and Dad. For the last time, I say thank you for having me, and thanks for making me the person I am today. I think.

My brother Mark. The middle brother, the middle man, and the mediator. You're always there for me when I need you. Liam, Maria, Kieran, and Diane, you've got a good man.

My brother Patrick. You're a straight shooter. Just don't write a book now.

James "Jimbo" Malhame. You've been there for me since day one. A true friend and a true believer.

Carlos Goffi. Your enthusiasm and belief rubbed off on me. Your friendship has been so important, and your favorite phrase, "Tough it out," still rings in my head.

Tony Palafox. You taught me how to play. You were a great coach, and you are an even nicer man.

Sergio "I've got to go to the bathroom" Palmieri. All these years you stood by me through thick and thin, and made me feel at home in Europe.

Gary Swain. Still working tirelessly after all these years, trying to keep the Mac train rolling.

Bill Norris, ATP trainer and John Denver look-alike. You always brought a smile to work, and we players appreciate it.

Todd Snyder, ATP trainer. Thanks for keeping the body together, and for the locker-room support.

Lamar Hunt. Thanks for your immense contribution to tennis, and for the integrity you brought to the game.

All my friends at Tennisport: Fred and Andrea Botur, Daniel, Juan Carlos, Alex, Luis, and Mike, among others.

Vitas Gerulaitis. I still miss you.

Dr. Irving Glick. No, I don't need any more minerals, but I did always value your support.

Dr. Omar Fareed, Davis Cup doctor, probably the world's nicest man, with the world's nicest tan.

Other tennis thank-yous go to Peter Fleming, Peter Rennert, Yannick Noah, Pat Cash, Mel Purcell, Gary Muller, Tom Cain, Bill Maze, Andrew Gomez, Diego Perez, Mats Wilander, Matt Mitchell, David Dowlen, Dave Sherbeck, Guillermo Vilas, Brian Teacher, Jim "Rock" Courier, Andre Agassi, Hank Harris, Joe "Right-hand Man" Guiliano, Tony "Left-hand Man" Graham.

Marshall Coben. My old L.A. friend, always calm around the storm.

Patrick O'Neal. We're still friends—need I say more?

Eric Fischl. You helped me more in the art world than anyone else. And your enthusiasm for tennis continues to rub off on me.

Joe Namath and Rod Laver. My idols growing up, and two great, down-to-earth guys.

George Foreman. My new inspiration: to be the George Foreman of tennis.

Kenny Margerum. Once a buddy, always a buddy.

Eric Heiden. I tried to emulate your drive; your legs are a little too big.

Chris Mullin. Another Irish city boy who did good.

Steve Dinkes. For making my U.S. Opens more pleasurable, and for being a friend.

The John McEnroe Band: Chris Scianni, Rich Novatka, John Martarelli, Dave Borla, and Keith Mack. Rest in peace.

Chrissie Hynde and Martin Chambers, the last Pretenders. For teaching me about rock and roll.

To my friends in Sun Valley, particularly Tom Drougas and Adi Erber, for making me feel at home.

Other thank-yous for keeping my body and mind together go to Cynthia Tucker, Martin Barlow, Drew Francis, Dan Harvey, and especially Tony Medouri, for being there at a tough time.

My friends in L.A.: Lou and Paige Adler (for loving Emily so much), Chris Chelios, Fred Hoffman, Dennis and Caroline Miller. Dennis, our friendship was really strengthened when we were canned from ABC within a week of each other! And Jack Nicholson, for telling me not to change a thing.

Bill Acquavella. Thanks for the honest art advice.

Jerry Lee. My bus driver from Buckley, who made me feel special at an early age.

The lady from Nedick's in Penn Station, who, when I was in ninth and tenth grade, gave me more free hot dogs and Cokes than I could imagine. I wish I knew your name; I'd love to pay back your kindness.

Jordan Tinker. My gallery right-hand man—now it's time to be an artist.

Chuck Bennett of IMG. For kick-starting my TV career.

Richard Lynch. A fellow tennis player who lived on my block in Douglaston when I was growing up, and who perished in the World Trade Center disaster.

The New York City firefighters. The real heroes.

—*John McEnroe*

I would like to acknowledge the following people for providing invaluable background information on John McEnroe's life and career: Mary Carillo, Bud Collins, Jim Delaney, Peter Fleming, Andrew Franklin, Dick Gould, John and Kay McEnroe, Mark McEnroe, Patrick McEnroe, Bill McGowan, Tony Palafox, Sergio Palmieri, Stacy Margolin Potter, Peter Rennert, Doug Saputo, Eugene Scott, Patty Smyth, Gary Swain, and Richard Weisman.

I would also like to thank Philippe Dore, Jim McManus, and Greg Sharko of the Association of Tennis Professionals for providing essential ranking data.

I am most grateful to Ted Panken for his superbly intelligent transcription.

And to Joy Harris, for taking me through the dark forest, and bringing me out of it.

Last, I would like to express gratitude beyond measure to Karen Cumbus and Robert Wennik-Kaplan.

—*James Kaplan*